LAND-LOCKED STATES AND INTERNATIONAL LAW

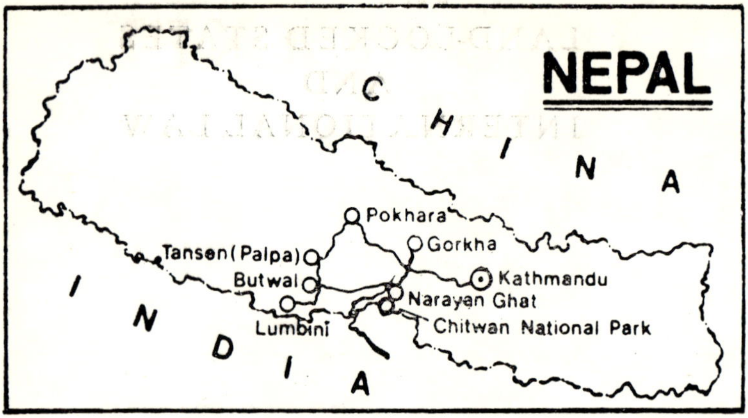

EXCLUSIVE DISTRIBUTORS IN NEPAL
RATNA PUSTAK BHANDAR KATHMANDU

LAND-LOCKED STATES AND INTERNATIONAL LAW

With Special Reference to
The Role of Nepal

ALMEEN ALI
Banaras Hindu University, Varanasi 221005

South Asian Publishers
New Delhi

This publication was financially supported by the ICSSR. The responsibility for the facts stated, opinions expressed, or conclusions reached, is entirely that of the author and the ICSSR accepts no responsibility for them.

ICSSR Research Consultant : Dr. L.S. RATHORE

ISBN 81-7003-102-8

SOUTH ASIAN PUBLISHERS PVT. LTD.
36 Netaji Subhash Marg, Daryaganj, New Delhi 110002

Exclusive Distributors in Nepal
RATNA PUSTAK BHANDAR,
Post Box 98, Bhotahity, Kathmandu

Published by South Asian Publishers Pvt. Ltd.,
36 Netaji Subhash Marg, Daryaganj, New Delhi 110002
and printed at Prabhat Press, 20/1 Nauchandi Grounds,
Meerut 250002. Printed in India.

To

MY PARENTS

Preface

This study is an outgrowth of an interest in the question of access to the sea of the land-locked states. The problem of the land-locked states has become more critical since the Second World War as the emphasis on trade and economic development has grown and at the same time many new land-locked states have come into existence. The state having no direct access to and from the sea are described as land-locked. One-fifth of the nations of the world are land-locked, that is, they are deprived of the sea and the sea resources. Such states have no direct access to the sea unless permitted by their coastal neighbour states. Therefore, the study of the land-locked states poses interesting and important questions. The main objective of the present study is to discover the rightful role of the land-locked states as a whole in general and of Nepal in particular.

The problem of the land-locked states is a burning question in the development of international law. If we did not deal with the problem of the land-locked states, we would be ignoring the problem of one-fifth of the total members of the world community which is solely dependent upon the facilities as offered by the transit country.

The question of free and unimpeded transit to the third states and of the right of access to and from the sea is very important for the rapid development of Nepal and its policy of trade diversification. Due to its natural handicap she has to suffer a great deal in pursuing an independent foreign trade policies.

The present study makes a broad as well as critical study of the relationship between the land-locked state and the transit state, and Nepal's policy for the access to the sea. The book aims at defining and explaining the Nepalese attitudes in international forums for access to the sea and transit facilities for her progress and advancement.

So far as my knowledge goes, little work has been done on this problem. The pioneering works on this problem are: Martin Ira Glassner, Access to the Sea for Developing Land-locked States (The Hague, 1970); Abdul Hakim Tabibi, The Right of Transit of Land-locked Countries (Kabul, 1970); and A. Mpazi Sinjela, Land-locked States and the Contemporary Ocean Regime (New York, 1983). Regarding Nepal, no specific book has been written on this problem. The present work deals with the general survey of the land-locked states of the world and their basic problems, as well as with the conventions of the land-locked states which were adopted in the various international conferences. Nepal's role and attitude as a land-locked state in the different international forums have been described. Therefore, the present work would be comprehensive and useful for understanding of the problems of land-locked states in general as well as the problems of Nepal in particular.

The methodology adopted in the book is mainly descriptive and analytical in the context of historical evolution of the system. At places an attempt has been made to explain the position of the land-locked states through the help of tables.

This work has been divided into seven chapters. The first chapter is introductory which deals with the definition of land-locked states, and the development of international law with respect to land-locked states and the concept of sovereignty.

The second chapter deals with Nepal as a land-locked state. Nepal's geographical structure, historical and political background and economic development have been discussed. The third chapter discusses Nepal's trade and transit problems. In the fourth, fifth and sixth chapters an attempt has been made to examine the international conferences on the land-locked states and Nepal's role in these conferences. These chapters have been divided into different periods. The last chapter deals with conclusion. The conclusions drawn from such analysis are my own.

The study reveals that while much progress has been made, much remains to be done, in assuring free access to the sea for the land-locked states, and in many related matters as well.

My wife Hazara and daughters Pinki and Roli helped me in many ways during the completion of this work. I am thankful to them.

Varanasi 221005 ALMEEN ALI
October 1988

Contents

PREFACE vii

ACRONYM xi

1. INTRODUCTION 1
2. NEPAL AS A LAND-LOCKED STATE 44
3. NEPAL'S TRADE AND TRANSIT PROBLEMS 66
4. INTERNATIONAL CONFERENCES ON LAND-LOCKED STATES—I 100
5. INTERNATIONAL CONFERENCES ON LAND-LOCKED STATES—II 124
6. INTERNATIONAL CONFERENCES ON LAND-LOCKED STATES—III 159
7. CONCLUSION 196

SELECT BIBLIOGRAPHY 215

INDEX 231

Acronyms

AALCC	Asian-African Legal Consultative Committee
CPT	Calcutta Port Trust
CTD	Customs Transit Declaration
EEC	European Economic Community
ECAFE	Economic Commission for Asia and Far East
ESCAP	Economic and Social Commission for Asia and Pacific
ECLA	Economic Community of Latin America
GAOR	General Assembly Official Records
GDS	Geographically Disadvantaged States
GATT	General Agreement on Tariffs and Trade
GDP	Gross Domestic Product
HMG	His Majesty's Government
LLS	Land-Locked States
LDC	Least Developed Countries
LAFTA	Latin American Free Trade Association
NTWC	Nepal Transit and Warehousing Corporation
NTL	National Trading Limited
NTC	Nepal Transport Corporation
NAM	Nonaligned Movement
NIEO	New International Economic Order
OAS	Organization of American States
RNAC	Royal Nepal Airlines Corporation
RNCG	Royal Nepalese Consul General
RSNT	Revised Single Negotiating Text
SNT	Single Negotiating Text
TPC	Trade Promotion Centre
TDB	Trade and Development Board
UN	United Nations
UNCTAD	United Nations Conference on Trade and Development
UNCLOS	United Nations Conference on the Law of the Sea
UNDoc	United Nations Document

1. Introduction

LAND-LOCKED STATES: THEIR BASIC PROBLEMS

Many countries of the world, do not have direct access to the sea. It is axiomatic that all states, though at different stages of their economic development, need access to the sea through which international trade is carried. This need is particularly urgent in case of the least developed and the developing countries which are determined to bring about rapid economic growth with a view to raising the standard of living of their peoples. They have initiated programmes of trade diversification in post-war years with considerable vigour.

The term land-locked states, which generally indicates the physical position of a state, is commonly used in legal, political and economic contexts. Since the time when this term was first introduced, it has been a touchy and sensitive concept. Perhaps, it was due to this sensitive nature of the concept that there was a long delay incorporating it in international law.

The term "Land-locked States means any state which has no sea-coast."[1]

The term "Traffic in Transit" means the passage of goods, including unaccompanied baggage, across the territory of a contracting state between a land-locked state and the sea when the passage is a portion of a complete journey which begins or terminates within the territory of the land-locked state. It also includes sea transport directly preceding or following such passage. The trans-shipment, warehousing, breaking bulk, and change in the mode of transport of such goods, as well as the assembly, disassembly or reassembly of machinery and bulky goods shall not render the passage of goods outside the definition of "traffic in transit", provided that any such operation is undertaken solely for the convenience of transportation. Nothing in this paragraph shall be construed as imposing an obligation on any contracting state to establish or permit the establishment of permanent facilities on its territory for such assembly, disassembly or reassembly.[2]

The term "Transit State" means any state with or without a sea-coast, situated between a land-locked state and the sea, through whose territory "traffic in transit" passages.[3]

The term means of "Transport" includes:

1. Any railway stock, sea-going and river vessels and road vehicles.
2. Where the local situation so requires porters and pack animals.
3. Land-locked states and transit states may by agreement between them, include as means of transport pipelines and gaslines.[4]

The land-locked states have two important objectives to achieve. First, access to the sea, second, the right to extract natural resources from the sea. The land-locked states have faced double obstacles in reaching to the sea for trade purposes: over land distance, which makes exporting costly and the potential or actual hostility of the coastal states, customary and codified international law have recognized the access and exploitation rights to the land-locked states, but have not required coastal states to respect such rights.

CHARACTERISTICS OF THE LAND-LOCKED STATES

Geographical Characteristics. The land-locked states are characterized by the absence of a sea-coast. They have, therefore, no direct access to the sea. Approximately one-fifth of the nations of the world, i.e., as many as thirty-one states are land-locked. They have to depend upon transit facilities provided by their coastal neighbours.[5] This geographical disadvantage stemming from the land-locked situation tends to isolate these countries from the global mainstream of trade exchange of goods, people, and ideas. Thereby they are deprived of having the "windows on the world".

The land-locked states are situated in Asia, Africa, Europe, and South America. These states are:

Africa: Botswana, Burundi, Central African Republic, Chad, Lesotho, Mali, Malawi, Niger, Rwanda, Swaziland, Uganda, the Uppervolta, Zambia and Zimbabwe.

Asia: Afghanistan, Bhutan, Laos, Mangolia and Nepal.

Europe: Andora, Austria, Czechoslovakia, Hungary, Luxembourg, San Marino, Switzerland, Liechtenstein and the Vatican City.

South America: Bolivia and Paraguay.

These countries have no access to the sea unless granted by the coastal states.[6]

The dates when the land-locked states acquired independent statehood, such as, Austria and Hungary, are historic, the states which have assumed in the past many territorial shapes and include sea-coasts. Switzerland and San Marino can claim over three centuries of independent statehood, while Afganistan and Nepal, too, are relatively old independent states. The rest, however, in their present form at least, have emerged in the nineteenth and the twenteenth centuries. Bolivia and Paraguay were colonial territories of Spain, Luxembourg acquired independence only in 1839. Czechoslovakia, Hungary and Austria in their reduced forms, are 'successor' states of the Austro-Hungarian empire which collapsed in 1918. Laos, formerly part of French Indo-China, is a creation of recent years.[7]

The land-locked developing countries are not only without direct access to the sea, but in many cases they are also very remote from the sea. For example, the shortest route from Chad to the sea, from Fort Lamy to Lagos, is 2,050 km. The other three alternative routes (Fort Lamy-point Noire, Fort Archambault-Point Noire, and Abecheport-Sudan) are substantially longer, ranging from 2,400 km to 3,000 km.[8]

Most of the land-locked states have their alternative routes through one or more states. The European land-locked states, i.e. Switzerland, Austria, Czechoslovakia, Hungary, and Luxembourg have much developed economies and are having access to the sea-ports of their transit neighbours through navigable rivers and joint transport system. Most of the fourteen African land-locked states are economically underdeveloped, politically unstable and lacking well developed transport systems. In Asia Nepal and Bhutan have only one alternative route through India.

The final aspect of location is the latitude of the world's land-locked states. Most of them are located entirely or largely within the tropics, but in very few of them is the core area located in a region with a tropical climate. Only Mangolia and the land-locked states of Europe are located at any great distance from the tropics, a matter of considerable importance in their economic geography.[9]

Most of the land-locked states occupy mountainous regions. Their internal transport facilities are not well developed. They use different modes of transport to reach to the sea. Most of the European land-locked states are well provided with many rivers. The African and the Asian land-locked states use road and rail transport to reach to the sea.

The human geography of the land-locked states reveals more common characteristics than their physical geography. In population all the land-locked countries are considered small, though the most populous of them, Afghanistan and Czechoslovakia, could conceivably be considered as middle sized. Of the twenty-five land-locked states in world, however, only two (Botswana and Lesotho), except Luxembourg and the micro-states in Europe, have fewer than one million people and most of them range in population between one and five million. Thirteen states come under this category.[10]

Most of the land-locked states are 'buffer states.' A 'buffer state' is a small state situated between the two large states, to prevent the chance of hostilities.[11] The Himalayan kingdom of Nepal appeared to be a 'buffer' between China and India. But the occupation of China over Tibet and its efforts in 1962 to rectify its boundaries with India indicated that its buffer function was lessening.

Historical Characteristics. In terms of age as independent sovereign state in their present forms, the land-locked states of the world come into four categories. The first and oldest are those countries which are essentially the remains of fragmented medieval Europe, although formal sovereignty may have been acquired rather recently. In second category come those land-locked states which have emerged after the collapse of the Spanish American empire, for example Bolivia and Paraguay. Under the third category come those states which emerged a century later as successor states of the old Austro-Hungarian empire to which belong Czechoslovakia, Austria and Hungary. The fourth category consists of those states which were the former colonies and protectorates of European powers in Africa and Asia who became independent in the mid-twentieth century.

Generally, as pointed out by Eric Fischer, the urge of states to have sea-coast works continuously even today and tends to diminish the number of the land-locked states. This works commonly either by the extension of corridors to the sea, a process which has lost favour as nationalism has intensified, or by some kind of federation or merger with the coastal states. Bolivia and Peru were briefly federated in the nineteenth century, Austria and Hungary have reached the Adriatic sea at various times, Serbia became the principal unit in the new state of Yugoslavia, Ethiopia absorbed Eritrea, etc. This process is likely to continue:

"If experience from other continents, where developments had more time to progress, are of any indication, it appears that the two continents with the oldest organized political life, Europe and Asia, have the lowest percentage of their area or population in land-locked countries. Africa has the largest percentage in both respects. This seems to confirm the view that there is a tendency of land-locked states to be reduced."[13]

Economic Characteristics In economic terms the land-locked states of the world fall into two categories: The developed and the developing countries. The land-locked developing countries are generally among the poorest of the developing countries. Out of the 21 land-locked developing countries 15 are also classified by the United Nations as the least developed countries.[14] Most of the land-locked developing and the least developed countries are in Africa, Asia and South America.

The economic performance of the land-locked developing countries was on average very weak during the 1970s. During that period the annual rate of growth of Gross Domestic Product (GDP) per capita income for these countries as a group was less than 1 per cent, reaching an average level of $ US 362 in 1980 for the group as a whole. Of the 19 countries for which data are available for the year 1970–1980, only seven led the average per capita income growth rate of 3 per cent or more while nine actually experienced a decline in their per capita income during this period.[15]

The major land-locked developed countries of Europe stand in sharp contrast, enjoying generally high per capita incomes and are highly industrialized. Even Hungary, the poorest of the European Mediterranean states has a per capita income which is more than double of her Comecon partner Mangolia, the richest of the non-European land-locked states.[16]

The performance of the foreign trade sector of the land-locked developing countries was sluggish, with exports growing more slowly than imports during the period of 1970–1980. During the years 1980–81 the situation deteriorated sharply as the value of exports fell by some seven per cent while import values stagnated. The purchasing power of exports declined by 1.3 per cent during the 1970s and was eroded even further in 1980–81 when it fell by almost seven per cent, following a deterioration in the terms of trade combined with the lower rates of growth of export volumes. The balance of payments constraints resulted in a significant decline in imports in many of these countries. The growth rate for the volume of imports of the group as a whole was less than 1 per cent between 1980–81.[17]

In addition, despite the seemingly low population densities in some of the developing countries, they all have current or incipient population problems. Much of their sparsely populated land remains so for obvious reasons—poor soils, aridity, high altitude, steep slopes, rugged terrains for transportation routes, lack of exploitable minerals and distance from markets. Nepal and Malavi are so poor that they must export some of their population as labourers or soldiers in order to earn money denied to them for lack of accessible natural resources.[18]

The foreign trade position of the land-locked developing countries and, to a considerable extent, that of their transit neighbours also is marked by several features. Thus, for eleven of the sixteen land-locked developing countries foreign trade is only 15 per cent or less of their GDP. The main reason for this is that many of their main export products are also produced by their neighbours, while their land-locked position adds to the difficulties in trading with the overseas markets The other significant hindering factor in the trade is the very low percentage ratio which manufactured goods bear to the total exports. In only four of the eighteen land-locked countries do manufactures constitute more than 5 per cent of total exports in marked contrast to the position of the four European land-locked countries.[19]

Because of the similar production patterns of the land-locked developing countries and of their neighbouring transit countries, some of the land-locked developing countries are more heavily dependent on trade with overseas countries than on trade with their neighbours. The three Asian land-locked countries (Afghanistan, Laos, and Nepal) carry on a considerable proportion of their trade with neighbours although the volume of trade is small. Again, within the average for Africa and South America, there is considerable variation from one country to another. In the case of western Europe about 70 per cent of the exports of European countries are exports to other European countries, and these are carried largely on the internal European transport system.[20]

Political Characteristics. The land-locked states differ in their political status. Of the thirty-one land-locked states in the world, some states are republic, some are kingdom, some are of other political status, while one is a grand duchy, another a principality, and the Papal state is unique. Most of the land-locked states are members of the United Nations. In Europe, Liechtenstein and Andora are principalities, Luxembourg is a grand duchy and the Vatican City is a Papal State. San Marino. Austria are republics, Czechoslovakia is a socialist republic, while Switzerland is a federal republic. In Africa, Lesotho and Swaziland are kingdoms and the others are republics. In Asia, Bhutan and Nepal are kingdoms while the other three are republics. In south America both states (Bolivia and Paraguay) are republics.[21]

The political functions of the land-locked states would be according to their idealogical frameworks. Czechoslovakia, Hungary, and Mangolia are currently aligned with the USSR. Bolivia, Paraguay and Luxembourg are clearly aligned with the United States. Austria and Switzerland are neutral by tradition or treaty. Afghanistan, Nepal, Bhutan and all the African land-locked states are non-aligned.

All of the land-locked states in the world are members of the United Nations, except Liechtenstien, San Marino and Switzerland and even they have participated in many United Nations activities. All but Liechtenstein and Chad of the existing states participated in the 1965 conference on Transit-trade of the land-locked states, at the UN Headquarters (New York) along with Byelorussia and the Holy Sea (Vatican City).[22]

All of the land-locked states may be considered militarily weak, even when compared with the middle rank powers such as Canada or Israel. While some of the land-locked states are useful to the larger coastal states because of their location, minerals or votes in the United Nations, in terms of the traditional indicators of national power they are uniformly weak. Their bargaining power in bilateral negotiations with the transit states for transit rights derives principally from International Law, and the possibilities of reciprocity and mutual economic advantages.

The land-locked states from all other states, large or small, rich or poor, strong or weak, old or new, that is the fact that these states are not only dependent upon transit states for their access to the sea, but also that they know they are dependent. There is a distinct psychological factor involved which must always be taken into account when considering the land-locked states in terms of history, politics, economics, geography or International Law.

DEVELOPMENT OF INTERNATIONAL LAW WITH RESPECT TO THE LAND-LOCKED STATES

The land-locked territories from ancient times have frequently had to face obstructions, restrictions, tolls or heavy transit dues on goods and persons passing between them and the sea through more advantageously placed territories. As trade grew in importance, the commercial advantages of free rights of way gradually began to loom large than the need to maintain absolute territorial sovereignty. As early as the eleventh and twelfth centuries, territories in Europe, particularly Italy, began giving treaty rights to the land-locked territories and began the internationalization of rivers, the first means of assuring access to the sea for the land-locked states. By the late eighteenth century, however, restrictions and heavy tolls on transit were still common. The principle of free transit was reinvigorated by the armies of France which in 1792 reopened the mouth of the river Scheldt closed by the Dutch in 1648, and by the diplomacy of Thomas Jefferson which resulted in the treaty of San Lorenzo el Real of 1795. This treaty gave the Americans the right to navigate the Mississippi river and other rivers under Spanish colony to the sea, conceding in fact, if not in principle, Jefferson's claim that, "the ocean is free to all men, and their rivers to all their inhabitants."[23]

International Law has long faced the question whether the "community" of states which enjoyed the benefits of freedom of the sea was confined to the coastal states excluding the land-locked states, or whether the "community" embraced this last category also. If one accepts the later view, then, clearly, it becomes possible to view the refusal by other states to accord the necessary transit rights across their territory as an 'abuse of rights'.

The father of International Law, Hugo Grotius, was the first among the Jurists to defend the right of freedom of the sea for all nations in his famous work "Mare Liberum". He states, "Even overland which has been converted into private property, either by state or individual unarmed and innocent passage is not justly to be denied to persons of any country exactly as the right to drink from a river is not to be denied."[24]

The international legal experts have built up many theories in respect to access to and from the sea. According to Charles De Visscher, "Access to the sea is a right conferred by nature on every country."[25]

George Scelle also maintains that the sea is an international public domain (Par excellence). He affirms that it should be accessible for navigation even to the nationals of a land-locked state.[26]

President Wilson, addressing the Senate in January 1917 said that "so far as practicable...every great people now struggling towards a full development of its resources and of its powers should be assured a direct outlet to the highways of the sea...with a right comity of arrangement no nation need be shut away from free access to the open paths of the world's commerce."[27]

Wilson followed these remarks by including among his fourteen points provisions for "a free and secure access to the sea," for Serbia (point 11) and for Poland (point 13).[28]

The framers of the covenant of the League of Nations did not deal specifically with the question of access to the sea, but rather with the broader one of freedom of transit including that between inland points. Article 23(e) of the covenant is significant because it was the first attempt to deal with the matter on a world wide basis. It provides that the members of the League "will make provision to secure and maintain freedom of communications and of transit and equitable treatment for the commerce of all members of the League."[29]

The problem of access to the sea has become more critical since the Second World War as the emphasis on trade and economic development has grown while at the same time many new land-locked states have come into being. The United Nations and its subsidiary bodies did specify many provisions of access to the sea for the land-locked states.

There are a few judicial decisions regarding the transit of the land-locked states. The provisions of innocent passage has been described in the North Atlantic coast fisheries case. The case has indicated that a country without a sea-coast is the beneficiary of a servitude of passage across a country having a sea-coast.[30] The international Court of Justice entertained the case submitted by Portugal against India concerning the right of passage over Indian territory. The court by 11 votes to 4, found that Portugal in 1954, before the change of situation in the enclaves, had a right of passage over intervening Indian territory between the enclaves of Dadra and Nagar Haveli and the coastal district of Daman and between these enclaves to the extent necessary for the exercise of Portuguese sovereignty over the enclaves.[31]

However, the late nineteenth century and the first two decades of the twentieth century were perhaps the period when the concept of "free and secure access to the sea" enjoyed its widest acceptance.

Thus, it came to be accepted in many quarters that a state has a right of access to the shores of oceans and that such access is necessary for the development of commerce and industry and is sanctioned by natural law.

In fact, access to the sea can be and is obtained in one of three distinct ways, i.e., by obtaining, (1) the right to use an international river, (2) the possession of a "corridor" to the coast and, (3) transit rights access to another country, with or without the rights of a free zone in a port of the latter.

THE PROBLEMS OF THE LAND-LOCKED STATES

The emphasis in consideration of the special problems of the land-locked states has shifted markedly since the First World War and even more markedly since the Second World War. Their geographical isolation leads to special problems connected with their transit trade such as difficulties in bulk transaction, high transport costs and other invisible costs. All these adversely affected their competitive position.

The degree to which the land-locked states are handicapped with respect to the sea varies greatly. In Europe the land-locked states are developed and have access to the seaports of the neighbouring coastal states through navigable rivers or joint transportation systems. In Africa and Asia, however, the land-locked states are economically poor, politically new and lack developed transportation systems.

A very important problem confronted by the land-locked countries relates to the question of transit. In these countries suitable transit facilities provided by their transit neighbours hold the key to the expansion of foreign trade which is an important goal of economic development. Almost all the land-locked countries have entered into various bilateral agreements for the purpose of obtaining transit facilities. While most transit countries show a full awareness of the problems and afford facilities to the land-locked developing countries through existing transit agreements, a number of problems and bottlenecks arise from time to time in respect of administrative procedures and practices governing different stages of goods in transit from the port of entry to its destination in the land-locked country. In order that many such problems that are involved in the process may be overcome with relative ease, the relations of the land-locked countries with their transit neighbours usually assume an overwhelming significance. Indeed, the transit so urgently needed for the promotion of foreign trade of these countries is largely determined by the state of political relations between the land-locked developing countries and their transit neighbours.

The land-locked states are handicapped with respect to access to the sea, because the land-locked states are not given good transit-transport facilities by their neighbouring coastal states. The land-locked countries become the worst sufferers on account of a poorly developed transport system. The key problems for all the land-locked developing countries is the lack of an adequate transport infrastructure, including adequate rail, road, inland water, air, pipeline and port facilities. Such conditions lead not only to difficulties with regard to their industrial development, but also to differences in prices between one region and another and to local shortages and gluts.[32]

The absolute costs of transport, for both imports and exports of the land-locked developing countries are usually high compared with the costs incurred by trades in the coastal transit states, owing to the factors of distance, inadequacy of transport facilities, transhipment and topography. In addition, there are other factors having the same effect. The long duration of journeys raises costs. Insurance costs are usually high, not only because of the period for which the goods are at risk, but also because of the risks of loss by damage or pilferage in transit-shipment.

The high transport costs, by lowering the receipts from exports and increasing the cost of imports, have an adverse effect on the terms of trade of a land-locked developing country. The balance of payments of the land-locked developing countries are adversely affected by their land-locked position, as the costs of transport include the payment, usually in foreign currency, for transit transport in addition to the payments for ocean transport.

The land-locked states are handicapped in respect of both the sea-bed resources and the continental shelf resources (EEZ resources). None of the land-locked states presently possesses technology necessary to tap the assets of the deep sea-bed. A real threat exists in that these minerals, viewed by many as a valuable future supply will be exploited exclusively by the powerful coastal states. Since the economies of some of the land-locked states, depend upon mineral exportation, they could be adversely affected by the future impact of the sea-bed minerals on the world market.

The transit-transport problems have a number of dimensions. As mentioned earlier, the remoteness and isolation from world markets and the lack of territorial access to sea of the land-locked developing countries compounded by the poor transit-transport infrastructures give rise to a heavy burden of high transportation costs which these countries have to bear. This burden is a serious constraint on the external trade development of these countries. It should, however, be underlined that the transport cost factor is not the only dimension to the transit problem. The fact that the land-locked countries must traverse foreign territory to gain access to ocean ports has not only economic but also legal, administrative, and political implications, whose treatment requires bilateral and/or regional and multilateral involvements.

THE CONCEPT OF SOVEREIGNTY AND THE LAND-LOCKED STATES

The modern concept of sovereignty was first formulated in the latter part of the sixteenth century with reference to the new phenomenon of the territorial state. It referred in legal terms to the emerging political fact of that age—the appearance of a centralized power that exercised its law making and law enforcing authority within a certain territory. Sovereignty has also been subject to reinterpretations, revisions and attacks, especially in the field of international law.

International law is a decentralized legal order in a dual sense. In the first place, its rules are, as a matter of principle, binding only upon those nations which have consented to them. In the second place, many of the rules that are binding by virtue of the consent given are so vague and ambiguous and so qualified by conditions and reservations as to allow the individual nations a very great degree of freedom of action whenever they are called upon to comply with a rule of international law. While the latter type of decentralization puts its imprint upon the judicial and executive functions of international law, the former is of paramount importance in the field of legislation.

While discussing sovereignty in the field of law enforcement, two situations must be distinguished. The sovereignty of the nation as a law-enforcing agent is identical with the sovereignty in the judicial field, i.e., the ultimate decision as to whether and how to engage in a law-enforcing action lies with the individual nation. On the other hand, the sovereignty of the nation as indeed the object of a law-enforcing action, manifests itself in what is called the "impenetrability" of the nation.[33] This is another way of saying that on a given territory only one nation can have sovereignty, supreme authority, and that no other state has the right to perform governmental acts on its territory without its consent.

The major obstacle to development of a guaranteed right of access to the sea for the land-locked states has been the claim of territorial sovereignty by the coastal states. The transit states have consistently argued that the principles of state, sovereignty allow them to regulate all transit through their territories. Their position is that the right of access to the sea for the land-locked states cannot be properly resolved through a single international rule, but, instead, it is a matter for bilateral or regional agreements. The transit states argue that sovereign jurisdiction over all activities within their territories includes the prerogative of denying the traffic to the land-locked states as a matter of security. Furthermore, it was stated that the rights of transit need be granted and enforced only on a reciprocal basis.[34]

The transit states argue that granting unrestricted transit rights through their territory to the land-locked states leads to serious problems of security and economic malpractices, like deflection of trade and smuggling. Therefore, it is essential that the adequate arrangement for the control of transit and inspection of goods be made so that dangers involved in them may be avoided. The land-locked states counter the argument by maintaining that the transit states want to reduce them to their economic colonies. The transit state should not have unrestricted rights to regulate their transit trade. There must be some impartial international agency to decide the reasonability of restrictions imposed by the transit states.

The fact is that the principle of sovereignty, as enunciated by John Austin, is no longer absolutely applicable. The scientific, technological and socio-economic political changes in modern times have led to erosion of the sovereignty of the state. With the ever increasing technological capabilities, the world is shrinking and the countries of the world are becoming increasingly inter-dependent. With the number of international agencies which made international cooperation on the one hand and international regulation on the other hand, the possibility is increasing day by day and states have accepted their authority in many fields, and thus compromising their sovereignty to some extent. The land-locked states feel that only international authority for the regulation of trade and transit relationship between them and their transit neighbours can solve their problems.

TABLE 1.1 The land-locked states.

Name of state	Political status	Date of independence	Area (in sq km)	Population (in millions) (1980)	Surrounded by
1	2	3	4	5	6
Asia					
Afghanistan	Republic	1747	647,497	15.9	Soviet Union (N), Iran (W.). China (E), Pakistan (S.E.)
Bhutan	Kingdom		47,000	1.3	India (S.W.E.), China (N.)
Laos	People's Democratic Republic	1949	236,880	3.7	Vietnam (E.), Thailand (W.), Combodia (S.), China (N.)
Mangolia	People's Republic	1921	1,565,000	1.7	Soviet Union (N.), China (E.W.S.)
Nepal	Kingdom	1769	147,141	14.3	India (S.W.E.), China (N.)

Table 1.1 Contd.

1	2	3	4	5	6
Africa					
Botswana	Republic	1966	600,327	0.8	South Africa (S.E.), Namibia (W.), Zimbabwe (N.E.), Zambia (N.)
Burundi	Republic	1962	27,834	4.2	Zaire (W.), Rwanda (N.), Tanzania (E.S.)
Central African Republic	Republic	1960	622,984	2.3	Chad (N.), Sudan (E.), People's Republic of the Cango and Zaire (S.), Camroon (W.)
Chad	Republic	1966	1,284,000	4.5	Libya (N.), Sudan (E.), Central African Republic (S.), Camroon and Niger (W.)
Lesotho	Kingdom	1966	30,355	1.3	South Africa (N.S.W.E.), Enclave by S.A.
Malawi	Republic	1964	118,784	6.2	Tanzania (N.E.), Mozambique (E.S.), Zambia (W.)

Table 1.1 **Contd.**

1	2	3	4	5	6
Mali	Republic	1960	1,239,998	6.9	Algeria (N.), Mauritania and Senegal (W.), Guinea and Ivory coast (S.), Upper Volta and Niger (E.)
Niger	Republic	1960	1,267,000	5.3	Algeria and Libya (N.), Chad (E.), Nigeria and Benin (S.), Upper-Volta and Mali (W.)
Rwanda	Republic	1962	26,338	4.8	Zaire (W.), Uganda (N.), Tanzania (E.), Burundi (S.)
Swaziland	Kingdom	1968	17,363	0.6	South Africa (N.W.S.), Mozambique (E.)
Uganda	Republic	1962	241,139	13.2	Sudan (N.), Zaire (W.), Rwanda and Tanzania (S.), Kenya (E.)
Upper Volta	Republic	1960	274,200	6.9	Mali (N.W.), Niger (E.), Benin, Togo, Ghana and Ivory coast (S.)
Zambia	Rcpublic	1964	752,620	5.8	Tanzania (N.E.), Zaire (N.), Botswana and Zimbabwe (S.), Malawi and Mozambique (E.), Namibia and Angola (W.)

Table 1.1 Contd.

1	2	3	4	5	6
Zimbabwe	Republic	1980	390,272	7.4	Mozambique (E.), Zambia (N.W.), Botswana (S.W.), South Africa (S.)
South America					
Bolivia	Republic	1825	1,098,581	5.6	Brazil (N.E.), Paraguay (E.), Argentina (S.), Chile and Peru (W.)
Paraguay	Republic	1811	406,752	3.2	Bolivia (N.), Brazil (E.), Argentina (S.W.)
Europe					
Austria	Republic	1919	83,853	7.51	W. Germany, Switzerland and Liechtenstein (W.), Czecho-slovakia and W. Germany (N.), Hungary (E.), Italy and Yugoslavia (S.)
Andora	Principality	1278	464	0.03	Situated between France and Spain

Table 1.1 Contd.

1	2	3	4	5	6
Czechoslovakia	Socialist Republic	1919	127,877	15,32	Poland (N.E.), GDR (N.W.), FRG (W.), Austria, Hungary (S.), USSR (E.)
Hungary	People's Republic	1918	93,033	10.71	Czechoslovakia (N.), Yugoslavia (S.), Austria (W.), Romania and USSR (E.)
Liechtenstein	Principality	1866	160	0.03	Situated between Austria and Switzerland
Luxembourg	Grand Duchy	1839	2,586	0.36	FRG (N.E.), Belgium (N.), France (S.W.),
Switzerland	Federal Republic	1648	41,293	6.37	FRG (N.), Italy (S.), Austria (E.), France (W.)

Table 1.1 Contd.

1	2	3	4	5	6
San Marino	Republic	1631	61	0.02	Situated and surrounded by Italy
Vatican City	Papal	1929	0.4	726	An independent state situated in Italy near Rome

Sources: i) The Statesman's Year-book, 1982–83, Macmillan, London.
ii) United Nations Demographic Year-book, 1958.
iii) Manorama Year-book, 1982.
iv) UNCTAD Secretariat, based on data from the United Nations Statistical Office. The United Nations population division, 1981 (E/1982/75).
v) UNCTAD—VI, TD/279, June 1983.
vi) Demographic Year-book, 1980 (United Nations).

TABLE 1.2 Main access to the sea for land-locked developing countries.

Land-locked States	Originating Point	Transit: Port	Transit: Country or Territory	Distance in km	Means
1	2	3	4	5	6
Asia					
Afghanistan	Kabul	Karachi	Pakistan	2,000	Road and Rail
	Kabul	Bendar Abbas	Iran (Islamic Republic)	2,000	Road
	Kabul	Hamburg (via USSR)	Germany (FRG)	10,600	Road, River and Rail
	Kabul	Leningrad	USSR	9,000	Road, River and Rail
Bhutan	Thimphu	Calcutta	India	800	Road and Rail
Laos	Vientiane	Bangkok	Thailand	670	Road, Water, Rail

Table 1.2 Contd.

1	2	3	4	5	6
Mangolia	Oulan-Bator	Tientsin	China	775	Road Rail
Nepal	Kathmandu	Calcutta	India	890	Road and Rail
Africa					
Botswana	Gaborone	Capetown	South Africa	1,400	Rail
	Gaborone	Maputo (Via S. Africa)	Mozambique	1,100	Rail
	Gaborone	Port Elizabeth	South Africa	1,200	Rail
	Gaborone	Durban	South Africa	1,100	Rail
Burundi	Bujumbura	Dar-es-Salaam	United Rep. of Tanzania	1,455	Rail and Water
	Bujumbura	Mombasa	Kenya	1,850	Road and Rail

Table 1.2 Contd.

1	2	3	4	5	6
Central African Republic	Bangui	Pointe-Noire	Cango	1,815	Rail and Water
	Bangui	Douala	United Rep. of Cameroon	1,400	Road and Rail
Chad	N'Djamena	Lagos	Nigeria	2,000	Rail and Road
	Moundou	Port Harcourt	Nigeria	1,750	Water and Road
	N'Djamena	Douala	United Rep. of Cameroon	2,000	Rail and Road
	Moundou	Douala	United Rep. of Cameroon	1,715	Rail and Road
	Sarh	Douala	United Rep. of Cameroon	2,015	Rail and Road
Lesotho	Maseru	Durban	South Africa	740	Rail
	Maseru	East-London	South Africa	800	Rail

Table 1.2 Contd.

1	2	3	4	5	6
Malawi	Blantyre	Beira	Mozambique	560	Rail
	Blantyre	Nalala	Mozambique	700	Rail
Mali	Bamako	Dakar	Senegal	1,289	Rail and Road
	Bamako	Abidjan	Ivory coast	1,250	Road and Rail
	Bamako	Abidjan	Ivory coast through Uppervolta	1,170	Road and Rail
Niger	Niamey	Cotonou	Benin	1,060	Road and Rail
	Zinder	Abidjan	Ivory coast	2,690	Road
	Niamey	Abidjan	Ivory coast	1,690	Road and Rail
	Zinder	Cotonou	Benin	1,700	Road and Rail
	Niamey	Lome	Togo	1,225	Road
	Zinder	Lome	Togo	225	Road
Rwanda	Kigali	Dar-es-salaam	United Rep. of Tanzania	1,750	Road, Water and Rail
	Kigali	Mombasa	Kenya	1,790	Road and Rail

Table 1.2 Contd.

1	2	3	4	5	6
Swaziland	Mbabane	Maputo	Mozambique	220	Rail
	Mbabane	Durban	South Africa	500	Rail and Road
Uganda	Kampala	Mombasa	Kenya	1,450	Rail and Road
Uppervolta	Ouagadougou	Abidjan	Ivory coast	1,210	Road
	Ouagadougou	Abidjan	Ivory coast	1,150	Rail
	Ouagadougou	Lome	Togo	1,000	Road
	Ouagadougou	Tema	Ghana	900	Road
Zambia	Lusaka	Beira and Nacala	Mozambique (Via Malavi)	2,570	Rail
	Lusaka	Dar-es-salaam	United Rep. of Tanzania	2,000	Road
Zimbabwe	Harare	Beira	Mozambique	592	Rail
	Harare	Necala	Mozambique	2,000	Rail
	Harare	Maputo	Mozambique	1,269	Rail

Table 1.2 **Contd.**

1	2	3	4	5	6
South America					
Bolivia	La Paz	Aricca	Chile	450	Rail
	La Paz	Antofagasta	Chile	1,130	Rail
	La Paz	Matarani	Peru	800	Rail and Water
	Sicasica	Aricca	Chile	350	Pipeline
	Camiri	Yacuiba	Argentina	250	Pipeline
	Sauta-cruz-corambe	Santos	Brazil	2,550	Rail
	Sauta-cruz-Yacuiba	Buienos Aires	Argentina	2,470	Rail
Paraguay	Asuncion	Buienos Aires	Argentina	1,600	River and Rail
	Asuncion	Montevideo	Uruguay	1,700	River and Rail

Table 1.2 Contd.

1	2	3	4	5	6
Europe					
Austria	Vienna	Trieste	Italy	225	Rail, Road
	Vienna	Humburg	FRG	460	Road, Rail
Andorra	Andorra Lavella	Barcelona	Spain	75	Road , Rail
Czechoslovakia	Prague	Trieste	Italy	325	Rail, Road
	Prague	Hamburg	FRG	310	Road, Rail
Hungary	Budapest	Trieste	Italy	275	Rail, Road
Liechtenstein	Vaduz	Genoa	Italy	200	Rail, Road
	Vaduz	Rotterdam	Netherland	425	Rail, Road
Luxembourg	Luxembourg-ville	Antwerp	Belgium	125	Road, Rail

Table 1.2 **Contd.**

1	2	3	4	5	6
San Marino	San Marino	Rimini	Italy	10	Road, Rail
Switzerland	Berne	Genoa	Italy	175	Road, Rail
	Berne	Rotterdam	Netherland	375	Road, Rail, River
Vaticancity	Vaticancity	Rome	Italy	—	—

Sources: a) A transport strategy for land-locked developing countries. Report of the expert group on the transport infrastructure for land-locked developing countries. (TD/B/453/Add. 1/Rev. 1) United Nations Publication, Sales No. E. 74-II. D5 adopted by the UNCTAD Secretariat.

b) Martin Ira Glasner, "Access to the sea for developing land-locked states" (Martin Nijhoff, The Hague, 1970).

TABLE 1.3 Economic structure of land-locked developing countries.

Land-locked developing countries	Levels (1980)		Growth rates (% per annum)			% Shares (1980)		
	Population (Millions)	Per capita GDP ($)	Population 1970–1980	Real GDP Per capita 1970–1980	Real GDP Per capita 1980–1981	Agriculture labour force as percentage of total labour force	Agriculture in total GDP	Manufacturing in total GDP
1	2	3	4	5	6	7	8	9
Afghanistan	15.9	240[a]	2.6	=0.9	—	78	55[e,f]	11[a]
Bhutan	1.3	80[b]	2.2	—	—	93	54[e]	8[a]
Bolivia	5.6	989	2.6	1.9	—3.2	50	16	14
Botswana	0.8	1107	2.6	8.4	2.9	80	16	7
Burundi	4.2	210	2.0	0.8	1.3	83	51	8
Central African Republic	2.3	320	2.1	−1.3	−7.5	87	34	14

Table 1.3 Contd.

1	2	3	4	5	6	7	8	9
Chad	4.5	227	2.0	−1.6	−9.2	84	41	9
Laos	3.7	100[c]	2.3	—	—	74	60[a]	4[g]
Lesotho	1.3	278	2.4	4.5	1.0	84	27	5
Malawi	6.2	252	3.2	3.8	0.1	84	38	16
Mali	6.9	173	2.6	−0.5	1.5	87	36	13
Mangolia	1.7	780[c]	2.9	3.1[b,d]	—	49	—	—
Nepal	14.3	139	2.3	−0.2	—	93	58[c]	4[e]
Niger	5.3	438	2.9	1.5	−1.6	88	49	5
Paraguay	3.2	1404	3.2	5.1	5.2	49	29	16
Rwanda	4.8	239	3.0	3.9	−0.8	90	46	12
Swaziland	0.6	823	2.6	4.7	1.9	73	35	24
Uganda	13.2	280[b]	3.0	−3.0	−2.7	81	75	5
Uppervolta	6.9	170	2.5	−0.7	4.2	81	36	14

Table 1.3 Contd.

1	2	3	4	5	6	7	8	9
Zambia	5.8	668	3.1	—2.5	—1.3	67	17	15
Zimbabwe	7.4	684	3.4	—0.4	8.4	59	14	24
Total above	115.9	362	2.7	0.4	(1.0)	80	36	13

Sources: UNCTAD Secretariat, based on data from the United Nations statistical office, the United Nations population Division, the world bank, the Economic Commission for Africa, the OECD Secretariat and the United Nations Economic and Social Council, Economic Survey of Latin America, 1981, (E/1982/75).

a) 1978
b) GNP (World Bank Atlas Method)
c) Per capita GNP in 1979
d) 1970–1978
e) 1979
f) Percentage of GNP
g) 1977

TABLE 1.4 Exports and Imports of land-locked developing countries: basic comparisons.

Land-locked Developing countries	Exports in 1980		
	Value $ Mill	As percentage of GDP	Value per capita ($)
Afghanistan	729	19.1[a]	45.7
Bhutan	—	—	—
Bolivia	1033	18.8	185.5
Botswana	503	56.1	623.3
Burundi	65	7.3	15.3
Central African Republic	115	15.7	50.1
Chad	65	6.4	14.6
Laos	37	9.9[b]	9.9
Lesotho	45	12.1	33.6
Malawi	295	19.0	47.9
Mali	175	14.6	25.2
Mangolia	343[c]	26.3[b]	211.5[c]
Nepal	80	4.0	5.6
Niger	577	24.8	108.5
Paraguay	314	7.1	99.1
Rwanda	76	6.6	15.8
Swaziland	340	74.2	610.4
Uganda	345	9.2[e]	26.1
Uppervolta	90	7.7	13.0
Zambia	1402	36.4	243.1
Zimbabwe	1423	28.1	192.4
Total above	8051	19.2	70.3

Table 1.4 Contd.

Land-locked Developing countries	Growth rates (% per annum)			
	Export value		Export purchasing power	
	1970–80	1980-81	1970–80	1980–81
Afghanistan	23.8	5.6	9.7	6.9
Bhutan	—	—	—	—
Bolivia	18.4	—11.9	5.2	—9.4
Botswana	36.7	—17.9	19.9	—17.7
Burundi	10 5	9.2	—3.1	9.5
Central African Republic	14.0	11.3	1.5	15.9
Chad	8.0	—7.7	—4.6	—8.3
Laos	18.1	—5.4	3.6	—5.1
Lesotho	22.3	0.0	7.3	0.2
Malawi	17.3	—3.7	3.6	—3.2
Mali	18.2	—11.4	4.1	—10.9
Mangolia	16.9[d]	—	—	—
Nepal	5.2	52.5	—7.7	52.9
Niger	33.7	—22.0	17.8	—22.7
Paraguay	17.2	—5.4	0.4	—10.8
Rwanda	11.8	—7.9	—1.1	—7.1
Swaziland	17.0	20.6	2.6	20.9
Uganda	2 0	—10.1	—9 6	—6.5
Uppervolta	17.5	—16.7	3.8	—16.2
Zambia	3.4	—21.5	—9.6	—23.6
Zimbabwe	14.5	3.3	0 4	3.5
Total above	12.5	—6.9	—1.3	—6.8

Table 1.4 Contd.

Land-locked Developing countries	Imports in 1980		
	Value $ Mill	As percentage of GDP	Value per capita ($)
Afghanistan	924	24.2[a]	58.0
Bhutan	—	—	—
Bolivia	833	15.1	149.6
Botswana	691	77.0	856.3
Burundi	168	16.9	39.6
Central African Republic	80	10.9	34.9
Chad	160	15.8	35.9
Laos	120	32.3[b]	32.3
Lesotho	320	86.0	238.6
Malawi	439	28.2	71.2
Mali	417	34.7	60.1
Mangolia	560	43.0[b]	335.5
Nepal	342	17.2	23.9
Niger	570	24.5	107.2
Paraguay	431	9.7	136.0
Rwanda	243	21.2	50.7
Swaziland	596	130.1	1070.0
Uganda	293	7.8[e]	22.2
Uppervolta	358	30.5	51.8
Zambia	1090	28.3	189.0
Zimbabwe	1322	26.1	178.7
Total above	9957	23.7	86.9

Table 1.4 Contd.

Land-locked Developing countries	Growth rates (% per annum) Import value 1970–80	1980–81	Import volume 1970–80	1980–81
Afghanistan	23.5	8.2	9.4	9.5
Bhutan	—	—	—	—
Bolivia	18.1	1.6	4 8	4.4
Botswana	30.3	14.2	14.3	14.4
Burundi	22.5	—0.6	7.5	—0.4
Central African Republic	8.9	25.0	—3.0	30.1
Chad	10.1	—6.3	—2.6	—6.9
Laos	0.5	—16.7	—11.8	—16.5
Lesotho	26.1	—6.2	10.4	—6.0
Malawi	17.7	—17.5	4.0	—17.1
Mali	24.4	—16.1	9.6	—15.6
Mangolia	16.6	—	—	—
Nepal	15.1	11.4	0.9	11.7
Niger	25.7	—3.5	10.8	—4.3
Paraguay	21.0	17.4	3.7	10.8
Rwanda	23.7	—9.5	9.5	—8.6
Swaziland	25.8	—7.7	10.3	—7.5
Uganda	5 5	—14.7	—6.6	—11.2
Uppervolta	22 0	—5.6	7.9	—5 1
Zambia	8.6	—8.3	—5.0	—10.7
Zimbabwe	14.9	5.9	0.8	6.1
Total above	16.5	0.0	2.4	—0.4

Sources: United Nations, Monthly Bulletin of Statistics, various issues, National Sources and Preliminary Estimates of the UNCTAD Secretariat.

a) As percentage of GDP in 1978.

b) As percentage of GNP in 1979.

c) 1979.

d) 1970–79.

e) As percentage of GNP.

TABLE 1.5 Net flows of external resources to land-locked developing countries. (net disbursements 1980).

Land-Locked developing countries	ODA		
	Total	Percapita	As percentage of imports
	$ mill.	($)	(%)
Afghanistan	41.6[b]	2.6[b]	4.5
Bhutan	8 3	6.4	—
Bolivia	175.5	31.5	21.1
Botswana	106.5	132.0	15.4
Burundi	130.0	30.7	77.4
Central African Republic	110.0	48.0	137.5
Chad	36.4	8.2	22.8
Laos	40.1	10.8	33.4
Lesotho	90.3	67.3	28.2
Malawi	143.3	23.2	32.6
Mali	255.1	36.7	61.2
Mangolia	—	—	—
Nepal	161.6	11.3	47.3
Niger	171.3	32.2	30.1
Paraguay	30.5	9.6	7.1
Rwanda	155.3	32.4	63.9
Swaziland	49.9	89.6	10.7
Uganda	111.9	8.5	38.2
Uppervolta	217.0	31.4	60.6
Zambia	350.5	60.8	32.2
Zimbabwe	162.7	22.0	12.3
Total above	2547.7	22.0	27.1

Table 1.5 Contd.

Land-Locked developing countries	ODA by category		
	Loans	Technical assistance	Other grants
Afghanistan	3.9	20.3	6.6
Bhutan	—	7.4	0.9
Bolivia	80.7	43.8	45.5
Botswana	5.7	53.9	44.2
Burundi	25.2	50.2	33.7
Central African Republic	19.0	35.9	54.0
Chad	1.9	13.5	19.9
Laos	10.1	13.9	16.1
Lesotho	10.3	38.0	41.9
Malawi	57.3	39.6	45.1
Mali	48.0	81.4	95.1
Mangolia	—	—	—
Nepal	27.0	65.4	63.8
Niger	49.8	66.7	45.1
Paraguay	—	20.9	9.6
Rwanda	25.8	57.2	65.0
Swaziland	15.6	23.3	11.0
Uganda	30.9	25.9	55.3
Uppervolta	44.9	78.9	81.6
Zambia	134.5	88.3	69.9
Zimbabwe	—34.4	70.2	121.6
Total above	556.2	894.7	925.9

Table 1.5 **Contd.**

Land-Locked developing countries	by main sources			
	DAC	OPEC	Socialist countries of Eastern Europe	China
Afghanistan	30.8	4.3	—	6.7
Bhutan	8.3	—	—	—
Bolivia	170.0	—	5.5	—
Botswana	103.8	2.7	—	—
Burundi	109.1	9.6	—0.2	11.5
Central African Republic	108.9	2.1	—1.0	—
Chad	35.3	0.0	—0.4	1.5
Laos	40.1	—	—	—
Lesotho	90.2	0.1	—	—
Malawi	142.0	1.3	—	—
Mali	224.5	20.0	—0.7	11.3
Mangolia	—	—	—	—
Nepal	156.2	5.4	—	—
Niger	161.6	8.9	—	0.8
Paraguay	30.5	—	—	—
Rwanda	148.0	7.3	—	—
Swaziland	49.9	—	—	—
Uganda	112.1	0.3	—0.5	—
Uppervolta	205.4	6.4	—	5.2
Zambia	292.7	2.7	46.3	8.8
Zimbawe	157.4	5.0	—	—
Total above	2376.8	76.1	49.0	45.8

Table 1.5 Contd.

Land-locked developing countries	Non-concessional[a] flows	Total external resources
Afghanistan	2.0[b]	43.8[b]
Bhutan	—	8.3
Bolivia	—13.0	162.5
Botswana	—53.2	53.3
Burundi	0.4	130.4
Central African Republic	16.4	126.4
Chad	—1.4	35.0
Laos	—1.0	39.1
Lesotho	—0.1	90.2
Malawi	32.8	176.1
Mali	5.7	260.8
Mangolia	—	—
Nepal	—1.6	160.0
Niger	81.3	252.6
Paraguay	44.2	74.7
Rwanda	0.4	155.7
Swaziland	20.2	70.1
Uganda	19.6	131.5
Uppervolta	28.6	245.6
Zambia	13.0	363.5
Zimbabwe	1.3	163.7
Total above	195.6	2743.3

Sources: UNCTAD Secretariat, based on data from the United Nations Statistical Office, the OECD/DAC Secretariat and the World Bank.

a) Including private flows from DAC member countries.

b) Excluding flows from socialist countries of Eastern Europe.

TABLE 1.6 The economic structure of the main European land-locked countries main indicators (1967).

Country	Population (million)	GNP at factor cost (million dollers)	GNP percapita (dollars)	Share of manufacturing in GDP (per cent)	Ratio of foreign trade GNP (per cent)	Share of export of manufacture in total export (per cent)
Austria	7.3	8,196	1,119	37.6[b]	25	77
Czechoslovakia	14.3	13,721[a]	964[a]	64.5[c]	20	84[a]
Hungary	10.2	7,787[a]	765[a]	56.0[d]	22	69
Switzerland	6.1	13,111	2,167	60.0[e]	29	88

Sources: Column (1): United Nations, Statistical Yearbook, 1968, E/F. 69. Table 18.
Column (2), (3) and (4): IBRD, World Table, 1968.
Column (5): Computed as mean of exports and imports expressed as percentage of GNP original data from United Nations, national and unofficial sources.
Column (6): Computed from United Nations Yearbook of International Trade Statistics, 1967.

a) 1966
b) Includes mining
c) Includes mining, quarrying, electricity and gas
d) Includes mining and quarrying
e) Estimated

TABLE 1.7 The international trade pattern of land-locked developing countries compared with that of the main European land-locked countries.

Land-locked countries of	Ratio of foreign trade to GDP	Exports		Imports	
		Total exports (million dollars)	Exports to neighbours (per cent)	Total imports (million dollars)	Imports from neighbours (per cent)
Africa[b]	23	1055	7	889	15
Asia	8	95	53	214	57
South America	19	222	14	212	15
Europe[a]	24	9871	49	10895	59

Sources: UNCTAD Documents, Country Reports, 1968

a) GNP of the European countries

b) Excluding Botswana, Lesotho and Swaziland

NOTES

1. UNCTAD, Convention on Transit-Trade of Land-locked State. Second Session, Annexes and Agenda 6, 1965, p. 3. TD/B/18.
2. Idid.
3. Ibid.
4. Ibid.
5. Martin Ira Glassner, "Access to the Sea for Developing Land-locked Statess," (The Hague, 1970), p. 12.
6. Abdul Hakim Tabibi, "The Right of Transit of Land-locked Countries," (Kabul, 1970), p. 216.
7. W.G. East, "The Geography of Land-locked States," Trans. and Papers, Ins. British Geographers, Publ. No. 28, 1960, p. 7.
8. Martin Ira Glassner, n. 5, p. 16.
9. Ibid., p. 18.
10. Ibid.
11. W.G. East, "The Geography of Land-locked States," Trans. Inst. British Geographers, No. 28, 1960, p. 9.
12. Martin Ira Glassner, n. 5, p. 32.
13. Eric Fischer, "Land-locked Countries of Africa," Unpublished Paper Read Before the Association of American Geographers in Denver, Calorodo, September 1963.
14. UNCTAD-VI, June 1983, p. 1, TD/279.
15. Ibid.
16. Martin Ira Glassner, n. 5, p. 35.
17. UNCTAD-VI, 1983, p. 1, TD/279.
18. Martin Ira Glassner, n. 5, p. 32.
19. UNCTAD-Third Session, Agenda Item 13, 1970–71, pp. 23-24.
20. Ibid.
21. Martin Ira Glassner, n. 5, p. 34.
22. Ibid.
23. G. Kaechenbeek, "International River" (London, 1918). p. 206.
24. Abdul Hakim Tabibi, n. 6, p. 16.
25. Ibid.
26. UN Conference on Law of the Sea, Official Records, Fifth Committee, Vol. VII, 1958, p. 20.
27. Narindra Mehta, "Political Geography" (Jullundur, 1971).
28. Encyclopedia Britannica, Vol. IX, 1965, p. 671.
29. League of Nations Document, 20/31/58, Third series, Vol. II, No. 1-2, 1921, pp. 83-124.

30. The North Atlantic Fisheries Case, Reference, "Revue General de droit International Public," Vol. XIX, 1912, p. 421.

31. Case Concerning Right of Passage Over Indian Territory, (Portugal v. India), International Court of Justice, Judgement of 12 April 1960, pp. 27-38.

32. UNCTAD-Transport Strategy for Land-locked Developing Countries, 1974, TD/B/453/Add/Rev. I.

33. Hans J. Margenthau and Kenneth W. Thompson, "Politics Among Nations: The Struggle for Power and Peace," (New Delhi, 1985), p. 328.

34. British Year Book of International Law, 167, 174, 1922–23.

2. Nepal as a Land-Locked State

GEOGRAPHICAL STRUCTURE

Nepal is a sovereign independent kingdom, situated on the southern slopes of the mid-Himalayas in central area. Nepal is bounded on the north by the Tibet region of the People's Republic of China, on the east by Sikkim and West Bengal and on the south and west by the states of Bihar and Uttar Pradesh of India. Nepal is located between 26° 12′ and 30° 27′ north latitudes and 80° 4′ and 88° 12′ east longitudes.[1] It has an area of 147,181 sq km Nepal's total population is 15,020,451 according to the 1981 census.[2]

The Himalayas form a natural boundary between China and Nepal. Towards north Nepal encounters not merely the barrier of the Himalayas but also the huge arid table-land of Tibet, which has an average altitude of 15,000 feet. Beyond that, there is the big Gobi desert. In fact, the main population centres of China are far away from Nepal. There is also no question of Nepal's gaining access to the sea from the northern side. That is perhaps why throughout history its relations with China have been occasional and formal. On the contrary, there is no natural frontier between Nepal and India, rather the former is a geographical extension of the latter as is evident from the contiguity of their settlements. Moreover, the Calcutta port is nearer not only to Nepal but to Tibet as well. Till the early 1950's the Chinese also preferred to go to Tibet via India.[3]

In terms of its geographical location, Nepal has some significant features. It extends for a distance of five hundred miles from east to west along the Himalayas, and its width varies from 80 to 150 miles. It, thus, does not have sufficient depth for its defence either from the north or from the south. This limits Nepal's role as a geographical buffer between India and China.

Nepal's border on the south is contiguous to the Indian plains, and the natural barriers and mountains and rivers (the river Kali on the west and the Tista on the east) extend into Indian territory.

Towards the north, the Himalayan range forms a natural boundary with the Tibet region of China. In October 1961 a formal boundary treaty was signed between Nepal and China. Nepal is a land-locked state. The nearest sea-coast is 1120 km away in India (Calcutta).[4]

Nepal has a mountainous topography, steep mountains and rolling hills constitute over three-fourths of the territory. Nepal may be divided into three geographical regions.

THE HIMALAYAN REGION

This lies at an altitude of 4877 metres to 8839 metres above the sea level with the snow line running at 4877 metres. The Himalayan ranges like the Kumbhakarana, the Jugal, the Mustang, the Ganesh, the Annapurna, and the Machhapuchhare fan out from the east to the west. It covers nearly 38 per cent of the total area of the country.[5]

MOUNTAIN REGION

This region is formed by the Mahabharat range that soars upto 4877 metres. It is also known as the mid-Himalayas. To the south of it lies the Churia range whose altitude varies from 610 to 1524 metres. The two ranges enclose between them valleys of various width and altitude, from 610 to 914 metres. They are known as the Doons or the inner Tarai. The mountain region accounts for about 68 per cent of the total land area.[6]

THE TARAI REGION

The Tarai region which has a width of about 26 to 32 km and a maximum altitude of 305 metres occupies about 17 per cent of the total land area of the country. The eastern Tarai is wider and spreads continuously while the western Tarai is narrow and irregular. The forest of the Char Koshe Jhadi, famous for big games, lies east to west.[7]

The tarai is the most developed region of Nepal, the northern most areas are the least developed. The north region is also largely inaccessable.

RIVERS

Nepal has a large number of rivers. The river system of the country is made up of three main rivers and their tributaries. The greatest and most outstanding river is the Koshi river. It is actually a confluence of seven rivers—the Koshi, the Sunkoshi, the Arun, the Tamor, the Tamakoshi, the Indravati, and the Likhu. It is, therefore, known as th: Sapta Koshi or Seven Koshi. The river drains the eastern part of Nepal. The second river, the Gandaki, too is composed of seven rivers. Its tributaries are the Trishuli, the Kali, the Seti, the Madi, the Daraundi, etc. This river is also called the Narayani. This river drains the central Nepal. The third river is the Karnali which drains the western part of Nepal.[8] All the rivers flow into the Ganga river.

THE ETHNIC AND CULTURAL MOSAIC

Nepal is a land of diverse ethnic groups who speak different languages. The Nepali is Nepal's national language written in Devanagari script. The Nepali, Maithili, Bhojpuri are of the Indo-Aryan group of languages while the rest mostly belong to the Mangoloid or Tibetan—Burmese group.

The Maithili, Bhojpuri, speaking people mostly inhabit the tarai plains. Among the Tarai Hindus, as elsewhere in the country, the topmost rank of the social hierarchy is occupied by the Brahmins and at the bottom come the 'Dom Dusadh' (Scavengers).[9]

The majority of the Mangoloids are scattered among the hills and mountains of the country. Kathmandu valley is the traditional home of the Newars. The Newars are mainly traders by occupation and their trade network is spread out all over the country.[10]

It is obvious from the above description that the topographical features of Nepal have played an important role in shaping the country's social life. Owing to the vertical flow of almost all rivers through the Himalayas, the different regions are mutually insulted and each region has its own distinct social, cultural, and linguistic identity. There are then the difficulties of transport and communication across the rugged terrain restricting the flow of traffic for the major part of the country.

HISTORICAL AND POLITICAL BACKGROUND

Nepal is an ancient country with a long and varied history in the course of which different tribes attained political power and eminence and several ruling clans and dynastics changed hands. The Kirats, the Lichchhavis, the Thakuris, the Mallas, and the Gorkhas have moulded and influenced the character and pattern of Nepali life and culture. Political frontier-lines shifted quite often, but Nepal has had the distinction of retaining her independence through the centuries despite adverse and tangled circumstances.

Since the remote past and till the advent of the fourteenth century A.D. the valley of Nepal received all kinds of settlers most of whom came from the south and south-east. No precise information is available about the name of these settlers. But one thing is certain that no one race or tribe has dominated this territory which reflects distinct traces of composite influences.[11]

Originally, the Kathmandu valley was a single kingdom. But in 1457 King Yaksha Malla divided it into three kingdoms—Bhatgaon, Kathmandu, and Patan, Nepal remained divided into these three kingdoms upto 1769.[12]

This disunited Nepal was surrounded in the east and the west by a large number of independent states. Some of these states were ruled by the native hill tribes, but most of them were under the Kshatriya kings who had migrated from India during the Muslim invasions between the fourteenth and the seventeenth century. Of all these states, Gorkha was destined to play a very significant role in the history of modern Nepal.

The Malla family of the valley of Kathmandu and the Shahs of Gorkha emerged as the main contenders in the seventeenth century. The trans-Himalayan trade became a bone of contention between them too. Ram Shah annexed the Kerong pass, which was the most frequented of all the trade routes. Pratap Malla then conquered the Kuti pass to open an alternative route and also marched some distance into Tibet. Thus, for the first time perhaps, Nepalese authority extended upto these vital passes.[13]

By the middle of the eighteenth century certain developments in Nepal changed the existing power structure of the region and also affected the trans-Himalayan trade. The Raja of Gorkha, Prithvi Narayan Shah, succeeded in overthrowing the Mallas of the valley in 1769 and set out to consolidate the kingdom of Nepal. Kathmandu became the capital of modern Nepal by 1769.[14] King Prithvi Narayan Shah was in favour of adopting a closed-door policy with regard to the British. Not only his social and economic directives have guided the country's socio-economic strategies but also the fore-sighted policy of neutrality under the dictum "a yam between two boulders" in Nepal's geo-political context, formed the principal guideline of the country's foreign policy through centuries.[15]

After Prithvi Narayan Shah and his successor Pratap Singh, Bahadur Shah became the regent of the infant king. Although he was opposed by a number of factions, he managed to keep his control over the administration tight. He did not seem to think much of the idea of expanding in the southern direction. Instead, he preferred to push northwards. Incidently there were deep internal dissensions in Tibet at this time. In 1792 when the country became entangled in a war with China, following Nepal's armed attack on Tibet in 1788 and 1791 over a trade dispute.

At the beginning of the 19th century, the Prime Minister Bhimsen Thapa spurred progress in the country when he succeeded in consolidating the state by eliminating the dispersion which had been characteristic of the feudal regime. Bhimsen Thapa decided to conquer the rich and fertile plain in the south. Obviously this ran counter to the British plans and thus in 1814 Britain declared war on Nepal. After a protracted mountain warfare, the conflict ended with the signing of the Treaty of Segouli in 1816. Under this treaty, Nepal lost a large part of their territory, and were forced to accept a permanent British Resident.[17]

With the rise of Rana Jung Bahadur in 1846 a new era began in Nepal's internal as well as external relations. The Ranas ruled for more than a century and gave the country much needed political stability.

In keeping with the wishes of the British colonialists, the Ranas kept Nepal isolated from the rest of the world. But after the fall of Randip Singh, Nepalese foreign policy underwent another change. For Bir Shumsher friendship with the British was a political necessity. In addition, it brought large economic benefits to Nepal. Indo-Nepal trade increased both in volume and content. Nepal's economy became a part of India's economy. For the first time a treaty was signed between Nepal and British India in 1923, which gave Nepal the right to import, free of duty, all government goods through India.[18]

After India became independent a new treaty of peace and friendship and a treaty of trade and commerce were signed in July 1950 between Indian government and the last Rana Prime Minister Mohan Shumsher.[19]

Popular protest against the Ranas had started gaining some momentum in the early 1940's. The autocratic rule of the Ranas was broken, and the modern history of Nepal thus begins in 1951. As a result of a palace revolt in 1950, the king regained his position of authority, and in February, 1951 King Tribhuvan's proclamation of a constitutional monarchy ended the reign of the Rana oligarchy. The period between 1951 and 1959 was marked by political instability and a rapid succession of governments, but it was also a period of persistent efforts by the king and some of the political leaders for the development of democratic institutions.[20]

When Tribhuvan died on 13 March 1955, he was succeeded on the throne by his son, Mahendra Bir Bikram Shah Dev, who adopted a policy of opening the country to the outside world. In the same year, Nepal was admitted to the United Nations.

In 1961 King Mahendra instituted a system known as panchayat. A new constitution was proclaimed in 1962. King Mahendra was credited with having brought Nepal into the 20th century by having established relations with many countries. He pursued a policy of positive neutrality, nonalignment and struggle against colonialism.

In January 1972 King Mahendra died and was succeeded by his son Birendra Bir Bikram Shah Dev. Like his father, King Birendra pursued an open-door policy to the outside world and of promoting national development with foreign aid.

ECONOMIC DEVELOPMENT

Nepal is a small nation nesting on the top of the great Himalayas, having limited resources and many natural constraints. The rugged topography of the country, centuries of economic backwardness, and isolation from outside world have made planning of economic development a Himalayan task. Nepal is one of the least developed land-locked countries, the per capita income being 130 dollar in

1979. The other countries with less than 130 dollar per capita income are Kampuchea, Laos, Bhutan, Bangladesh and Chad.[21] The country's land-locked situation makes export to overseas countries difficult. The 500 miles long open border with India is both a curse and a blessing, on the one hand hindering the development of an independent economic policy and on the other providing Nepal with openings to the vast Indian market.

Nepal emerged as a unified kingdom in the late 1760's. Then for a long time it remained as a forbidden land. It was only after the political changes of 1951 that the kingdom stepped out of her isolation and started to initiate efforts for development and modernization. In 1956 the country ushered in the era of development planning and by 1980 it had already passed through four-five year plans and one three year plan.[22]

When Nepal aspired for development in the early 1950's, the kingdom was, by many indications, in a traditional way. The country had a poor resource base, domestic savings capacity was too low and modern technical know-how almost non-existent. The administrative and managerial system was in a rudimentary stage, the entire administration was virtually meant for the collection of taxes and the maintenance of law and order.

In the early 1950's, the country badly lacked economic infrastructure. The transport network consisted of about 376 km of motorable roads (mostly in Kathmandu valley). A World Bank report has summarized the economic problems of Nepal in the early 1950's as follows: "Few countries began their development as late and at such natural disadvantages as Nepal. The country emerged from a self-imposed isolation in the early 1950's, with practically no infrastructure. The country itself was only a very loosely linked services of mini-economics which most people paid little notice to what went beyond their own villages."[23]

Nepal did initiate planning of economic development in 1956. But many difficulties, such as lack of transport and communication facilities, absence of required data and skilled manpower, dearth of needed resources were on the way. In addition, the political climate was also not congenial to build up a favourable atmosphere for taking up planned economy on firm ground. Nepal, therefore, could streamline her development process only from 1962 when she launched her second development plan.

Nepal has a subsistence level agrarian economy. Over ninety per cent of the population is dependent on agriculture. Even this large manpower has not yet made agriculture productive enough to be a source of strength to the national economy. It is subsistence farming of small plots. Even in the cultivable area, which is not much, except in the Tarai, cultivation is undertaken by small families. Most of the land belongs to big land-owners. Hence most cultivators are tenants on the subsistence level of existence. The political system being feudal-cum-aristocratic, it does not force people to tighten their belts. In the name of land reforms certain measures have been passed, but these are insufficient to infuse the necessary interest in the tiller to work more and adopt new techniques.

While agricultural exports have declined, the demand for manufactured goods, machinery, transportation equipment, and fuel for development efforts has constantly increased and with it, the amount of imports. Thus, Nepal suffers the classical problem of the developing countries, export earnings from a stagnant agricultural sector provide an insufficient base to finance the growing consumer and industrial demands for imported food and manufactured products. Nepal's land-locked geographic location magnifies this problem, first, because the lack of an ocean port increases the costs and difficulties of foreign trade and second, because the long open border with India, combined with considerable dependence on India for both trade and transit of overseas trade, limits the possible economic growth strategies Nepal could pursue.

Nepal's predominantly agrarian economy does not mean that there is no trade. His Majesty's Government has adopted a policy of trade diversification and Nepal has, accordingly, entered into trade agreements with a number of countries. Most of the Nepal trade is confined to India and over ninety per cent of Nepal's international trade is with or through India. Despite the construction of Kathmandu-Kodari road, trade between China and Nepal still flows, in the main, through Calcutta because of comparatively cheap costs of transportation.[24]

The role of the industrial sector in Nepal's economy is not very significant, its contribution to the Gross Domestic Product (GDP) being only 5 per cent, as against 62 per cent of GDP contributed by agriculture.[25] It provides employment to just one per cent of the active labour force.

Immediately after the political change in 1951, rapid industrial development was expected. But only half a dozen industries were established between 1951 to 1956.

Despite the formulation of five development plans, industrial activities are still at infant stage. Industrial planning has not been effective in bringing about structural changes. The establishment of industries, however, did little to change the Nepalese economy.

The factories that were established were confined within the Tarai region. Owing to the proximity of that area to India, the factories here enjoyed better transport facilities, and they had, also, access to the markets in India.

Due to many constraints the industrial sector has played in Nepal a minor role. While for some of these problems there are no easy remedies, in other cases the problems can and must be resolved if industry is to play a major role. The two most formidable problems are the small size of the Nepalese market and the country's land-locked position.

Nonetheless, Nepal today has more than 1300 industrial houses, big and small, producing sugar, cement, ironpipes, cigarettes, jute, alcohol, furniture, biscuits, matches, soaps, shoes, wool and textiles. These industrial houses of Nepal employ little over 12,000 persons and produce goods worth about Rs. 600 million.[26]

Some of the major industries are located as follows:

1. Cigarette (Janakpur)
2. Sugar (Birganj and Bhairwa)
3. Agricultural tools (Birganj)
4. Leather and shoe (Kathmandu)
5. Brick and tile (Lalitpur and Bhaktapur)
6. Textile (Hatauda)
7. Drugs and medicines (Kathmaudu)
8. Brewery (Hatauda)
9. Cement (Kathmandu)
10. Tea—(Illam and Jhapa).[27]

In the industrialization process of Nepal, cottage and small industries play a pivotal role. The cottage industry, particularly handicrafts, has however, in recent years received a large boost. It accounts for almost 8 per cent of Nepal's total exports overseas.[28]

Blessed with geographical, historical, and cultural specialities, unique and individual, Nepal has wide prospects for tourism development. Tourism is one of the country's most important sources of foreign exchange earnings and it employs approximately 200,000 people, directly or indirectly, the year round.[29]

Nepal, which has a hydroelectric power potential of 83,000 mw is suffering from an acute power shortage which has apparently caused a great setback to industry and the whole kingdom. Electric power is basic to the economic development of the country.[30] The hydroelectric projects on Nepal's major river systems have been made possible almost entirely by Indian economic aid.

In spite of nearly a quarter of a century of economic planning, Nepal is still one of the world's poorest countries. Partly the reason for such unyielding poverty lies in the unfavourable geographic location of the country, particularly its land-locked position.

All of these factors have contributed to the present situation under which Nepal is a virtual adjunct of the Indian economy, badly exposed to developments in India that are beyond Nepal's capacity to influence, much less determine. Kathmandu's autonomy in devising economic policies is extremely limited, not only on such obvious matters as international trade but even with respect to internal questions such as land reform, currency, industrial policy and taxation.

TRANSPORT AND COMMUNICATION

Besides hindering the development of trade and industry, the lack of an interregional transport system is Nepal's great handicap in welding the country into one nation. It would be difficult to conceive of a pattern of internal transport that would more seriously hinder the achievement of political unity and coherence than does that of Napal. Most of the overland routes from Kathmandu to the outlying districts in the east and the west go across the Indian border, through Indian territory, and back into Nepal.

Being a land-locked mountainous country without any outlet to the sea, it has five means of transport: (1) Land routes, (2) Railways, (3) Ropeways, (4) Airways and (5) Inland waterways.

ROAD TRANSPORT

In Nepal some roads are useful for the whole year, some can be used only in winter and some are metallic roads laid with bitumen.

TABLE 2.1 Nepal's development plans (in millions of rupees).

Item	First Plan (1956–61)		Second Plan (1962–65)		Third Plan (1965–70)		Fourth Plan (1970-75)	
	Plan Outlay	Expenditure (Actual)	Plan Outlay	Expenditure (Actual)	Plan Outlay	Expenditure (Actual)	Plan Outlay	Expenditure (Actual)
1. Agriculture, Irrigation and Forest (including drinking water)	103.5	46.7	97.1	91.3	377.5	398.0	1171.6	720.0
2. Transport and Communications	111.5	94.9	143.5	93.5	615.0	873.0	1252.0	1364.0
3. Industry and Power	55.0	29.8	193.0	107.6	399.0	87.0	720.0	526.0
4. Social-services	44.0	37.2	78.7	95.3	272.5	239.0	381.5	621.0
5. Miscellaneous	16.0	5.9	87.7	209.1	76.0	182.0	14.7	84.0
Total	330.0	214.5	600.0	596.8	1740.0	1779.0	3540.0	3315.0

Source: 'Facts about Nepal', His Majesty's Government, Ministry of Communications, Department of Information, Nepal (Kathmandu), 1982, p. 105.

TABLE 2.2 The fifth plan (1975–80) (in millions of rupees). (Estimated outlay)*

Item	Minimum	Maximum
1. Agriculture, Irrigation, Forest, Land Reform and Erosion Control	3167.0	3570.8
2. Transport and Communications	2527.0	3385·4
3. Industry, Commerce, Power and Mines	1799.9	2040.4
4. Education, Health, Drinking Water, Panchayat and Other Social Services	1703·0	2007.4
Total	9197.0	11404.0

*Includes Public, Panchayat and Private Sector outlay.
Source: 'Facts about Nepal', His Majesty's Government, Ministry of Communications, Department of Information, Nepal (Kathmandu), 1982.

TABLE 2.3 The sixth plan (1980–85) (in millions of rupees).

Item	Public Sector	Panchayat Sector	Private Sector	Total Amount	Percentage
1. Agriculture and Forest	6260	490	3820	16570	31.1
2. Industry and Power	5280	30	3500	8810	26.0
3. Transport and Communications	4230	540	1100	5870	17.3
4. Social Services	4720	740	3230	8690	25.6
Total	20490	1800	11650	33940	100.0

Source: 'The Sixth Plan' (1980–85). A Summary, His Majesty's Government, National Planning Commission, Nepal (Kathmandu), 1981.

TABLE 2.4 Principal industrial production programmes to be undertaken in the public sector.

	Name	Unit	Target
1.	Agricultural Tools Factory (Production of different agricultural implements)	Rupees equivalent	45,000,000
2.	Agricultural Lime Factory		
	(a) Agricultural Lime	Metric Tone	10,000
	(b) Chemical Limestone	Metric Tone	55,000
3.	Birgunj Sugar Factory		
	(a) Sugar	Metric Tone	60,500
	(b) Spirit	Litre	5,300,000
4.	Janakpur Cigarette Factory		
	(a) Cigarette	Stick (in million)	12,467
5.	Bansbari Leather and Shoe Factory		
	(a) Shoes	Number	685,000
	(b) Sole Processing	Metric Tone	1,750
	(c) Leather	sq. ft.	3,700,000
6.	Harisidhi Brick and Tile Factory		
	(a) Brick	Number	132,500,000
	(b) Roofing tile	Number	3,000,000
	(c) Flooring tile	Number	1,500,000
7.	Bhaktapur Brick Factory		
	(a) Brick	Number	100,000,000
8.	Hetauda Textile Factory	Metre	34,200,000

Source: The Sixth Plan (1980–85), A Summary, His Majesty's Government, National Planning Commission, Nepal (Kathmandu), Jan., 1981, p.78.

Prior to 1956, the country had a total of 624 km of road of which only 259 km were all weather. Now the total is 3005 km. The cooperation from friendly countries like India, China, the USSR, the USA, and the UK have been significant in developing the roads in the country.[31]

Some important roads are as follows:

Tribhuban Raj Marg. This highway connects the Kathmandu valley with India in the south. This road is a vital life-line for Kathmandu because all imported or exported goods from or to India have to traverse this road.

Ariniko Raj Marg Highway. This highway links the Kathmandu valley with Tibet in the north. It was constructed with Chinese assistance. This highway is about 80 miles in length.

Sidhartha Raj Marg. The valley of Pokhra in western Nepal was accessible either, by air or by a long trek across the mountains. This highway is constructed with Indian cooperation. It will play a great role in the export of oranges and grain from the Pokhra valley.

Prithvi Raj Marg. This highway is constructed with Chinese aid, to link Pokhra with Kathmandu, the capital city. Its length is about 174 km. It is of great importance for the development of the tourist industry of Nepal.

Mahendra Raj Marg. This highway is also known as the East-West highway. The governments of Russia, India and the UK are rendering assistance in its construction. The great problems facing the construction engineers is bridge building as all the rivers in Nepal flow from the north to the south.

The other highways in the country are the Kathmandu-Trisuli (a part of Prithvi Raj Marg), the Bhakti Marg and Balabhadra Marg The Narayanghat-Gorakha highway has recently been completed. A 407 km long Surkhet-Pokhra Rajpath is also going to be constructed through Chinese aid. Similarly, Dharan-Dhankuta, Dhanagadhi-Dadeldhura and Nepalgunj-Jumla roads are also under construction. Until 1956 Kathmandu was an isolated capital having no modern surface transport link with the rest of the world.[32] A number of unpaved fair-weather roads serve the Tarai, linking the local trade marts with rail heads in India.

RAILWAYS

In Nepal there are only two narrow gauge railways. This mode of transport is in a most infantile stage and no progress has been made so far.

The Nepal Government Railway (NGR) runs from Raxaul-Birgunj to Amlekhgunj, a distance of 49 km. The other is the Nepal Jayanagar, Janakpur Railway (NJJR) starting from Jayanagar to Janakpur and Bijalpura, a distance of 54 km. The Amlekhgunj-Raxaul railway brings in goods imported from India and overseas to Amlekhgunj and carries back logs and timber. The Jankpur-Jayanagar railway carries food from Mahottari to Jayanagar and brings in goods imported from India to Janakpur. Besides that it carries pilgrimes visiting Janakpurdham. It will be splendid if this railway line can be extended as far as Sindhuli-Chisapani.[33]

This existing narrow gauge railway has not been able to cope with the increasing volume of the imports and exports of Nepal. So its extension as far as Hetauda is aimed at in the five-year plan. This plan, if it materializes, will greatly facilitate the exports and imports of Kathmandu.

The Russian experts have carried out a survey to run a railway in the Tarai region from the eastern to the western part. As hydro-electricity is being developed, it will be beneficial to Nepal, if the future railways are operated by electric energy.

ROPEWAYS (SKY CABLE WAY)

So far goods are transported by means of trucks, aeroplanes and ropeways. Among the means of transport, the ropeway is found to be cheap and easy. Formerly there was a ropeway line from Dharsing to Matatirtha in Kathmandu. At present the line runs from Hetauda to Tekudown. The United States has given aid for the development of ropeways. Another survey is being carried on to connect Dharan and Dhankuta by ropeway.

AIRWAYS

The importance of airways as a means of transport is increasing at present. As it saves a lot of time, is comfortable and also a quick means of transport, it is gaining popularity. Although it costs a lot initially it is the quickest means of transport for the country. Nepal's air transport began quite modestly with one DC-3 aircraft and a few fair-weather airfields in 1958. Air transport has developed considerably and has been instrumental in establishing regular links for many remote and inaccessible areas of the country. Nepal has one international airport—Tribhuvan airport, in Kathmandu and 39 airfields have been constructed in important parts of the country until 1980. Now more airstrips are being constructed in inaccessible hills like Darchula, Rukum, Salle, Kalikat and Mugu. The Royal Nepal Airlines Corporation (RNAC), a public undertaking, enjoys monopoly over internal and external services. RNAC operates its flights as follows:

External Flights.

1. Kathmandu–New Delhi (India)
2. Kathmandu–Patna (India)
3. Kathmandu–Calcutta (India)
4. Kathmandu–Dhaka (Bangladesh)
5. Kathmandu–Bangkok (Thailand)
6. Kathmandu–Colombo (Srilanka)

Internal Flights. In internal service RNAC has scheduled flights to Gorkha, Pokhra, Bhairwa, Biratnagar, Rajbiraj, Janakpur, Simra, Nepalganj, Dang, Bharatpur, Dhangadhi and Jhapa, etc.

The RNAC is operating small aircrafts and helicopters in its services for places with small or virtually no airstrips.

WATERWAYS

In Nepal most of the mountain rivers come down swirling, tumbling and rushing at a dangerous speed. Because of this rivers are not of any use as waterways for long distances. The rivers are crossed by means of canoes. In the west, ferry boats ply on the Buri Gandaki, the Banighat, the Garighat, the Narayani and in the east on the Kosi.

Of all the means of transport, waterways are the easiest and cheapest. Although navigation is out of the question in the mountainous region, in the plains of the Tarai, where the current is slow, the waterways of the Kosi, the Gandaki, the Karnali and other big rivers may be developed so that boats and small steamers can be plied. As all the rivers of Nepal join the Ganges which is navigable and connected with the Bay of Bengal, it is feasible to sail from the rivers of Nepal straight down to the Bay of Bengal. If this new inland waterway can be opened, the import and exports of goods can be effected easily and cheaply. The possibility of developing this waterway is receiving the attention of the government and the United Nations special fund is giving some assistance for this.

A survey, which suggests that most of the three major river (Kosi, Gandaki, Karnali) systems in the land are navigable for a part of the year upto the Ganges in Patna enjoying a year-round navigability to the mouth of the sea, notes that the cost of transport in the case of river-traffic would be brought down to one-eighth of its present cost by land route.[34]

Most of Nepal's internal and external trade is carried over by inadequate trucks. The airlines, therefore, is likely to have a big future role to play, and for non-local passenger transport, at least, air transport may become a serious competitor to road or river craft.

COMMUNICATIONS

In a country like Nepal where the bulk of the territory is mountainous, where air transport is still limited, telecommunication stands out head and shoulders above other means of communications.

Nepal's first telecommunication project was the telegraphic link of Kathmandu with Raxaul in India in 1914. The development in the field of telecommunication has been quite extensive over the years. In 1980 there were 80 wireless stations for public use in various parts of the country.[35]

A new dimension will be added in the international communication service of Nepal after the completion of the satellite communication earth station project jointly undertaken by His Majesty's Government and the British Government.

The earth station with a maximum of six channels will have

direct telecommunication link with Europe, Africa, the South-West Asian countries, Japan, and Australia through the Intelset 5 earth satellite over the Indian ocean.[36]

An Indo-Nepalese coaxial cable link was commissioned on 12 May 1983. The cable link connects Raxaul in India with Birganj in Nepal. The Patna-Muzaffarpur-Raxaul wideband microwave scheme was planned with the twin objectives of improving the national network and providing a link between India and Nepal which would be an important component of the Asian telecommunication network.[37]

Of all the available communication media the postal services and telephone exchanges have an important role in the context of diverse geographical conditions of the kingdom. Nepal has made greater progress in the postal services after the initiation of planned economic development of the country in 1956.

External communication links connect the country with many countries of the world through telegraphic, telex, or trunk telephone systems. Local and trunk telephone facilities are available in most of the large cities of the country.[38]

In Nepal economic planning and development may serve as a means of social mobilization. As economic and social development makes headway and as the means of transport and communication expand, a national economy will gradually take shape.

NEPAL'S ACCESS TO THE SEA

Nepal is one of the few countries in the world whose destiny has been determined by geography. Nepal is a land-locked state, the nearest sea-coast, approximately 575 km from the eastern border, is Calcutta in India. Nepal is surrounded on three sides by Indian territory, south, west and east, and her northern border is China (Tibet Region). The south-eastern border of Nepal is separated from Bangladesh by a narrow strip of 12 miles of Indian territory.[39]

The land-locked position of Nepal is unique. Nepal and Afghanistan the two land-locked countries of Asia are similar in many ways but different in terms of their access to the sea. While Afghanistan has four neighbours, Nepal has only two. Similarly, Switzerland, an European land-locked state can choose from among France, Austria, Italy and Germany for access to the sea. However, Nepal has no option in the choice of access to the sea. Nepal has two routes. These two routes are on the north through the People's Republic of China and on the south through India. Nepal's third option for access to the sea is through Bangladesh. China as a potential transit country is less attractive because the transport network in Tibet is not fully developed, and the major sea-ports, e.g. Sanghai or Gaungzhou are about 5,000 km away from Kathmandu. On the contrary, transit transport network in India is relatively advanced and the nearest sea-port, Calcutta is approximately 575 km from the nearest Nepalese border post. Consequently, India continues to be the sole transit country to facilitate Nepal's trade with third countries. Provisions to allow only Calcutta port as Nepal's outlet to the sea in India, limited routes and tran-shipments points represent additional constraints to the transit system.

Since 1978 Bangladesh has provided port facilities to Nepal. But Bangladesh and Nepal do not possess a common border. The two are separated by a small portion of Indian territory. Therefore, the third option of Nepal for access to the sea through Bangladesh is dependent upon India. In order to utilize the route through Bangladesh the government of India agreed to provide necessary overland transit facilities through Radhikapur. The points of entry and exit as designated by the government of the People's Republic of Bangladesh are Khulna-Chalna port, Chittagong port, Biral and Banglabandhu. There are more than three points of ports as available in Bangladesh.[40]

The three transit routes as mentioned above are related to India, China and Bangladesh. But China's route for access to the sea is not well developed. Nepal's access to the sea through China is negligible. The traffic in transit via Bangladesh is not independent, it is related to India. At last India is a potential transit country, which gives more transit facilities to Nepal for access to the sea. To facilitate Nepal's access to the sea, India and Nepal have concluded many trade and transit treaties.

For Nepal's trade with third countries, the port of Calcutta has been the entry and exit port since the 1950's. Almost all the India-Nepal border points are connected by meter-gauge railway and roads. Nepal's only means of reaching to the sea are through roads and railways. The air services which are expensive do not contribute much to trade, internal or external. The Royal Nepal Airlines Corporation (RNAC) was established as a national carrier in 1958. The

Tribhuvan international airport is the only international airport that can accommodate wide-bodied aircrafts (currently airbus) which directed linkage to Bangkok, Calcutta, Delhi, Colombo, Dhaka, Hongkong, Karachi, etc. Domestic air services of the RNAC is available at 38 places throughout Nepal. Domestic air services focus mainly on passenger traffic as is the case with the RNAC's external services, and therefore, serve very little to goods traffic.

Nepal has also a narrow gauge railway service operating in two sections—Janakpur to Jayanagar with a 29 km line and Birganj to Raxaul with a 25 km line. While the first is still in regular operation serving mainly passengers the latter is almost abondoned now due to the modern road transport available in that section.[41]

Although ropeway is regarded as a suitable transport means for a mountainous country like Nepal with potential hydro-power generations, it is still in infant stage. A bi-cable ropeway with a capacity of 25 tons per hour operates between Kathmandu and Hatauda covering a distance of 42 km. The Kathmandu-Hatauda ropeway service is potentially important and the cheapest transport to serve the Kathmandu-Birganj corridor through which majority of imports pass.[42]

Regarding the development of the inland waterways, the use of the Ganges has become a realistic possibility for Nepal. Barge transport could be the safest, as well as the least cost form of transport. Recently the Indian government announced that it is going to operate barges from Patna to Varanasi. After the completion of Farakka dam locks the route can connect Calcutta to Patna for barge traffic with possible extensions upto the Gandaki river. The inland waterways route could be cheaper by as much as about 50 per cent per ton per mile than railway freight, considering potential savings in time and damages. The Gandaki, the Koshi and the Karnali river have not yet been exploited for this purpose. So at present Nepal is not using river navigational facilities to reach out to the sea. But she is asking for such facilities to India for the access to the sea.

There are fifteen entry points on the Nepal-India border in addition to the Tribhuvan International Airport (for air route) and foreign post office, both located in Kathmandu. Nepal's trade with countries other than India passes through these fifteen border posts, which are well served by Indian railways and roads. The Birganj-

Raxaul entry points handles about 75 per cent of Nepal's imports from overseas. Most of Nepal's exports to the overseas destinations originate from the jute area of Biratnagar.[43]

Nepal is in a disadvantageous position in transit matter for access to the sea, because of its peculiar geographical conditions. In Nepal transport system is not fully developed. On account of this she has been provided with only one mode of transport, i.e. road and Indian railways. All the imported goods come from Calcutta by Indian railway upto Nepali borderpost, where from bulk imports are moved by trucks for onward transportation to Nepal.

Apart from this, Nepal's position as a landlocked state is unique in comparision with the other Asian land-locked countries. Nepal's access to the sea is only through roads and Indian railways.

NOTES

1. Facts about Nepal, HMG, Ministry of Communications, Department of Information, Kathmandu (Nepal, 1982), p. 3.
2. Ibid., pp. 3-11.
3. Ramakant, "Nepal-China and India (Nepal-China Relation)," (New Delhi, 1976), p. 31.
4. Facts about Nepal, n. 1, p. 4.
5. P.P. Karan, "The Himalayan Kingdoms: Bhutan, Sikkim and Nepal," (New Jersey, 1963), p. 81.
6. Facts about Nepal, n. 1. p. 4.
7. Ibid.
8. Ibid., p. 7.
9. Ibid., p. 13.
10. Ibid., p. 14.
11. Shriman Narayan, "India and Nepal: An Exercise in Open Diplomacy," (Bombay, 1975), p. 11.
12. Ibid., p. 12.
13. Ramakant, n. 3, p. 19.
14. Ibid.
15. Facts about Nepal, n. 1, p. 25.
16. Ibid., p. 26.
17. Ramakant, n. 3, p. 24.
18. G.P. Bhattacharjee, "India and Politics of Modern Nepal," (Calcutta, 1970), p. 204.
19. Ibid.

20. P.P. Karan, n. 5, p. 89.
21. Facts about Nepal, n. 1, p. 101.
22. Ibid.
23. The World Bank, Nepal: Development Performance and Prospects, (Washington, DC, 1979), p. I.
24. Shriman Narayan, n. 11, p. 69.
25. The Illustrated Weekly of India (Bombay, 1982), 29 August 1982, p. 11.
26. Vedanand Jha, "Nepal's Economic Development," Occasional Papers, Centre for the Study of Nepal, Department of Political Science, BHU, Varanasi, 1982, p. 7.
27. Facts abobt Nepal, n. 1, p. 122.
28. Ibid., p. 126.
29. Ibid.
30. The Sixth Plan (1980–85), A Summary, HMG, National Planning Commission, Kathmandu (Nepal, 1981), p. 92.
31. Facts about Nepal, n. 1, p. 132.
32. New York Times, 21 February 1962.
33. N.B. Thapa and D.P. Thapa, "Geography of Nepal, (Physical, Economic, Cultural and Regional)," (Bombay, 1969).
34. Manjoor World, "The Feasibility and Necessity of Waterways in Nepal," South Asia Forum, No. 4, August 1982, pp. 33-80.
35. Facts about Nepal, n. 1, p. 135.
36. Nepal News, Royal Nepalese Embassy, (New Delhi, 1982), 5 July, p. 10.
37. Times of India (New Delhi, 1983), 13 May.
38. Facts about Nepal, n. 1, p. 136.
39. Sita Shrestha, "Nepal and the United Nations," (New Delhi, 1974), p. 135.
40. Indo-Nepal Treaty of Trade-Transit Agreements of Cooperation, Trade Promotion Centre, (Kathmandu, 1978), March 1978, p. 30.
41. Kesheb P. Kaphley, "Trade Channells Systems and Procedures Country Study: Nepal," CEDA, Tribhuvan University, Kathmandu, May 1984, p. 86.
42. Ibid., pp. 86-87.
43. Ibid., pp. 80-81.

3. Nepal's Trade and Transit Problems

NEPAL'S TRADE PROBLEMS

Foreign trade plays a significant role in a country's economic development. Nepal, a small underdeveloped country is very much dependent on a single country, India for her trade and transit facilities. Except in the larger population centres, internal commerce in Nepal is largely on a barter basis. Nepal has little foreign trade with nations other than India because of three factors: (1) unstable currency which necessitates payment in Indian currency; (2) small size of Nepal's demand for goods manufactured outside India; and (3) its dependence on Indian railways and sea-ports for shipment from abroad.[1]

Historically, Nepal's trade was confined to India along the southern, eastern, and western borders and Tibet the autonomous region of China on the northern border. During the Rana regime Nepalese government representatives were stationed in Lhasa (Tibet) and Calcutta (India) for commercial counselling. The overseas trade was prohibited as a matter of policy to keep the country isolated from the world. Nepal's trade with the third countries started only in 1951 after the fall of the Ranas.[2]

More than 90 per cent of Nepal's export and imports were from India. Nepal's trade with Tibet account for only about 1 per cent of the total. Regarding the overseas trade, no separate account was available till 1961–62 because the goods were first exported to India and then re-exported to the overseas countries.[3]

TRADE DIVERSIFICATION

Nepal's real problem is that it is a land-locked state, and almost for its entire international trade it depends on the southern routes through India. As for industrialization, only some small beginnings have been made. Napalese leaders realize that if Nepal is to be really independent this utter dependence on India must be reduced. With the royal take over in December 1960, King Mahendra made a determined effort to diversify Nepal's foreign trade and thus reduce its dependence on India. Both for political and economic reasons, Nepal decided to follow a policy of trade diversification. Nepal, therefore, has established trade relations with a large number of countries, including her neighbours, China and Pakistan. Today Nepal has entered into bilateral trade agreements with 14 countries, such as Bangladesh, Bulgaria, China, Egypt, India, N. Korea, S. Korea, Pakistan, Poland, Srilanka, UK, USSR, USA and Yugoslavia.[4]

To some extent Nepal has became successful to diversify her foreign trade and has reduced the concentration of trade with India. Still the larger portion of her foreign trade is confined with India.

Since 1960 Nepal has been consistently insisting that she, as a land-locked country, should be given the right to enjoy unrestricted transit facilities. In his address to the 22nd session of the UN General assembly, King Mahendra observed: "A small land-locked country like Nepal... is particularly, handicapped in respect of trade and development. Unless we have proper facilities of trade and transit, we cannot develop even internally and we cannot certainly develop our international trade. It is our feeling that the understanding in this direction has to be faster and deeper."[5]

Nepal's main trade problems can be put as, firstly, a continuing trade concentration both in terms of market and commodity exports, and, secondly, increasing deficits in its balance of trade. Both of the problems are likely to linger for some time to come. Since they are structural in nature, they are long term problems that require long term remedies for their solution. In view of the trade concentration by market, trade diversification has been put forward as a solution to all problems and has been stressed as one of the cherished objectives in the past several development plans. However, it appears that there has not been any significant movement towards that goal and Nepal's foreign trade concentration in terms of both commodity and market has remained virtually the same.

EXPORTERS EXCHANGE ENTITLEMENT SCHEME

An important policy instrument adopted to diversify Nepal's trade was the "Exporters Exchange Entitlement Scheme" initiated in the year 1960.[6] The objective behind the scheme was to increase exports to third countries rather than India through the provision of generous incentives for exports to third countries. At the outset the exporters had complete freedom to import any commodity of their choice from overseas countries out of the foreign exchange earnings availabe to them. However, they were authorized to utilize only 25 per cent of export earnings for the purpose. Subsequently, these ratios underwent frequent modifications and ultimately Nepal introduced in January 1974 a new differential entitlement scheme under which 25 per cent of the bonus earned had to be used to import "development goods" needed for agriculture, transport and communication; 50 per cent entitlement was on "consumers goods", and 25 per cent on "luxury goods" like motor vehicles, etc.[7]

Though the "Exporter's Exchange Entitlement Scheme" gave an initial flllip to trade with overseas countries, for obvious reasons the policy failed to yield the desired results. The scheme stressed only the geographical aspect of diversification without consideration to commodity diversification. The incentives thus granted to the industries exporting to countries other than India also led to a distortion in the country's allocation of resources in unforeseen ways.

The year 1978 was very significant as many substantial changes were introduced in this year in Nepal's external trade system. They involved the abolition of the "Exporters Exchange Entitlement Scheme," the introduction of a system of two-tier exchange rates, the liberalization of the traffic of goods, and the devaluation of the Nepalese rupee vis-a-vis the US dollar, and various import duty charges. These steps reflected the government's determination to accelerate the country's industrialization and encourage the export of surplus products.

In the fifties almost all the Nepal's foreign trade was with India, and only nominally (around 1 per cent) with Tibet. The trade volume during the late seventies shows significant diversification. For example, in 1977–78 the total volume of trade with India was only 58 per cent.[8] As regards export trade, agricultural products account for over 75 per cent because of the fact that Nepal is an exporter of primary products and importer of manufactured goods and capital goods. The magnitude of trade deficit has been rising at an increasing pace. The trade deficit of Nepal for 1956–57 was around $ 6.22 million. This deficit increased to $ 67.71 million within twenty years. Imports exceeded exports by $ 199.38 million in the year 1979–80.[9]

According to statistics released by the Trade Promotion Centre (TPC), Nepal's exports amounted to Rs. 1131.04 million in 1982–83, and imports to Rs. 6106.34 million. Thus, leaving a record deficit of Rs. 4975.3 million. The report added, exports declined by 23.2 per cent in that year, whereas imports increased by 27.6 per cent, 25.6 per cent of the total exports trade, and 58.4 per cent of the total imports trade, was conducted with overseas countries.[10]

Nepal's trade with India and Tibet in 1982–83 was as given in Table 1.

TABLE 3.1 Nepal's trade with India and Tibet, 1982–83 (in million rupees).

	India	Tibet (China)
Exports	829.74 (73.4)*	11.6 (1)*
Imports	2519.96 (41.2)*	22.29 (0.4)*
Deficit Rs.	1690.21 mn.	10.69 mn.

*Percentage of total trade.
Source: Nepal Press Digest (Kathmandu), 23 January 1984, p. 35.

Nepal's trade with South Asian countries during the year 1982–83 is given in Table 2.

TABLE 3.2 Nepal's trade with South Asian Countries, 1982–83 (in rupees '000).

Country	Exports	Imports
India	829.748	2,519,961
Bangladesh	621	43,092
Pakistan	Nil	2,750
Srilanka	4	3,312
Bhutan	134	20
Maldives	Nil	1

Source: Nepal Press Digest (Kathmandu), 9 April 1984.

India is Nepal's largest trading partner. In 1981–82, out of Nepal's total imports of Rs. 4,930.3 million India's share was Rs. 2280.9 million, and out of Nepal's total exports of Rs. 1491.5 million, India's share was Rs. 994.4 million. Major Nepalese exports to India are raw jute and jute products, maize, medicinal herbs, dry-ginger and timber. Nepal imports are mostly manufactured goods, such as machines, transport equipments, drugs, petroleum products, coal, cement and iron-pipes, etc.

However, foreign trade of Nepal, more or less depends upon the economic relations with India. India could not set aside this fact even while Nepal wants to conduct her trade with the countries other than India. It is only that when India provides the free and unrestricted transit facilities that the trade diversification with other countries is possible.

NEPAL'S TRANSIT PROBLEMS

Nepal's transit problems are of recent origin because in the past her trade with overseas countries was negligible. Since 1960 she has been insisting for the recognition of the 'right of free transit' which is an integral part of the international law. Because of geographical position, Nepal does not have more access routes to the sea as other land-locked countries have. In north transit through China is still a hypothetical question as there is no transit agreement between Nepal and China. The Kathmandu-Kodari road, on which much hope for the growth of trade with Tibet had been based has practically not been used for commercial purposes. By contrast, the transit route to the sea-coast of India is relatively advanced and the closest sea-port Calcutta is approximately 575 km from the nearest Nepali border post.[11] Consequently, India continues to be the sole transit country to facilitate Nepal's trade with third countries.

All Nepal border points are served by the Indian metre-gauge railway whereas the Calcutta port is connected by the broad-gauge railway. That means all imported traffics in transit need to be transferred from one railway gauge to another requiring, thereby, double handling with charges of loss, pilferage, damage and delays. Compared to a normal journey time of seven days, the railway takes weeks and even months to complete the journey from Calcutta port to Nepal border.

TABLE 3.3 Direction of Nepal's foreign Trade (value in '000 Rs.).
F.Y. 1978–79 to 1983–84.

Fiscal	Export				Import			
Year	India	Overseas	Tibet	Total	India	Overseas	Tibet	Total
1978–79	650100	849515	25860	1525745	1581800	1448908	15316	3046024
	(42.62)	(55.69)	(1.69)	(100.00)	(51.93)	(47.57)	(0.50)	(100.00)
1979–80	520935	780605	23797	1325337	1786406	1885585	20262	3692253
	(39.31)	(58.90)	(1.79)	(100.00)	(48.38)	(51.07)	(0.55)	(100.00)
1980–81	992390	604659	68279	1665328	2179047	2397811	17282	4594140
	(59.59)	(36.31)	(4.10)	(100.00)	(47.43)	(52.19)	(0.38)	(100.00)
1981–82	994348	462307	16982	1473637	2280877	2516797	8745	4806419
	(67.48)	(31.37)	(1.15)	(100.00)	(47.65)	(52.17)	(0.18)	(100.00)
1982–83 ^{R}	843314	289692	11600	1144606	2499595	3564086	22295	6085976
	(73.7)	(25.3)	(1.0)	(100.00)	(41.0)	(58.6)	(0.4)	(100.00)
1983–84 ^{P}	598073	202214	20419	820706	1402279	1671128	20014	3093421
(First six months)	(72.9)	(24.6)	(2.5)	(100.00)	(45.3)	(54.0)	(0.7)	(100.00)

R = Revised.
P = Provisional.
Source: Nepal Overseas Trade Statistics (1982–83), Trade Promotion Centre and Nepal Rastra Bank.

Air transportation has not yet opened out the possibilities of Nepal's desire to have direct contacts with the third countries to promote her exports. Thus, air services which are expensive do not contribute much to the trade, internal or external. Various airlines like the Union of Burmese Airlines, the Thai International Airlines are operating their services, while the Royal Nepal Airlines has extended its services to Sri Lanka and Thailand. The possibility of carrying the goods with high value and less weight like handicrafts has not yet come out as expected.

The mode of river transport might be helpful in Nepal's trade. But the three major rivers the Gandaki, the Koshi, and the Karnali have not yet been expoilted for this purpose.

The Nepalese traders are still unhappy about the delay in the movement of the Nepalese goods bound for the third countries. The delay results from congestion at Calcutta port which requires the Nepalese traders to spend millions of rupees in demurrages and wharfages besides suffering damage to and loss of goods in transit. Nepal is not happy about the following transit procedures.[12]

1. Allocation of space for unloading and storing goods in transit is not satisfactory to meet the increasing requirements of Nepal, problems of storing come up when goods are received in excess of the availability. When goods are stored outside, shipments cannot be made immediately because it is difficult to locate the goods.

2. Under the prevalent transit systems, the Jogbani railway station which is the main transhipment point is not allowed to accept the goods from Nepal until such time it receives intimation to that effect, and until bookings of the Nepalese goods are allowed by the dock manager at the Calcutta port. When the permission for bookings is obtained from the docks it has to be submitted to the nearby Indian railway station by the exporters, which in turn asks for further permission from the district headquarters.

3. Shipping formalities are always lengthy.

4. Sometimes the exporters have to pay the shut-out rent if the goods are accidently unloaded in the shipping yard. The shut-out rent is generally 7 to 9 times higher than the normal rent on the goods kept in store shed allocated to Nepal. Thus, the Nepalese shippers have to pay additional charges for nothing. Even the Nepal warehouses and transit companies have not been much helpful to traders due to many reasons.

5. Another irritation is that the Nepalese exporters have to present the export licence at the Calcutta customs. Nepal's customs have also started to examine the licence.

6. Steamer agents reject the Nepalese goods on the grounds of low ocean freight export. This arises on such commodities as jute cuttings, oil cakes, etc. This results in the prolonged storage of the Nepalese goods which make the Nepalese traders to pay mounting rents.

7. Curriers and handicrafts sent to the overseas countries are examined by the Archaeology Department of the Government of India and by other officials of India.

8. Transport of goods by trucks, except in special circumstances, is not allowed. This has resulted in the dislocation of Nepal's foreign market because the delayed shipments are affecting Nepal's exports.

The primary source of transit problems is the inadequate and antiquated infrastructures and services along the transit corridors which reflect the developing status and resource constraints of transit countries. A number of direct charges such as demurrage, triple rent, port rent, removal changes, etc. are imposed on imports in addition to indirect charges in the form of delays, damages, losses and pilferages. All these amount to high cost of transit transport.[13]

Since India has never denied Nepal transit rights in conducting trade with the third countries, Nepal is seeking additional port feasible transit routes and other arrangements which would reduce her transit cost.

CHOICE OF TRANSIT ROUTES

Nepal and Afghanistan, the two land-locked countries of Asia, are similar in many respects but there is a difference between them in terms of their access to the sea. While Afghanistan has four neighbours, Nepal has only two. Similarly, Switzerland, an European land-locked state, can choose from among France, Austria, Italy and Germany for access to the sea. However, Nepal has no option in the choice of transit routes. In the north side China's transit transport network is not developed and the sea port is far away from the Nepalese Capital. So there is no question of transit routes through the northern side. On the contrary in south, India is a potential country and transit transport network is well developed and the sea port is nearer to the Nepalese capital. The third option as explored within a few years is through Bangladesh. Bangladesh is not touched by the borders of Nepal. There is a little distance to be covered in India in crossing from Bangladesh to Nepal. Therefore, the third option of Nepal for transit through Bangladesh is mostly related to India. In order to utilize the route through Bangladesh the government of India agreed to provide necessary overland transit facilities through Radhikapur.[14] Since 1978 Nepal is using Bangladesh seaport also. So Nepal's choice of transit route is only through India, although Nepal is using the Bangladesh sea port also but it is related to India's consent. So in the choice of transit routes Nepal is handicapped in comparison to the other land-locked states. Nepal is fully dependent upon India on the matter of transit facilities.

Transit Routes via Indian Ports. Nepal is carrying her overseas trade through the Indian port of Calcutta and Haldia.

Calcutta. Calcutta is the nearest sea port to Nepal's border and thus the most logical from a geographic standpoint for its export and imports with the third countries. Almost all the formally, authorized Nepal-India border points are connected with Calcutta by railway or roads. Many shortcomings make this port very costly for Nepal's exports and imports of goods in transit, for instance, serious congestion at port, labour unrest, inadequate storage and warehousing facilities, etc.

Haldia. The use of Haldia port for the Nepalese export and import to and from the third countries is formally accepted by India according to the treaty of trade and transit of 1978.

TRANSIT TRANSPORT VIA BANGLADESH

According to the treaty of trade and transit 1976 between Nepal and Bangladesh, the government of Bangladesh has agreed to provide the following entry and exit points by all available means of transportation for Nepal's transit goods.

(a) Khulna-Chalna port
(b) Chittagong port

(c) Biral
(d) Banglabandhu
(e) Chihati
(f) Bonapale

Road Distances from Calcutta to Nepal's Border Point, via Prevailing Routes, 1980

Calcutta–Bambasa	1464 km
Calcutta–Nepalganj	1238 km
Calcutta–Jarwa	1182 km
Calcutta–Nautanwa	1033 km
Calcutta–Raxaul	872 km
Calcutta–Jayanagar	788 km
Calcutta–Biratnagar	575 km
Calcutta–Kakavita	544 km
Calcutta–Pasupatinagar	604 km

Distance Bangladesh Routes[15]

From	*To*	*Via*	*km*
(a) *Railway* (*Meter-gauge*)			
Chittagong	Jogabani	Biral/Radhikapur	958
Chittagong	Raxaul	Biral/Radhikapur	1242
Narayanganj	Jogabani	Biral/Radhikapur	630
Tistamukhghat	Jogabani	Biral/Radhikapur	189
(b) *Broadgauge*			
Khulna	Katihar	Rohanpur/Singhabad	491
Goalundaghat	Katihar	Rohanpur/Singhabad	405
Paksey	Katihar	Rohanpur/Singhabad	256
Khulna	New Jalpaiguri	Rohanpur/Singhabad	630
Khulna	Narayanpur Anant	Rohanpur/Singhabad Farraka	680
Khulna	Narayanpur	Darsana/Gede	761
(c) *Broad-meter-gauge carb*			
Khulna	Jogabani	Parbatipur, Biral/ Radhikapur	664
Road:			
Khulna	Biratnagar	Bonapal Petrapal	664

Waterways:

Chittagong—Tistamukhghat, approx. 15 days round trip
Chittagong—Paksey, approx. 13 days round trip
Chittagong—Goalundaghat, approx. 8 days round trip

Chittagong—Narayanganj (Dacca), approx. 6 days round trip
Chittagong—Khulna, approx. 12 days round trip
Chalna—Khulna, approx. 5 hours (one way)
Chalna—Tistamukhghat, approx. 16 days round trip
Chalna—Narayanganj, 36–48 hours

The distance to the Chittagong port in Bangladesh by railway is longer by over 300 km than to Calcutta from the eastern Nepal border. The chief advantage of using the Chittagong port is that it does not require any transhipment as the route is entirely served by the metergauge railway upto Nepal borders. The other major attraction of the Bangladesh routes is that the port charges in Chittagong account for only about 13 per cent of the Calcutta port charges. On the whole, the Bangladesh route appears comparatively cheaper but is not at present used regularly on account of the other inconveniences, for instance, goods transfer from meter-gauge to broad-gauge, pilferage, damages and delays. Therefore, the route via the Calcutta port remains as the principal inlet for Nepal's imports.[16]

Table 4 shows the selected port charges at Calcutta, Chittagong and Chalna.

India being the only transit country, Nepal has concluded many trade and transit treaties with her for all round development.

TRADE AND TRANSIT TREATIES BETWEEN NEPAL AND INDIA

The Indo-Nepalese trade and economic relations are the product of the age-old cultural, geographic and economic ties that existed between the two countries ever since the dawn of civilization in this subcontinent. During the British rule of India, Nepal was given certain trade and transit facilities. There was no particular trade agreement between Nepal and British India before 1923.

THE 1923 TREATY

On 21 December 1923, a treaty was signed between Nepal and British India. According to this treaty, it was agreed that:

"The British government will grant in respect of all trade goods, imported at British Indian ports for immediate transmission to Kathmandu without breaking bulk in route of a rebate of the fully

TABLE 3.4 **Selected port charges*** Calcutta, Chittagong, Chalna (cost in Indian Rs. per million ton).

Heads of Expenditure	Commodities								
	Cement			Fertilizer			Iron Rod		
	Cal.	Chittg.	Chalna	Cal.	Chittg.	Chalna	Cal.	Chittg.	Chalna
River dues	—	2.79	2.46	—	2.79	2.46	—	2.79	2.46
Landing charge	28.00	3.57	4.13	32.00	3.57	4.13	114.30	3.57	4.13
Londing/Unloading charge	17.00	12.40	12.40	17.00	12.40	12.40	80.00	12.40	12.40
Crane & hoisting	—	—	—	—	—	—	157.00	7.14	7.14
Port rent per day	15.00	5.81	5.81	15.00	5.81	5.81	15.00	5.81	5.81
Stevedoring charge	99.20	8.27	6.26	99.20	8.27	7.82	131.00	13.63	6.26

*In effect Jan. 1974 at Calcutta, mid-1973 at Bangladesh Ports.

Source: A.K. Shrestha, "Transit Treaty Provisions and Their Impact on Nepal's Transit Trafic Costs," UNDP/UNCTAD, Kathmandu, August 1984, p.37, NEP/82/002.

duty paid, provided such goods may break bulk for repacking at the entry under customs supervision in accordance with such rules as may from time to time be laid down on this behalf.[17]

This was perhaps for the first time that Nepal was given the right to import, free of duty, all goods through India. Article 5 of the treaty granted the right to import from or through British India, whatever arms, ammunition, machinery, warlike material or stores Nepal needed, provided the intentions of the government are friendly and there is no immediate danger to India from such importations.

Article 6 stipulated that no customs duty shall be levied at the British Indian ports on goods imported on behalf of the Nepal Government for immediate transfer to that country. It was further arranged that a certificate has to be presented on behalf of the Nepal government at the port of import and that such goods are not meant for 'state monopoly' or 'state trade' but for 'public services'.

After the treaty of 1923 between Nepal and British India, Nepal could not develop any significant international trade, and even with India its trade did not exceed Rs. 8.2 crores till 1945.[18] The reason was that the general policy of the Rana government was to avoid close economic contacts with the British government. The Ranas feared that such contacts would bring British influence into the Kingdom. For this reason, they did not even pay attention to the improvement of communication and transport links with her southern neighbour.

INDO-NEPAL TREATY OF TRADE AND COMMERCE, 1950

After India became independent a new treaty of trade and commerce was signed between Nepal and India on 31 July 1950. The new treaty favoured Nepal to enjoy the "full and unrestricted right of commercial transit of all goods and manufactures through any Indian port and territory" (Article I). It agreed to "allow all goods at any Indian port and intended for re-export to Nepal to be transmitted to such place or places in Nepal as may be approved by the two governments, without breaking bulk 'enroute' and without payment of any duty at any 'Indian port' " (Article II). Furthermore, it was agreed to give every reasonable facility for the import and export of commodities and in particular to facilitate the use of routes and methods of transportation which were most economical and convenient.[19]

Although the spirit of the treaty was most favourable to Nepal as far as commercial transit was concerned, Nepal could hardly utilize the advantages given by the treaty in the absence of adequate means and policies to conduct any significant amount of international trade. In the light of this factor there was no specific provisions regarding 'traffic in transit', no prescribed procedures, documentary requirements and regulations were laid down. Thus, the treaty of 1950, in effect, remained as a treaty of trade only.

INDO-NEPAL TRADE AND TRANSIT TREATY (1960)

This treaty was signed on 11th September 1960 and replaced the previous treaty. The main objectives of the treaty were to expand the mutual trade, to encourage collaboration in economic development and facilitate Nepal's trade with the third countries. This treaty was more complex and restrictive in comparision to its predecessor. In order to regulate freedom of transit through Indian territory specific details regarding the terms 'traffic in transit' and related procedures, documents and regulations were added.[20]

The key clauses of the treaty fell into three broad categories. Articles I to IV regulated the Indo-Nepalese trade procedure, while Articles V and VI were related to Nepal's trade with the third countries. The remaining Articles were meant to regulate transit facilities provided by India to Nepal.[21]

The treaty was indeed a marked improvement over the treaty of 1950 and proved beneficial to both the countries in several ways. The treaty of 1950 had put limitations on Nepal's trade with the third countries, whereas the treaty of 1960 recognized that Nepal could conduct its international trade without India's intermediary role. Nepal was also given better transit facilities at the Calcutta port. The government of India agreed to arrange for more space at the Calcutta port where Nepal could store all such goods which were in transit to or from Nepal.[22]

Hardly a few months after the operation of the treaty of trade and transit, the Royal take-over took place, which created a political dead-lock between New Delhi and Kathmandu for about two years. In May 1961, discussions were held between the officials of the two countries in New Delhi to remove certain difficulties arising out of the working of the treaty of 1960.[23] One of the difficulties of the Nepalese traders was regarding the 'Bond System'.

THE BOND SYSTEM

Under this system, the Nepalese importer or his agent was required to furnish a bond to the Indian customs house in the form prescribed by the Collector of Customs with the surety of a bank of standing, binding him to pay the duty and penalty for 'Contraven Importing Trade Control Restrictions' on any portion of the consignment that was not proven to have duly entered Nepal.[24] The bond amount asked from the Nepalese importers in some cases was as much as 600% of the value of the goods imported. This naturally created resentment among the Nepalese traders and they demanded modification in the system. Ultimately, with effect from 1 December 1963 the Bond System had to be abolished in view of the growing Nepalese demands.

SPACE AT THE CALCUTTA PORT

Nepal needed self-contained area at the sea-port where Nepal could protect her goods against loss and damage. The existing space at the Calcutta port was insufficient, although India had promised to give a separate shed to Nepal as stated in the trade and transit treaty of 1960. It was agreed to provide a separate shed, the central storage shed at Calcutta wherein all goods in transit (other than hazardous goods) might be stored. As a matter of fact, there was no sufficient warehousing facilities at the Calcutta port. Other commodities lay outside the warehouse exposed to the vagaries of the weather.[25] Studies had been made by Indian and Nepalese representatives regarding facilities on European ports of Roterdam and Hamburg, but no action has been taken.

PROCEDURES AND DOCUMENTATION

The 1960 Treaty in its memorandum set forth detailed procedures and documentation for transit goods at the entry/exit points. The principal provisions are as follows:

1. Clearance of goods in transit was permitted only against

import/export licences issued by His Majesty's Government (HMG) of Nepal and supplied to the Collector of Customs with the specimen signature of His Majesty's Government (HMG) officers who are authorized to sign them. Thus, the copy of the licence produced by the importer/exporter at Calcutta is compared with the copy received from His Majesty's Government (HMG), Nepal.

2. Four copies of the invoice, bill of entry, and import licence were required by the customs house, Calcutta for examining goods to check whether they matched descriptions in the documents. After extensive examination of the packages, they were then sealed with Indian customs seals. The wagons carrying transit goods were also sealed by the railways and the customs. The invoice and the import licence were endorsed by the Calcutta customs and forwarded to the border customs post. On arrival of goods at the transfer points and border customs post, they were again reinspected thoroughly. After such examination of goods, the traffic in transit was allowed to proceed and the copies of the invoice were signed accordingly. Finally, the invoice and the import licence were endorsed by the Nepal customs certifying the arrival of goods in Nepal. Thus, a series of endorsements on the invoice was necessary making the procedure complicated and time consuming.[26]

SEARCH FOR ALTERNATIVE ROUTES

On 19 October 1962 Pakistan assured Nepal of port and transit facilities for its trade with the third countries through Pakistan territory.[27] But the diversification of trade depends on India's co-operation. In August 1963, Nepal officially demanded the transit facilities at Radhikapur and Waga on India's border with the then East and West wings of Pakistan.[28] In the first meeting India had agreed in principle to provide such facilities and requested the Nepalese government to indicate the expected volume of trade, requirements of wagons, and the points of destination so as to enable authorities in India to determine the nature and quantum of facilities to be provided.[29]

In a meeting held on 27 November 1964, India agreed to provide transit facilities to Nepal, if the latter was ready to bear the cost of such facilities. However, the Nepalese delegation took an uncompromising stand and maintained that like Calcutta, no service charges should be levied at all for the supervision and handling.

This resulted into a deadlock between the two sides.[30] Ultimately, India compromised and during the visit of the Indian Commerce Minister, Manubhai Shah to Nepal in January 1965, it was agreed that the desired facilities would be provided to Nepal at Radhikapur for nominal rail service charges.[31] But before any such movement of goods could start Radhikapur route was dislocated due to the disruption of railway lines during the Indo-Pak war of September 1965. Hence, Nepal-Pak trade virtually did not operate at all through these transit channels.

SMUGGLING

Nepal has 500 miles of open border with India. There is no restriction on movement of men and commodities between them. This procedure was good as long as Nepal was not given the option to trade with the third countries. But according to the treaty of 1960 Nepal was given this facility and it was decided that goods 'originating' in Nepal were only permissible in India. However, the Bonus voucher scheme introduced by Nepal encouraged deflection of trade. The scheme was technically known as an 'Import Entitlement Scheme' for Nepalese exporters to trade with the third countries other than India.

Indian goods of various kinds were smuggled on a large scale into Nepal via such border towns as Biratnagar. Moreover, a number of articles, such as transistors, silk cloth, terylene garments, watches, pens, cameras, etc. began to appear in the Indian market from Nepal which were actually manufactured in China, Japan, Hongkong and other countries. These items are smuggled by Indian merchants. It was reported that jute, rice, wheat, petrol, pulses, kerosene oil, etc. are smuggled into Nepal from India. This appeared to be an insurmountable point with regard to the export of synthetic fabrics and stainless steel from Nepal which Nepal was actually importing and whose import was banned in India by the Indian government. Large quantities of these commodities imported by Nepal found their way into India through smuggling. The smuggling problems were raised and discussed in a number of Indo-Nepalese trade conferences, but they continued to plague the friendly political relations of the two countries.

The 1960 treaty of trade and transit marked a definite improvement upon its predecessor in so far as it made provision for a special shed in the port of Calcutta for the temporary storage of Nepalese customs officers in Calcutta and Barauni, the major transhipment points between the Indian broad-gauge and meter-gauge railways. However, the provision for the requirement the importer and exporter post 'a bond with suitable guarantee' that the goods will not be diverted enroute turned out to be a hindrance for the promotion of Nepal's trade. Ultimately, on the persistent demand of the Nepalese the bond system was abolished three years later. The 1960 treaty sought to meet the criticism against the earlier treaty.

THE TREATY OF TRADE AND TRANSIT, 1971

The treaty signed on 13 August 1971 was similar to the previous treaty of 1960 in several respects and formalized additional restrictions.

According to a joint communique published after its being signed said that "the new treaty embodies the desire of the two governments to strengthen mutual economic cooperation and develop their economies for their several and mutual benefit as well as to facilitate transit of trade with third countries."

In the field of 'Trade' the treaty aims at the expansion and diversification of the mutual trade of the two countries in goods produced in their territories. Most favoured nation treatment will be accorded by both countries to each other's products. The primary products of Nepal will have unrestricted entry into the Indian market, without any obligation to pay customs duties. In order to promote the industrial development of Nepal, India has extended special favourable treatment on a non-reciprocal basis to goods manufactured in Nepal with Nepali or Indian raw materials. Such manufactured goods will have access to the entire Indian market without any quantitative restriction and without the obligation to pay customs duties. Concessions in excise duties available to small industrial units in India will be made available also to products imported from similar units in Nepal. Other manufactured goods which may have third country materials will receive favourable treatment if the value of Nepali materials and labour added is at least 50% of the ex-factory value of the product. The nature and extent of excess to the Indian market and tariff reference to be given to such products will be decided on the merits of each case after taking all relevant factors into consideration.[32]

The treaty permitted HMG to impose duties on Indian products on most favoured nation basis. Excise and other duties collected by the government of India on goods exported to Nepal would be refunded directly to HMG to the extent of the import duty chargeable on similar goods in Nepal. With regard to the problem of deflection of trade, both countries have agreed to cooperate effectively with each other to prevent infringement and circumvention of foreign exchange and foreign trade laws and regulations. An understanding has been reached on the areas of cooperation to prevent deflection of trade. Each country will prohibit the export from its territory of the products of the other country as well as of products made mainly from raw materials of the other country. Each country will take effective measures to enforce the ban. Similarly, re-exports to the other country of goods imported from the third countries and all goods which contain materials from third countries in excess of 50% of the ex-factory value of products are prohibited. Provisions were made for mutually acceptable overland routes to be used by the two countries within the framework of regional co-operation arrangements among the concerned countries. Provisions were also made for the transport of goods between Calcutta and Nepal by road. The communique, in addition, stated that the warehousing and other facilities available to Nepal would be considerably augmented and that customs procedures had been simplified.[33]

The 'Transit' provisions of the treaty were that both Nepal and India shall accord to traffic in transit freedom of transit across their respective territories through routes mutually agreed upon. Each side shall have the right to take all indispensable measures to ensure that such freedom does not in any way infringe its legitimate interests of any kind. Such traffic in transit shall be exempted from customs duties and all transit duties or other charges except reasonable charges for transportation and other services. The government of India will provide warehouse or sheds for the storage of Nepal's transit cargo. Passage of goods from one place to another in the territories of each side through the territories of the other shall be subject to such arrangements as may be mutually agreed upon. Both sides shall prohibit and take effective measures to prevent re-export of goods imported from the other side or from the third countries, as well as of products which contained imports from the third countries exceeding 50% of the ex-factory value. Merchant ships sailing under the flag of Nepal shall be accorded, subject to India's laws and regulations, treatment no less favourable than that accorded to ships of any other foreign country. But this provision shall not extend to coastal trade.

During the negotiations Nepal placed emphasis on securing a number of gains such as, (1) that there should be separate treaties covering trade and transit, (2) that there should be a trade route to East Pakistan (now Bangladesh) through the Indian territory of Radhikapur in Dinajpur district of West Bengal, (3) that qualitative and quantitative restrictions on Nepal's imports from the third countries and its export to India should be removed, (4) that the customs procedures should be simplified, (5) that the additional warehouse space in the port of Calcutta should be treated as a free port zone and should be placed under Nepali supervision, (6) that there should be facilities for operating barges in the Calcutta port and for transporting commercial goods from the Calcutta port to the destination in Nepal by sealed container trucks, and (7) that there should be the same kind of treatment to ships with Nepali flags in the Indian port as that given to the Indian ships.[34]

Freedom of transit was conditioned by taking all indispensable measures to ensure that such freedom did in no any way infringe on India's legitimate interests of any kind (Article VIII). Furthermore, the provision to comply with 'procedures prescribed' again appeared in Article XII as in the treaty of 1960. The intent was to prevent the diversion of transit goods enroute, but varied interpretations subsequently resulted in unnecessary delays which in practice made the transit system more restrictive and costly. In addition to such vague provisions, the following changes were made in the 1971 Treaty.

TRANSIT ROUTES

Transit routes and modes were more clearly prescribed. Nepal's traffic in transit was allowed to use only one access port, Calcutta. The use of road transport was restricted to goods belonging to HMG agencies and Nepal had to rely on the services of Indian railways for the bulk of her trade with the third countries. Border stations permitted to service transit goods (via Calcutta) included,

Galgalia, Jogbani, Bhimnagar, Jayanagar, Raxaul, Nautanwa, Barhni, Nepalganj Road, Gauriphanta, Banbasa and Sukhia Pokhari.

TABLE 3.5 Authorized Indo-Nepal Trade Routes and Points (entry and exit).

S.No.	Land customs station	Routes
1.	Jogbani	Road connecting Jogbani and Biratnagar in Nepal
2.	Jayanagar	Railway line connecting Jayanagar and Janakpur in Nepal
3.	Raxaul	Road and railway line connecting Raxaul and Birganj in Nepal
4.	Galgalia	Road connecting Galgalia and Bhadrapur in Nepal
5.	Nirmali	Road connecting Nirmali Kanhauli and Raj Biraj in Nepal
6.	Bairgania	Road connecting Bairgania and Gaur in Nepal
7.	Bikhanathori	Road connecting Bikhanathori and Thori in Nepal
8.	Sonbarsa	Road connecting Sonbarsa and Sarlahi in Nepal
9.	Nautanwa	Road connecting Nautanwa Sonauli and Bhairwa in Nepal
10.	Nepalganj	Road connecting Nepalganj road (Rupaidhia) and Nepalganj in Nepal
11.	Tanakpur	Road connecting Tanakpur, Banbasa, Mahendra Nagar in Nepal
I2.	Pithoragarh	Road connecting Pithorgarh and Jhulaghat in Nepal
13.	Tikonia	Road connecting Tikonia and Rajapur in Nepal
14.	Barhani	Road connecting Barhani and Krishnanagar in Nepal
15.	Shoharatgarh	Road connecting Shoharatgarh and Taulihwa in Nepal

16.	Gauriphanta	Road connecting Gauriphanta and Triagar in Nepal
17.	Jarwa	Road connecting Jarwa and Koilabas in Nepal
18.	Sukhiapokhari	Road connecting Sukhiapokhari and Phalehung in Nepal
19.	Bhimanagar	Road connecting Bhimanagar and Bhantawari in Nepal
20.	Naxalbari	Road connecting Naxalbari and Kakarbhita in Nepal
21.	Sursand	Road connecting Sursand, Bhitamore and Jaleswar in Nepal
22.	Katarniaghat	Road connecting Katarniaghat and Rajapur Mandi in Nepal

Source: N.P. Banskota, "Indo-Nepal Trade and Economic Relations," B.R. Publishing Corporation, Delhi, 1981, pp.65-66.

STORAGE SPACE

The Government of India designated transit goods storage on the first floor of 7 Calcutta Jetty shed (approximately 62,775 sq ft), first floor of 25 Berth Kidderpore Dock shed (approximately 48,000 sq ft), half of first floor of 2 Garden Reach Jetty shed (approximately 47,000 sq ft) and open space west of the New Traffic building in King George's Dock area abutting Circular Garden Reach Road (approximately 10,000 sq ft) covered sheds located on first floors require double handling of transit goods.[35]

FOREIGN EXCHANGE AUTHORIZATION

Para 8.4 of the protocol, specified that Nepal should not issue any import licences on the basis that the foreign exchange required by it would be arranged by the importer himself. Thus, evidence of appropriate foreign exchange authorization from the Central Bank of Nepal was required by the Indian authority. Since this provision effectively abridges Nepal's options to pursue her own policies, it was no longer included in the subsequent Treaty of 1978.

RAILWAY RISK RATE

Provision of the bond with suitable guarantee required under the previous treaty was dropped, and replaced by booking transit goods at railway Risk Rates or insuring the goods, if such booking was not accepted by the Railways. The amount for which the import/export goods were booked or insured were equal to the market price of such goods in India with a stipulation that in the event of the goods specified in the Customs Transit Declaration (CTD) not being imported/exported from India, the CIF price of the goods should be payable to the importer, exporter and the balance to the Collector of Customs, Calcutta or the Indian Customs Officer-in-charge of the Indian border station. The railway risk rate was a standard 20 per cent above the owner's risk rate. A record of the amount of transit goods carried on railway's or owner's risk rates is not readily available. In essence risk rates have been replaced by duty insurance requirements.[36]

PROCEDURES AND DOCUMENTATION

Procedures and documentation remained essentially as before. The invoice form required in the previous treaty was replaced by the Customs Transit Declaration (CTD) containing detailed particulars of goods declared for transit purposes. In addition to a series of endorsements being required at different points, the CTD form required a certificate of ratification from the Royal Nepalese Consul General or Consul (RNCG) to ensure that the goods specified in the CTD had been permitted by HMG to enter Nepal under appropriate import licensing.

The Trade and Transit Treaty of 1971 is a marked improvement on that of the treaty of 1960. It is a symbol of cooperative bilateral relationship between India and Nepal. While the earlier treaty had adopted the goal of a 'common market' between the two countries, the new treaty was concluded on the basis of 'Most favoured nation treatment' on a reciprocal basis. Nepalese goods now had access to the market of India without any restriction. The treaty also intended to increase the industrial production of Nepal. India agreed to import the products of Nepal's large scale industries subject to payment of customs duties and quantitative restrictions, as well as to a 25% concession in payment of excise duties on

Indian goods of similar categories. Nepal's industrial goods containing not more than 50 per cent of the third country materials also could be exported to India on comparatively favourable conditions. The goods containing the third country materials to the extent of more than 50 per cent might be exported to the third countries. India agreed to make arrangements for storage facilities at Haldia, a concession which was not given to Nepal in the treaty of 1960. The new treaty also entitled Nepal to use an overland route from the Calcutta port, for which it was decided to transport Nepalese goods in sealed containers through the Indian railways or by trucks so that loss or leakage during the transit could be eliminated.

The new Nepal-India Trade and Transit Treaty was debated at the National Panchayat on 22 August 1971. Five members participated in the debate, one of whom expressed dissatisfaction that separate treaties had not been concluded for trade and transit despite the assurances given repeatedly by HMG. Another member pointed out that "the provision to check a certain percentage of our imports at the Calcutta port in order to verify whether or not they are in accordance with the particulars contained in the customs transit declaration (CTD) form may create difficulties in the transit of goods." There were also complaints that the treaty would make Nepal dependent on the Indian market and Indian materials for the development of trade and industry. However, other members welcomed the trade and transit facilities provided to Nepal under the treaty.[37]

THE TREATY OF TRADE AND TRANSIT OF 1978

The Janata Government which came to power in India in 1977 gave particular attention to consolidate this country's relations with her immediate neighbours in pursuance of its declared foreign policy objective of 'beneficial bilateralism'. Among the bilateral issues pending solution between Nepal and India, the most important was the question of trade and transit. Though the 1971 Treaty of Trade and Transit had lapsed in 1976, it was kept in operation till March 1978 when the new separate treaties on trade and transit were signed. This delay was due to some differences in approach between two governments on the issue. It was a longstanding Nepalese demand to have two separate treaties on trade and transit. The underlined objective behind the demand was Nepal's desire to de-link the problems of her trade with India from her general overseas trade that had to go through India in transit because of Nepal's land-locked position. India was unwilling to accede to such a demand as the previous government of Indira Gandhi felt that the question of trade had been inseparably linked with transit between India and Nepal, because of the very nature of geographical contiguity and economic linkage between them. The Indian apprehension was that separation of the provision of trade from transit would further aggravate the already existing problem of illegal and deflected trade. Ultimately, the Janata Government conceded the Nepalese demand for two separate treaties during Prime Minister Morarji Dasai's visit to Kathmandu in December 1977. Accordingly, on 17 March 1978 two separate treaties on trade and transit and an agreement on cooperation in controlling unauthorized trade on the border were signed between Nepal and India in New Delhi. They came into operation with effect from 25 March 1978 replacing the 1971 composite treaty of trade and transit.

Under the 'Treaty on Trade', India agreed to enlarge the market for Nepal's manufactured products in India in order to assist in the industrial development of Nepal. The two governments also agreed to finalize necessary arrangements to maintain supplies of essential commodities needed by each other. In keeping with the efforts of the two countries to promote mutual trade, preferential treatment was accorded to primary products on a reciprocal basis. The goods manufactured in Nepal would have access to the Indian market free of basic customs duty and quantitative restrictions. Those goods were to contain not less than 80 per cent of Nepalese raw materials or Nepalese and Indian raw materials. In the case of other manufactured goods, in which the value of Nepalese and Indian materials and labour added in Nepal was alteast 50 per cent of the ex-factory prices, the government of India determined the goods on an ad-hoc basis for preferential treatment in the Indian market.[38]

The 'Treaty on Transit' and the annexed protocol laid down the procedures be followed for Nepal's traffic in transit through India. The new facilities included movement of bulk cargo both by rail and road. India also agreed to provide to Nepal overland route for its trade with Bangladesh as well as with the third countries through Bangladesh. Procedural arrangements in this regard were to be negotiated by the government of India with the Bangladesh government. The agreement to control unauthorized trade reconfirmed the right of both countries to pursue independent foreign trade policies, and the need to ensure that the economic interests of either country were not adversely affected through unauthorized trade.[39]

On 14 August 1978 Bangladesh and India signed a memorandum of understanding providing Nepal with transit facilities to Dacca and the third countries through their respective territories from 15 September 1978. Under the memorandum Dacca and New Delhi agreed to open a railway route connecting Bangladesh and Nepal through a short corridor of Indian territory. The route between the Biral and Radhikapur railway stations, when opened, would have three terminating points for entry and exit of Nepal's export and import cargo, at Raxual, Galgalia, and Jogbani on the Nepal-India border. The memorandum thus provided Nepal with access to the sea through the ports of Chittagong and Chalna in Bangladesh. Nepal's only access to the sea at present is through Calcutta in India. It also provided for the movement of traffic in transit through the agreed rail route and outlined customs and other procedures. The two sides agreed that the procedures applicable under the Indo-Nepal transit treaty should apply to Nepal's traffic in transit in Indian territory, and the procedures envisaged in the Nepal-Bangladesh Transit agreement to Nepal's traffic in transit in Bangladesh territory.[40]

PRINCIPAL TREATY PROVISIONS

(a) *Storage Space.* This treaty provides 25 years lease on agreed terms, separate sheds for storage of transit cargo at 'A' Shed Kidderpore Dock (approx. 3,315 sq m) on the ground floor, shed No. 25 Kidderpore Dock (approx. 4,424 sq m) on the first floor, Calcutta Jetty shed No. 8 on the ground floor and open space land at Circular Garden Reach Road (approx. 4,332 sq m). The Calcutta Jetty shed No. 8 was not used by Nepal because it was not in good condition. A request to lease ground floor space at 25 KPD or GR Jetty shed is still pending.[41]

(b) *Port Facilities.* According to the current treaty of transit between Nepal and India, the freedom for Nepal's cargo in transit to exit ports is limited primarily to Calcutta only. Although in the treaty of 1978 the government of India has agreed to arrange for suitable facilities at the Haldia port so that Nepal can use it for its transit goods, but to date this has not materialized.

(c) *Transit Routes and Mode of Transport Railway Facilities.* In addition to the railway routes agreed on in the 1971 treaty, the border stations authorized to handle transit traffic were Tikonia, Jarwa, Bhitamore and Naxalbari.

All traffic in transit shall pass only through the following routes:

Calcutta—Galgalia
Calcutta—Jogbani
Calcutta—Bhimanagar
Calcutta—Jayanagar
Calcutta—Raxaul
Calcutta—Nautanwa
Calcutta—Barahni
Calcutta—Nepalganj Road
Calcutta—Gauriphanta
Calcutta—Banbasa
Calcutta—Tikonia
Calcutta—Jarwa
Calcutta—Bhitamore (Sitamarhi).[42]

As no broad-gauge lines directly serve Nepalese border points, goods moving by railways have to be transhipped between road and meter-gauge systems or from and to trucks. Transhipments points, viz., Narayanpur Anant, Katihar, New Jalpaiguri, Gorakhpur and Gonda have been added in order to relieve the prevailing congestion at Barauni. Narayanpur Anant, New Jalpaiguri and Gorakhpur broad-gauge terminals are available for bulk imports, (principally cement and fertilizers), but no facilities exist to tranship from broad to meter-gauge and trucks are used for onward movement. To facilitate Nepalese trade with Bangladesh and beyond, India has opened the Birat/Radhikapur railway line to transit traffic.

Road Facilities. According to the provisions of the Transit Treaty, all trucks shall have pilfer-proof containers which are capable of being locked and sealed. The container shall be locked and individual packages shall be sealed by the Indian customs.

Duty Insurance. To compensate for any goods diverted or lost in transit, the treaty of transit entitles the Indian customs authorities to impose an insurance policy on goods in transit for the following valuations:

1. An amount equal to the Indian customs duty on goods moving by rail.
2. An amount equal to the Indian customs duty and in addition an undertaking by NTWC (Nepal Transit and Warehousing Corporation) to pay the difference between the market value of goods in India and their CIF value plus customs duty on goods moving by road in trucks belonging to NTWC or NTC (Nepal Transport Corporation).
3. An insurance policy of an amount equal to the difference between market value of the goods in India and their CIF value on goods moving by roads in trucks other than NTWC or NTC.

Import Licensing. To the treaty of transit 1978, one copy each of import licenses issued by HMG, Nepal and the specimen signature of official/officials who sign HMG's import licenses are sent to the Collector of Customs, Calcutta. Indian customs authorities, in turn, compare this copy with the one presented by importers and make a percentage examination of the goods to check whether the goods are in accordance with those specified in the import licence.

Procedures and Documentation. Procedures and documentation are basically the same as in the Treaty of 1971. For import goods, the Calcutta customs requires an import licence (issued by HMG, Nepal), bill of loading, invoice, certificate of origin, packing list, insurance certificate, personal bond and Customs Transit Declaration (RNCG should furnish a certificate to validate CTDS).

Customs Transit Declaration. The importers have to produce the Customs Transit Declaration (CTD) form in quadruplicate. After a through examination of goods, the Calcutta customs authority endorses all the copies of the CTDS and hands over the original copy to the importer. The duplicate and triplicate are sent to the Indian border customs post. At the border post, goods are checked by the Indian officer who would then certify the copies of the CTDS for goods destined for Nepal.

Export Procedure. Nepal's export goods face similar procedures and documentation requirements except that duty insurance coverage and personal bond requirements are normally waived, except for goods prohibited for import to India. There is no record of any duty insurance paid for Nepalese export to the third countries.[43]

THE TREATY OF TRADE AND AGREEMENT OF COOPERATION TO CONTROL UNAUTHORIZED TRADE BETWEEN NEPAL AND INDIA, 1983

Nepali-Indian officials held talks in New Delhi on the Nepal-India Trade and Transit treaties and the agreement on control of unauthorized trade. Nepal had concluded separate treaties on trade and transit with India in 1978. The term of the Trade Treaty expired in March 1983, while that of the Transit Treaty would expire two years later. However, the New Delhi meeting has discussed the transit treaty too. The transit treaty comes up for renewal in March 1985. Both Nepal and Indian officials, at their talks in New Delhi, have decided to extend the term of the treaty on trade and agreement of cooperation for control of unauthorized trade by another five-years. Both Nepal and India renewed the treaty of trade and agreement of cooperation for control of unauthorized trade for a further period of five years through the exchange of letter on 21 March 1983.[44]

Nepal and India have realized the need to promote the bilateral trade. Nepal's growing trade deficit with India for the past few years has naturally become a matter of concern for Nepal. Against this background, the report that in course of the same talks the Indian officials have announced a concession allowing the entry of ten more Nepali products into the Indian markets without payment of customs duty, in addition to the 26 products that have been already provided such concession.

The authorities of both the countries had exchanged views also on ways and means to check the activities of people engaged in clandestine activities on both sides taking advantage of the open border. Given mutual cooperation and goodwill among border officials of both sides, it is possible to control such illegal and undesirable activities too. As a large volume of Nepal's trade with the third countries is carried through India, the extension of the term of the trade agreements highlights the greater understanding shown by the Indian officials towards Nepal.

India showed much cordiality in extending the trade treaty for another term of five-years. The number of the Nepali items exempted from export duty was raised to 36, and India agreed to continue to provide transit facilities for Nepali goods. It underscores India's goodwill, spirit of cooperation and understanding towards Nepal. Nepal, on her part, has demonstrated its goodwill by agreeing to adopt vigilance and promote contacts between the border officials of both countries to stop smuggling and unauthorized trade.

To facilitate movement of Nepalese transit cargo, insurance premium on it has been reduced and further reduction is being considered. The scope of insurance would be widened by including the Nepalese insurance companies. Railway transit and transhipment points are being increased to include Gonda and Katihar to facilitate speedy movement of transit cargo to the western and eastern regions of Nepal. Nepal suggested to India to extend the Raxaul railway line upto Birganj to facilitate direct delivery of transit cargo.

As regards unauthorized trade, the Nepalese government agreed to strengthen its watch and ward and customs patrol guards and border security police. The two countries agreed to exercise greater vigilance in respect of the third country goods.[45]

TRADE AND TRANSIT RELATIONS OF NEPAL WITH COUNTRIES OTHER THAN INDIA

Nepal has traditionally been much dependent on India for her trade and transit facilities. Nepal's trade with the countries other than India has risen significantly in the last few years. Since 1960 Nepal has adopted a policy of trade diversification and reduce economic dependence on India. Nepal has established trade relations through bilateral-agreements with a number of countries including China, Pakistan and Bangladesh, her neighbours.

China comes on the first place in Nepal's trade relations. Nepal had traditionally trade relations with Tibet. Prior to 1956, there were no formal diplomatic relations between China and Nepal. In September 1956, Nepal and China signed a comprehensive treaty of trade and friendship in which both the governments expressed their desire to develop their traditional economic and trade relations on the principles of equality and mutual benefit. New trade agreements were concluded between the two governments in 1964, 1966, 1968, 1974 and 1981, but these served more to change the directions and terms of trade than to increase its volume.[46] There is no transit agreement between Nepal and China.

The trade relations between Nepal and Pakistan began when diplomatic relations were established in March 1960. Nepal and Pakistan signed a trade and transit agreement by their respective Commerce ministers in 1963. The agreement provided on a reciprocal basis freedom of transit for goods intended for import into or export from the territories of either country from or to a third countary.[47] By 1963 treaty of trade and transit India gave transit facilities to Nepal to carry her trade through East Pakistan. But it was not operated due to Indo-Pak war of 1965.

With the emergence of Bangladesh in 1971, and when Nepal recognized Bangladesh in 1972, Pakistan restored its normal relations with Nepal. There was no agreement between both countries till 1976. In 1976, an air agreement was signed between Pakistan and Nepal. [48]

Another trade agreement between Nepal and Pakistan was signed in 1982. This agreement replaced the trade agreement between Pakistan and Nepal of 1962 and came into force from the date of its signing. It would remain in force for a period of five years and would be renewable automatically for similar periods thereafter, unless terminated by either contracting party giving three months written notice to the other.[49]

After 13 years the Pakistan President General Zia-ul-Haq visited Nepal on 24 May 1983. A ministerial level joint economic commission has been established. This will, according to its terms, seek to improve bilateral ties in the field of trade, agriculture, hydro-electric, power, water management, industry, communication and tourism.[50]

The main channel of communication between Nepal and Pakistan has been the airline service between Kathmandu and Karachi. Its economic importance is very limited.

Bangladesh emerged as a new nation in South Asia in 1971. There were no agreements between Nepal and Bangladesh till 1976. For the first time a treaty of trade and transit was signed between Nepal and Bangladesh in 1976. According to the trade agreement both the countries will be extended the most favoured nation treatment for the mutual benefit of both, excepting border trade, customs union and free trade zone. According to the transit treaty freedom of transit to traffic and transit from and to Nepal to port facilities will be available in Bangladesh.[51]

The treaty with Bangladesh does not contain any route or transport mode restrictions and Nepal has access to the two principal ports of Chittagong and Chalna. Bangladesh has been encouraging Nepal transit traffic by allowing a rebate of 25 per cent on railway freight, and availability of waterfront sheds (land on negotiable terms at Chittagong and Chalna ports). To date only imports via Chittagong have taken advantage of the Bangladesh route as numerous institutional and some technical problems remain to be solved in order to generate more interest in shipping transit goods via Chittagong or Chalna.[52]

Despite its best efforts in the past decade, India still accounts for at least 90 per cent of Nepal's total trade. Further diversification is being sought, but Nepal is now more concerned with improving the trade system with India, and particularly with gaining access to markets in India for Nepali products. Trade with India has been increasing rapidly since 1960, indeed in absolute terms for more than with the rest of the world. Nepal is thus still a part of the broader Indian economic and commercial system.

NOTES

1. Karan and Jenkins, "The Himalayan Kingdoms: Bhutan, Sikkim and Nepal," (New Jersey, 1963), p. 110.
2. Nirmal K. Bista, "Imports-exports Structure and Trade Expansion in South Asia (Nepal)," CEDA, Tribhuvan University, (Kathmandu, 1981), p. 10.
3. S.D. Muni, "Foreign Policy of Nepal," (Delhi, 1973).
4. M.K. Malwan, G.P. Pokhral and M.R. Shakya, "The Transit Transport Network of Nepal," United Nations Development Programme: Least Developed Land-locked countries Programme in Nepal, (UNCTAD/ESCAP), Kathmandu, Nov. 1981.
5. Annual Report 1967–68, HMG, Ministry of Foreign Affairs, Kathmandu (Nepal), p. 91.
6. N.P. Banskota, "Indo-Nepal Trade and Economic Relations," (Delhi, 1981), p. 98.

7. Ibid., p. 99.
8. Nirmal K. Bista, n. 2.
9. Ibid.
10. IDSA, News Review, on South Asia/Indian ocean, Vol. 17, No. 2, Feb., 1984, p. 12.
11. A.K. Shrestha, "Transit Treaty Provisions and their Impact on Nepal's Transit Traffic Costs," United Nations Development Programme, Project on Development Logistics. (UNDP/UNCTAD), Kathmandu, 1984, p. 1, NEP/82/002.
12. Udyog Barijaya Patrika, April-May, 1977.
13. Keshab P. Kaphley, "Trade channels systems and procedures country study: Nepal," CEDA, Tribhuvan University, Kathmandu (Nepal), May 1984, p. 96.
14. "Nepal-India Treaty of Trade—transit agreement of cooperation," Trade Promotion Centre, Kathmandu, March 1978, p. 30.
15. Transit Transport Network of Nepal, Trade Promotion Centre, Kathmandu (Nepal, 1981), No. 083, p. 94.
16. Keshab P. Kaphley, n. 13, p. 83.
17. For the text of the Treaty see, Appendix 1.
18. P.N. Pant, "Nepal's foreign trade," The Motherland, (Kathmandu, 1963), 28 January 1963.
19. For the full text of the Treaty see, Appendix II.
20. A.K. Shrestha, n. 11, p. 2.
21. For the full text of the Treaty see, Appendix III.
22. A.S. Bhasin, "Documents on Nepal's Relations with India and China," (New Delhi, 1970), pp. 128-29.
23. The Times of India, (New Delhi, 1961), 20 May 1961.
24. Sita Shrestha, "Nepal and the United Nations," (New Delhi, 1974), p. 157.
25. H.R. Sharma, "Nepal's Trade with and Through India," The Rising Nepal (Kathmandu, 1969), 5 July 1969.
26. A.K. Shrestha, n. 11, p. 4.
27. Udyog Banijya Patrika, December-January 1967.
28. A.S. Bhasin, n. 21, p. 132.
29. Asian Recorder, 10-16 September 1963, p. 5407.
30. The Motherland (Kathmandu, 1963), 24 October 1963.
31. The Hindustan Times, (New Delhi, 1965), 8 January 1965.
32. Gorakha Patra (Kathmandu, 1971), 14 August 1971.
33. Ibid.
34. Rishikesh Shaha, "Nepali Politics: Retrospect and Prospect," (Delhi, 1978), p. 131.

35. Indo-Nepal Treaty of Trade and Transit, 1971, Ministry of Commerce & Trade, Government of India, (New Delhi, 1971), p. 8.
36. A.K. Shrestha, n. 11, pp. 5-6.
37. Gorakha Patra, (Kathmandu, 1971), 23 August 1971.
38. Nepal Press Digest, (Kathmandu, 1978), Vol. 22, No. 12, 20 March 1978.
39. Ibid.
40. Gorakha Patra, (Kathmandu, 1978), 15 August 1971.
41. Indo-Nepal Treaties of Trade, Transit and Agreement for Cooperation to Control Unauthorized Trade, 1978 Department of Commerce, Ministry of Commerce, Civil Supplies and Cooperation, Government of India, (New Delhi, 1978), p. 20.
42. Nepal-India Treaty of Trade, Transit and Agreement of Cooperation, 1978, Trade Promotion Centre, (Kathmandu, 1978), pp. 19-20.
43. A.K. Shrestha, n. 11, p. 14.
44. Nepal's Trade and Transit Agreements, Trade Promotion Centre, Kathmandu, 1983, pp. 59-105.
45. The Times of India (New Delhi, 1983), 22 March 1983.
46. Leo E. Rose, "Nepal Strategy for Survival," (Bombay, 1971), p. 267.
47. Asian Recorder, (New Delhi), Vol. IX No. 11 March 1963, p. 5088.
48. P.K. Mishra, "India, Pakistan, Nepal and Bangladesh," (Delhi, 1979), p. 144.
49. Nepal's Trade and Transit Agreements, Trade Promotion Centre, (Kathmandu, 1983), p. 127.
50. Nepal News Royan Nepalese Embassy, (New Delhi, 1983), Vol. XXII, No. 15, 31 May 1983, p. 8.
51. P.K. Mishra, n. 47, p. 171.
52. A.K. Shrestha, n. 11, p. 15.

4. International Conferences on Land-Locked States–I

There is a long history of attempts made to solve the problems of land-locked states through international conventions and bilateral as well as multilateral agreements. The first such attempt can be traced back to the peace of Westphalia in 1648, which divided the central Europe into a large number of states, some of which did not have a sea-coast. It laid down certain rules and regulations regarding free navigational facility and traffic charges which contributed to the development of international law on free access to the sea for the land-locked states.[1]

BILATERAL AGREEMENTS

A bilateral agreement designed to facilitate the transit of a land-locked state was signed on 16 March 1816, between Sardinia, the Swiss Confederation, and the Canton of Geneva. Article V of the agreement exempts from all transit duties, goods and products from the free-port of Geneva to the State of Geneva.[2]

One may also mention the convention of 24 July 1890 between Great Britain and Portugal and of 2 August 1929 between Italy and Ethiopia. In Latin America treaties were signed between Bolivia, a land-locked state, and Argentina on 9 July 1868, and 26 March 1947 with Brazil, 27 March 1867, 12 August 1910 and 25 February 1938 with Chile.[3]

In Asia the trade conventions between the Great Britain and Afghanistan on 5 June 1923, the Soviet Union and Afghanistan on 28 June 1955, Nepal and India on 31 July 1950, and between Thailand and Laos, are some of the examples of the many bilateral agreements reached at for the solution of transit problems.[4]

MULTILATERAL AGREEMENTS AFTER THE FIRST WORLD WAR

There have been numerous attempts to find a general solution to this vast question, especially vigorous efforts made after the First World War under the auspices of the League of Nations, which had received instructions to that effect under the treaty of Versailles of 1919. The powers which met at Versailles after the war of 1914–1918 attached great importance to the solution of the problem of freedom of transit. Several articles of the treaty of Versailles refer to that problem and the future League of Nations was entrusted with the task of its solution. Article 23(e) of the covenant was the first attempt to deal with the question on a universal level. It stated that the member of the League "will make provision to secure and maintain freedom of communication and of transit and equitable treatment for the commerce of all members of the League."[5]

In pursuance of this provision a series of conferences took place during the 1920's which produced both multilateral conventions and bilateral treaties aimed at the facilitation of free transit. Among these the most important were the convention and statute on freedom of transit and the convention and statute on the regime of navigable waterways of international concern which was adopted in Barcelona in 1921.

BARCELONA CONVENTION AND STATUTE ON THE FREEDOM OF TRANSIT

In 1921, at a conference held at Barcelona, a number of conventions were adopted (such as on railways, ports, navigable waterways and flags of states having no sea-coast), the most important of which was the convention and statute on the freedom of transit. This sought to guarantee and facilitate transit traffic free from discrimination or excessive charges.[6]

The system established by the Barcelona convention on freedom of transit provides a clear proof of the firm determination of the states represented at the conference, (more than forty nations, thirty-two of whom ratified the convention) to recognize the right of the land-locked states to transit through surrounding territories. It was supported by strong guarantee regarding the equality of treatment and permanent enjoyment, as well as, by establishing a machinery for the settlement of disputes which its implementation might give rise to.[7]

The Barcelona convention testified to the progress of the idea of free access to the sea for the land-locked countries. The practice of states based on the convention of Barcelona and Geneva (1923) resulted in the evolution of a number of principles which found expression in multilateral and bilateral treaties.[8]

The states represented at the Barcelona conference and were the signatories to the conventions were, Albania, Austria, Belgium, Bolivia, Brazil, Bulgaria, Chile, China, Colombia, Costa Rica, Cuba, Denmark, the British Empire (with New Zealand and India), Spain, Esthonia, Finland, France, Greece, Guatemala, Haiti, Honduras, Italy, Japan, Lativia, Lithuania, Luxembourg, Norway, Panama, Paraguay, the Netherlands, Persia, Poland, Portugal, Rumania, the Serb-Croal-Slovene state, Sweden, Switzerland, Czechoslovakia, Uruguay and Venezuela.[9]

Nepal did not participate in the Barcelona conference.

The Barcelona resolution stated that it is well to proclaim the right of free transit and to make regulations, thereon as being one of the best means of developing cooperation between states without prejudice to their rights of sovereignty or authority over routes available for transit. The high contracting parties declare that they accept the statute on freedom of transit annexed hereto, adopted by the Barcelona conference on 14 April 1921.[10]

STATUTE ON FREEDOM OF TRANSIT

Under article I of this convention, as adopted at Barcelona, the contracting parties, declare that they accept, 'the statute on freedom of transit' annexed to and deemed to constitute an integral part of the convention.

Article I of the statute, which repeats almost verbatim the article I of the original draft of the convention, explains that the following shall be deemed to be in a transit across the territory of the contracting states.

Article 1: Persons, baggage and goods and also vessels, coaching and goods stock and other means of transport, shall be deemed to be in the transit across territory under the sovereignty or authority, with or without transhipment, warehousing breaking bulk, or change in the mode of transport, is only a portion of a complete journey, beginning and terminating beyond the frontier of the state across whose territory the transit takes place.

Traffic of this nature is termed in this statute 'traffic in transit'.

Article 2: Subject to the other provisions of this statute, the measures taken by contracting states for regulating and forwarding traffic across territory under their sovereignty or authority shall facilitate free transit by rail or waterway on routes in use convenient for international transit. No distinction shall be made which is based on the nationality of persons, the flag of vessels, the place or origin, departure, entry, exit or destination, or on any circumstances relating to the ownership of goods or of vessels, coaching or goods stock or other means of transport.

In order to ensure the application of the provisions of this article, contracting states will allow transit in accordance with the customary conditions and reserves across their territorial waters.

Article 3: Traffic in transit shall not be subject to any special dues in respect of transit (including entry and exit). Nevertheless, on such traffic in transit there may be levied dues intended solely to defray expenses of supervision and administration entailed by such transit. The rate of any such dues must correspond as nearly as possible with the expenses which they are intended to cover, and the dues must be imposed under the conditions of equality laid down in the preceding article, except that on certain routes such dues may be reduced or even abolished on account of differences in the cost of supervision.

Article 4: The contracting states undertake to apply to traffic in transit on routes operated or administered by the state or under concession, whatever may be the place of departure or destination of the traffic, tariffs, which having regard to the conditions of the traffic and to considerations of commercial competition between routes, are reasonable as regards both their rates and the method of their application. These traffic shall be so fixed as to facilitate international traffic as much as possible. No charges, facilities or restrictions shall depend, directly or indirectly, on the nationality or ownership of the vessel, or other means of transport on which any part of the complete journey has been or is to be accomplished.

Article 5: No contracting state shall be bound by this statute to afford transit for passengers whose admission into its territories is forbidden or for goods of a kind of which the importation is prohibited, either on grounds of public health or security, or as a precaution against diseases of animals or plants.

Each contracting state shall be entitled to take reasonable precautions to ensure that persons, baggage and goods, particularly goods which are the subject of a monopoly and also vessels, coaching and goods stock and other means of transport, are really in transit, as well as to ensure that passengers in transit are in a position to complete their journey and to prevent the safety of the routes and means of communication being endangered.

Nothing in this statute shall affect the measures which one of the contracting states may feel called upon to take in pursuance of general international conventions to which it is a party, or which may be concluded hereafter particularly conventions concluded under the auspices of the League of Nations, relating to the transit, export or import of particular kinds of articles, such as opium or other dangerous drugs, arms or the produce of fisheries or in pursuances of general conventions intended to prevent any infringement of industrial, literary or artistic property, or relating to false marks, false indications of origin, or other methods of unfair competition.

Any haulage service established as a monopoly on waterways used for transit must be so organized as not to hinder the transit of vessels.

Article 6: This statute does not of itself impose on any of the contracting states a fresh obligation to grant freedom of transit to the nationals and their baggage, or to the flag of a non-contracting state, not to the goods, nor to coaching and goods stock or other means of transport coming or entering from, or leaving by, or destined for a non-contracting state, except when a valid reason is shown for such transit by one of the other contracting states concerned. It is understood that for the purposes of this article, goods in transit under the flag of a contracting state shall, if no transhipment takes place, benefit by the advantages granted to that flag.

Article 7: The measures of a general or particular character which a contracting state is obliged to take in case of an emergency affecting the safety of the state or the vital interests of the country may in exceptional cases, and for as short a period as possible, involve a deviation from the provisions of the above articles, it being understood that the principle of freedom of transit must be observed to the utmost possible extent.

Article 8: This statute does not prescribe the rights and duties of belligerents and neutrals in time of war. The statute shall, however, continue in force in time of war so far as such rights and duties permit.

Article 9: This statute does not impose upon a contracting state any obligations conflicting with its rights and duties as a member of the League of Nations.

Article 10: The coming into force of this statute will not abrogate treaties, conventions and agreements on questions of transit concluded by contracting states before 1 May 1921.

In consideration of such agreements being kept in force, contracting states undertake, either on the termination of the agreement or when circumstances permit to introduce into agreements so kept in force which contravene. The provisions of this statute the modifications required to bring them into harmony with such provisions, so far as the geographical, economic or technical circumstances of the countries or areas concerned allow.

Contracting states also undertake not to conclude in future treaties, conventions or agreements, which are inconsistent with the provisions of this statute, except when geographical, economic or technical considerations justify exceptional deviations therefrom.

Furthermore, contracting states, may, in matters of transit, enter into regional understandings consistent with the principles of this statute.

Article 11: This statute does not entail in any way the withdrawal of facilities which are greater than those provided for in the statute and have been granted, under conditions consistent with its principles, to traffic in transit across territory under the sovereignty or authority of a contracting state. The statute also entails no prohibitions of such grant of greater facilities in the future.

Article 12: Any dispute which may arise as to the interpretation or application of this statute which is not settled directly between the parties themselves shall be brought before the permanent court of international justice, unless, under a special agreement or a general arbitration provision, steps are taken for the settlement of the dispute by arbitration or some other means.

Proceedings are opened in the manner laid down in article 40 of the statute of the permanent court of international justice.

Article 13: In order to settle such disputes, however, in a friendly way as far as possible, the contracting states undertake, before resorting to any judicial proceedings and without prejudice to the powers and right of action of the Council and of the Assembly, to submit such disputes for an opinion to any body established by the League of Nations, as the advisory and technical organization of the members of the League in matters of communications and transit. In urgent cases, a preliminary opinion may recommend temporary measures intended, in particular, to restore the facilities for freedom of transit which existed before the act or occurrence which gave rise to the dispute.

Article 14: In view of the fact that within or immediately adjacent to the territory of some of the contracting states there are areas or enclaves, small in extent and population in comparison with such territories, and that these areas or enclaves from detached portions or settlements of other parent states, and that it is impracticable for reasons of an administrative order to apply to them the provisions of this statute, it is agreed that these provisions shall not apply to them.

The same stipulation applies where a colony or dependency has a very long frontier in comparison with its surface and where in consequence it is practically impossible to afford the necessary customs and police supervision.

The states concerned, however, will apply in the cases referred to above a regime which will respect the principles of the present statute and facilitate transit and communications as far as practicable.

Article 15: It is understood that this statute must not be interpreted as regulating in any way rights and obligations *inter se* of territories forming part or placed under the protection of the same sovereign state, whether or not there territories are individually members of the League of Nations.[11]

The Barcelona convention came under criticism for, it was only confined to the European states and not for other land-locked states of Asia, Africa and Latin America. The Barcelona convention indeed, despite its weeknesses, came to be regarded as a datum plane, a minimum standard to be used thenceforth in negotiations for bilateral and multilateral agreements on transit, including those involving access to the sea. It retained its value and prestige for more than forty years, a not inconsiderable accomplishment in the twentieth century.

Although Nepal did not participate in the Barcelona Convention, but she was satisfied with the conventions which were adopted in the conference. During the British rule of India Nepal was given certain trade and transit facilities mostly by convention. The Barcelona convention is still in force and can be acceded to by any country willing to do so.

GENERAL AGREEMENT ON TARIFFS AND TRADE (GATT), 1948: ARTICLE V, ON FREEDOM OF TRANSIT

Shortly after the end of the Second World War, the major trading states of the world undertook, on the initiative of the United States, a commitment to reduce tariffs and other barriers to trade for their mutual benefit. The general principles of liberalized trade and the participants' specific undertakings (123 bilateral trade agreements) are embodied in the General Agreement on Tariffs and Trade (GATT) adopted at Geneva on 30 October 1947. The agreement came provisionally into force on 1 January 1948.[12] Article V of GATT entitled, 'Freedom of transit', while not referring specifically to land-locked states, however, reaffirms the principle of the Barcelona convention.

On 18 February 1946, the Economic and Social Council of the United Nations, pursuant to a proposal submitted by the representative of the United States, resolved 13(I) to convene an international conference on trade and employment. The council at the same time, provided to establish a preparatory committee composed of one representative each of Australia, Belgium, Brazil, Canada, Chile, Cuba, Czechoslovakia, France, India, Luxembourg, the Netherlands, New Zealand, Norway, South Africa, USSR, UK and USA.[13]

The second session of the preparatory committee in Geneva in fact undertook two entirely separate functions. In addition to completing the draft charter for an international trade organization, it also sponsored the negotiations for the reduction of tariffs and the discussions which led to the formulation of the General Agreement on Tariffs and Trade (GATT). It was considered that this would promote the objectives of the proposed international trade organization. This part of its work began on 10 April 1947 in Geneva and concluded on 30 October 1947, when the final act of GATT was signed.[14]

Recognizing that their relations in the field of trade and economic endeavour should be conducted with a view to raising standards of living ensuring full employment and a large and steadily growing volume of real income and effective demand, developing the full use of the resources of the world and expanding the production and exchange of goods.

Being desirous of contributing to these objectives by entering into reciprocal and mutually advantageous arrangements, it was directed to the substantial reduction of tariffs and other barriers to trade and the elimination of discriminatory treatment in international commerce.[15]

The provisions which have most bearing on the subject under discussion are contained in Article V of the General Agreement which provides:

ARTICLE V: FREEDOM OF TRANSIT

1. Goods (including baggage) and also vessels and other means of transport shall be deemed to be in transit across the territory of a contracting party when the passage across such a territory, with or without transhipment, warehousing, breaking bulk, or change in the mode of transport, is only a portion of a complete journey beginning and terminating beyond the frontier of the contracting party through whose territory the traffic passes. Traffic of this nature is termed in this article "traffic in transit".

2. There shall be freedom of transit through the territory of each contracting party, via the routes most convenient for international transit, for traffic in transit to or from the territory of other contracting parties. No distinction shall be made which is based on the flag of vessels, the place of origin, departure, entry, exit or destination, or on any circumstances relating to the ownership of goods, of vessels or of other means of transport.

3. Any contracting party may require that traffic in transit through its territory be entered at the proper custom house, but, except in cases of failure to comply with applicable customs laws, and regulations, such traffic coming from or going to the territory of other contracting parties shall not be subject to any unnecessary

delays or restrictions and shall be exempt from customs duties and from all transit duties or other charges imposed in respect of transit, except charges for transportation or those commensurate with administrative expenses entailed by transit or with the cost of services rendered.

4. All charges and regulations imposed by contracting parties on traffic in transit to or from the territories of other contracting parties shall be reasonable, having regard to the conditions of the traffic.

5. With respect to all charges regulations and formalities in connection with transit, each contracting party shall accord to traffic in transit to or from the territory of any other contracting party treatment no less favourable than the treatment accorded to traffic in transit to or from any third country.

6. Each contracting party shall accord to products which have been in transit through the territory of any other contracting party treatment no less favourable than which would have been accorded to such products had they been transported from their place of origin to their destination without going through the territory of such other contracting party. Any contracting party shall, however, be free to maintain its requirements of direct consignment existing on the date of this agreement, in respect of any goods in regard to which such direct consignment is a requisite condition of eligibility for entry of the goods at preferential rates of duty or has relation to the contracting party's prescribed method of valuation for duty purposes.

7. The provisions of this article shall not apply to the operation of aircraft in transit, but shall apply to air transit of goods (including baggages).[16]

Article V of the general agreement restates to a large extent the principles adopted at the Barcelona Conference (1921) and incorporated in the Barcelona Convention.[17] The point to be noted here, however, is that both the General Agreement, the Barcelona Convention, and the statute on freedom of transit prescribe favourable treatment only for traffic proceeding to or from a contracting party. This seems to show that the signatories regarded freedom of transit less as a rule of the law of nations than as a right to be affirmed in multilateral or bilateral treaties.

The GATT provision on 'freedom of transit' made no specific reference to the land-locked countries. The Havana Charter made an express reference to them. But the Havana Charter never came into force, as it was not ratified, while GATT was binding on most of the trading nations.

Nepal did not participate in the GATT Conference. But she was satisfied with the trading system of the world to some extent.

HAVANA CHARTER

The purpose of the conference which opened in Havana in November 1947, the month following the adoption of GATT, was to establish an international trade organization (ITO) which would supervise a vastly expanded world trading system based on the freest possible trade in accordance with the principle of competitive private enterprise. The conference produced a charter which was never ratified by more than one state (Australia, with reservations) and never came into effect. Nevertheless, Article 33 of the Havana Charter of 24 March 1948 is considered to have been a step forward on the road to a free and secure access to the sea for land-locked states.[18]

The Havana Charter reaffirmed and, in some respects, strengthened the Barcelona Convention's provisions for freedom of transit. In seven of its eight paragraphs Article 33 of the Havana Charter was virtually identical with the seven paragraphs of the Article V of the GATT. However, two differences are significant. GATT established a multilateral most-favoured-nation system with respect to transit traffic in paragraph 5, the Havana Charter includes this identical provision in its own paragraph 5, but an interpretative note provides specifically that if "a member grants to a country which has no direct access to the sea more ample facilities than those already provided for in other paragraphs of the Article 33, such special facilities may be limited to the land-locked country concerned, unless, the organization finds, on the complaint of any other member that the withholding of the special facilities from the complaining member contravenes the most favoured nation provisions of this charter."[19]

By admitting this principle the Havana Charter clearly intended to facilitate the conclusion of agreements favourable to land-locked countries.

Since the Havana Charter never came into force, the Barcelona Convention and Article V of the GATT remained the yardstick by which facilities of transit trade of land-locked states could legally be measured.

THE ECONOMIC COMMISSION FOR ASIA AND THE FAR EAST (ECAFE) AND THE LAND-LOCKED COUNTRIES

In January 1956 the United Nations Economic Commission for Asia and the Far East (ECAFE) considered the problems of its land-locked members (Afghanistan, Laos and Nepal). After discussion on the issues it approved a resolution in which it recommended "that the needs of land-locked member states and members having no access to the sea in the matter of transit trade be given full recognition by all member states and that adequate facilities thereof be accorded in terms of international law and practice in this regard."[20]

At its twelfth session (2 to 14 February 1956) ECAFE approved the committee's resolution.[21] The Secretariat of the Commission then prepared a report entitled "Problems of trade of land-locked countries in Asia and the Far East."[22]

In its report to the Commission the committee on industry and trade recommended that the land-locked countries should be given transit facilities in accordance with the provisions of the Barcelona Statute and the GATT, irrespective of membership, and recognized that this was a constructive step forward.

The Commission also took note of the General Assembly resolution 1028(XI), cited in paragraph I of the present memorandum.

GENERAL ASSEMBLY RESOLUTION 1028(XI), 1957

The distinctive position of the land-locked countries and "the need for adequate transit facilities in promoting international trade" was recognized in General Assembly resolution 1028(XI) of 20 February 1957. This resolution invited the cooperation of all member states in according "adequate facilities in terms of international law and practice...bearing in mind the future requirements resulting from the economic development of the land-locked countries."[23]

In chapter II of the report on the work of the eighth session (23 April to 4 July 1956), the International Law Commission submitted draft articles on the law of the sea and, being of the opinion that its work had sufficiently prepared the ground, recommended that the General Assembly should summon an international conference of plenipotentiaries to examine the law of the sea. The draft article did not, however, contain any provision regarding the land-locked countries.[24]

The Commission's report was considered by the sixth committee of the General Assembly at its 481st meeting on 21 November 1956 and by its 485th to 505th meetings (28 November to 20 December 1956).

Nepal together with five other land-locked states—Afghanistan, Austria, Bolivia, Czechoslovakia and Paraguay—moved an amendment to the joint draft resolution on convening a conference of plenipotentiaries. The text appears, with only slight amendments, as operative paragraph 3 of the resolution 1105 (XI) adopted by the General Assembly on 21 February 1957. The paragraph reads: "Recommends that the conference should study the question of free access to the sea of land-locked states, as established by international practice or treaties."[25]

During the debate several references were made, particularly by representatives of land-locked states, to the need for giving recognition in any future convention to the right of such countries, including not only the right of navigation on the high sea, but also "a right of free passage without restrictions in the territorial sea and the free passage over land."

The major arguments were put forth during the debate in the sixth committee by the advocates of the right of free access to the sea. The representatives of Paraguay stated: "all states including those with no sea-coast of their own, were entitled freely to engage in trade and to have access to the world's market and to the raw materials necessary for their economic prosperity."[26]

At the 499th meeting, the repressentative of Afghanistan contended "that no convention on the law of the sea would be complete unless it guaranteed the rights of states which had no sea-coast"; indeed he said without such a guarantee it would be valueless, because:

(i) No state could survive without an outlet to the sea.
(ii) Maritime communications were indispensable to all states.
(iii) The right of innocent passage had been recognized for centuries and the treaty of Versailles, like other bilateral

agreements in force, had established the right of states which had no sea-coast.

(iv) No country could claim absolute sovereignty over historic sea laws.[27]

At the 499th meeting the representative of Nepal also took side with those who had demanded guarantees of the right of land-locked states.[28]

Under the terms of that resolution 1028(XI) the General Assembly recognized "the need of land-locked countries for adequate transit facilities in promoting international trade and invited the governments of member states... to give full recognition to the needs of land-locked states in the matter of transit trade and, therefore, to accord them adequate facilities in terms of international law and practice in this regard, bearing in mind the future requirements resulting from the economic development of the land-locked countries."[29]

NEPAL'S PARTICIPATION

After becoming a member of the United Nations in December 1955, Nepal along with two other land-locked states of Asia, Afghanistan and Laos, took the initiative in acquainting the Committee on Industry and Trade of the ECAFE with the problems of land-locked states. The efforts made by Nepal (with the cooperation of Afghanistan and Laos) through ECAFE to draw the attention of the members of the United Nations to the problems confronting the land-locked states were crowned with success with the resolution adopted by the General Assembly on 20 February 1957. Nepal also mobilized the opinion in the General Assembly in favour of the rights of the land-locked countries to free access to the sea. Nepal along with other five land-locked countries—Afghanistan, Austria, Bolivia, Czechoslovakia, and Paraguay—moved an amendment to the joint draft resolution on convening a conference of plenipotentiaries.[30]

THE FIRST LAW OF THE SEA CONFERENCE, 1958 (GENEVA) AND LAND-LOCKED STATES

In accordance with the resolution 1105(XI) of the General

Assembly on 21 February 1957, the first conference on the sea law was held at Geneva from 24 February to 27 April 1958.[31]

A preliminary conference of states without direct access to the sea was held at Geneva from 10 to 14 February 1958, on the invitation of the Swiss federal government. This conference was the sequel to a series of meetings held in New York between the representatives of the land-locked states, as well as members of the United Nations, many of whom had taken an active part in the discussions in the eleventh session of the General Assembly on the draft articles on the law of the sea presented by the International Law Commission contained no provisions dealing directly with the position of the land-locked states, and, further, that in proposing the establishment of a special committee in the conference on the law of the sea to give effect to the land-locked states.[32]

On the request of Afghanistan's representative the Secretary General of the General Assembly proposed to establish a Special Fifth Committee to consider the question of free access to the sea of the land-locked states.

The states invited to the preliminary conference were all the land-locked states and states members of specialized agencies by the United Nations. The land-locked states invited in the conference were: Afghanistan, Austria, Bolivia, Byelorussian, Czechoslovakia, Holysee, Hungary, Laos, Luxembourg, Nepal, Paraguay, San Marina, and Switzerland.[33]

At the beginning of the session, members of the conference were able to study with keen interest the question of free access of land-locked countries to the sea, prepared by the United Nations secretariat, which sets out in detail the current aspects of this problem and the history of earlier attempts to solve it.

The preliminary conference devoted the greater part of its meetings to hearing statements by the delegates of the different states represented on the situation of their particular countries. The majority of them were under bilateral on multilateral agreements on their needs and on their experiences.

After an exhaustive exchange of views, the group submitted its proposals for the formulation of "principles" at the final meeting of the preliminary conference, held on 14 February 1958. The preliminary conference approved the statement of seven principles which in the view of the participants gave expression to international law on the subject, under discussion. It was intended merely to state precisely a certain number of principles dealing with the status of the land-locked states. The following general principles are part of the existing international law.

PRINCIPLES ENUNCIATED BY THE PRELIMINARY CONFERENCE OF LAND-LOCKED STATES: PRINCIPLE I—RIGHT OF FREE ACCESS TO THE SEA

"The right of each land-locked state of free access to the sea derives from the fundamental principle of freedom of the high seas."

Principle II—Right to Fly a Maritime Flag. "Each land-locked state enjoys, while on a footing of complete equal treatment with the maritime state, the right to fly its flag on its vessels which are duly registered in a specific place on their territory."

Principle III—Right of Navigation. "The vessels flying the flag of a land-locked state enjoy, on the high seas, a regime which is identical to the one that is enjoyed by vessels of maritime countries in territorial and on internal waters, they enjoy a regime which is identical to the one that is enjoyed by the vessels flying the flag of maritime states, other than the territorial state."

Principle IV—Regime to be Applied in Ports. "Each land-locked state is entitled to the most favoured treatment and should under no circumstances receive a treatment less favourable than the one accorded to the vessels of the maritime state as regards access to the latter's maritime ports, use of these ports and facilities of any kind that are usually accorded."

Principle V—Right of Free Transit. "The transit of persons and goods from a land-locked country towards the sea and vice versa by all means of transportation and communication must be freely accorded subject to existing special agreements and conventions.

"The transit shall not be subject to any customs duty or specific charges or taxes except for charges levied for specific services rendered."

Principle VI—Rights of States of Transit. "The state of transit while maintaining full jurisdiction over the means of communication and everything related to the facilities accorded shall have the right to take all indispensable measures to ensure that the exercise of the right of free access to the sea shall in no way infringe on its legitimate interests of any kind, especially with regard to security and public health."

Principle VII—Existing and Future Agreements. "The provisions codifying the principles which govern the right of free access to the sea of the land-locked state shall in no way abrogate existing agreements between two or more contracting parties concerning the problems which will be the object of the codification envisaged, nor shall they raise an obstacle as regards the conclusion of such agreements in the future, provided that the latter do not establish a regime which is less favourable than or opposed to the above mentioned provisions."[34]

This brief meeting had a dual importance—first, the general discussion gave an almost complete view of the problems and circumstances under which all the land-locked countries were living in various parts of the world, and, secondly, for the first time, in history all the land-locked countries of the world for a common cause and purpose exchanged views on the exercise of their right of free access to the sea. The views expressed by the representatives of the land-locked countries in Geneva during the preliminary conference showed that these states have obtained in International Law in general, a high degree of recognition for their right of free access to the sea.

Above all, the preliminary conference provided an outstanding example of cooperation and coexistence between the countries who had a common problem because of their special geographical position.

THE RECOGNITION OF THE RIGHT OF FREE ACCESS TO THE SEA BY THE FIRST LAW OF THE SEA CONFERENCE IN 1958

During discussion of the question of free access to the sea for the land-locked states in the fifth committee various proposals were introduced. Proposal submitted by Afghanistan, Albania, Austria, Bolivia, Bulgaria, Byelorussian, the Soviet Socialist Republic,

Czechoslovakia, Ghana, Hungary, Iceland, Indonesia, Laos, Luxembourg, Nepal, Paraguay, Saudi Arabia, Switzerland, Tunisia, and the United Arab Republic, were as follows.

Right of Free Access to the Sea. "Every state without a coast (land-locked state) has the right to free access to the sea. This right derives from the fundamental principle of the freedom of the high seas."

Right to a Flag. "Every state without a coast possesses on terms of complete equality of treatment with maritime states, the right to a flag in respect of such of its ships as are duly registered in a specific place in its territory that place shall be the port of registry for such ships."

Right to Sail in the Territorial Sea and in Internal Waters. "Every state without a coast has the right to claim that ships flying its flag shall enjoy in the territorial sea and the internal waters of any maritime state a regime identical to that accorded to the ships of other maritime states."

Regime Applicable in Ports of the Coastal State. "Every state without a coast shall be entitled to most favourable treatment and in no event shall such treatment be less favourable than that accorded to ships of the coastal state, in maritime ports under the sovereignty or authority of the coastal state as regards freedom of access to the ports, the use of the ports and the full enjoyment of the facilities of all kinds generally granted."

"The expression 'coastal state' means for the purposes of this article, any state whose territory can, in the light of the geographical and economic circumstances, be reasonably regarded as constituting the means of access to the sea for the specific state without a sea coast."

"For the purposes of this article the expression 'Maritime ports' means ports normally used by merchantships and open to international trade."

Right of Free Transit to the Sea. "Transit from a land-locked state towards the sea and vice-versa by all means of transportation and communication shall be freely accorded, subject to existing special agreements and conventions."

The transit shall not be subject to any customs duty or special charges or taxes levied by the coastal state or by the state of transit except for charges levied for specific services rendered.

Form of the Exercise of the Right of Access to the Sea. "The form in which the land-locked state is to exercise the rights mentioned in Articles IV and V shall, in so far as it is not determined by existing international treaties, be laid down by agreement between the land-locked state and the coastal states and states of transit."

Right of Protection of the State of Transit. "The coastal state or state of transit, maintaining full sovereignty over its territory and in particular over the means of communication and all matters relating to the facilities accorded, shall have the right to take all indispensable measures to ensure that the exercise of the rights mentioned in the Articles IV and V shall in no way infringe any of its legitimate interests whatsoever, especially its interests in security and public health."

RELATION OF THE NEW REGULATIONS TO PREVIOUS AGREEMENTS

"Articles I to VII neither abrogate nor affect agreements which are in effect between two or more of the contracting parties concerning questions regulated under the said articles, nor do they preclude the conclusion of similar agreements in the future provided that such future agreements do not institute a less favourable regime and do not conflict with the aforesaid articles."

EXCLUSION OF THE APPLICATION OF THE MOST FAVOURED NATION CLAUSE

The present provisions as well as those of multilateral and bilateral agreements concluded or to be concluded between land-locked states and countries of transit and coastal countries are excluded from the application of the most favoured nation clause.

It was on the basis of the work of the working group that the fifth committee finally succeeded in adopting unanimously to the conference draft articles to be adopted by the conference on the basis of the international law commission text. Articles 15, 27 and 28 read as follows.

Article 15. "Subject to the provisions of the present rules, ships of all states whether coastal or not, shall enjoy the right of innocent passage through territorial sea."

Article 27. "The high seas being open to all nations, no state may validly purport to subject any part of them to its sovereignty. Freedom of the high seas comprises, inter alia both for coastal and non-coastal states."

1. Freedom of navigation
2. Freedom of fishing
3. Freedom of laying submarine, cables and pipelines
4. Freedom to fly over the high seas.

These and others freedoms which are recognized by the general principles of International Law, shall be exercised by all states with reasonable regard to the interests of other states in their exercise of the freedom of the high seas.

Article 28. "Every state whether coastal or not has the right to sail ships under its flag on the high seas."
"Access to the sea for states having no sea-coast."

Article 29. 1. In order to enjoy the freedom of the seas on equal terms with coastal states, states having no sea coast should have free access to the sea. To this end states situated between the sea and a state having no sea coast shall, by common agreement with the latter, and in conformity with existing international conventions accord:

(a) To the state having no sea-coast on a basis of reciprocity, free transit through their territory, and
(b) to ships flying the flag of that state, treatment equal to that accorded to their own ships or to the ships of any other

states, as regards access to sea ports and the use of such ports.

2. States situated between the sea and the state having no sea-coast shall settle, by mutual agreement with the latter, and taking into account the rights of the coastal state or state of transit and the special conditions of the state having no sea-coast, all matters relating to freedom of transit and equal treatment in ports, in case such states are not already parties to existing international conventions.[35]

This proposal was adopted unanimously by the conference and was included as established rules of International Law as articles 2, 3, 4 of the high seas convention. This was indeed a legal milestone in favour of land-locked states.

NEPAL'S PARTICIPATION IN THE FIRST UNITED NATIONS CONFERENCE ON THE LAW OF THE SEA

Nepal, along with thirteen land-locked states participated in the first law of the sea conference held in Geneva in 1958. Nepal, with the other land-locked states submitted a memorandum to the conference on the law of the sea requesting affirmation of the seven principles formulated by it.[36]

Nepal actively participated in the deliberations of the preliminary conference and in the fifth committee of the conference on the law of the sea which dealt with the question of free access of the land-locked countries to the sea. The Nepalese delegate to the conference stated Nepal's views that the right of transit and the right of access to the sea should not be viewed solely from the point of view of a land-locked state's present requirements, but also from that of the country's subsequent economic development.[37] The Nepalese delegate pointed out that freedom of the high seas had no meaning for the land-locked states unless the right of access to the sea was first guaranteed. He stated that access of the land-locked states to the sea was bound up with the more general question of the right of transit. The Nepalese delegate described the right of free transit as vitally important to the land-locked countries as a condition of their economic survival. The Nepalese delegate suggested that the study of regulations for the carriage of passengers and goods to and from the ports of a coastal state and related questions entrusted to the economic and social council or to some other competent international body.[38]

The Nepalese delegation also maintained that the non-application of the most favoured nation clause, referred to in the preamble to the principles enunciated by the preliminary conference, might be mentioned among the principles themselves in the interests of the land-locked states and the coastal states. The Nepalese delegation took the view that the question of free zones and free ports should also be included among the principles. For the settlement of disputes concerning the interpretation and the application of the right of access of the land-locked states to the sea, Nepal suggested the formation of a special tribunal or a mixed commission.[39]

At last, the Nepalese delegation stressed that the question of the free access of the land-locked states to the sea merited the special attention of all coastal states and, in particular, that of the great powers and of coastal states adjacent to the land-locked states, which by cooperating in the effort to solve a problem so vital to the land-locked states would have an opportunity of fulfiling the solemn undertaking they had given under articles 55 and 56 of the United Nations charter.

Most of the coastal states supported the views of the Nepalese delegation, and the coastal states upheld that the principle of the freedom of the high seas and access to the sea should be granted to the land-locked states. But the coastal states stated that the freedom of the high seas and the right of access to the sea, depended on transit. The former right was in fact an established principle of international law whereas the latter was limited by the sovereignty of the coastal state.

NOTES

1. Fred L. Israel, (ed.) "Major Peace Treaties of Modern History" (1648-1967), (New York, 1967), Vol.I, p.35.
2. Abdul Hakim Tabibi, "The Right of Transit of Land-locked Countries," (Kabul, 1970), p.22.
3. Ibid.
4. Ibid.

5. League of Nations Documents, 20/31/58. 1921, p. 124.
   See also Sita Shrestha, "Nepal and United Nations,"(New Delhi, 1974).
6. UNCTAD, Doc. TD/B/308, 11 June 1970, p.1.
7. E/CN.14/INR/44, p.5.
8. Sita Shrestha, n.5.
9. League of Nations Treaty Series, Vol.VII, 1921-22, No.1-3, p.11.
10. Ibid., p.17.
11. Ibid., p.12.
12. Protocol of Provisional Application of the General Agreement on Tariffs and Trade (GATT), Signed at Geneva on October 30, 1947, p. 308.
    See also—United Nations Treaty Series, Vol. 55, 1950, No.814, p.194.
13. Yearbook of the United Nations, 1947-1948, p.976.
14. Ibid.
15. United Nations Treaty Series, Vol.55, 1950, No. 814, p.194.
16. Ibid.
17. See Barcelona Conference, 1921.
18. United Nations Conference on Trade and Employment, Final Act and Related Documents, Havana, March 1948, p.27.
19. UNCTAD, Text of International Instrument and Certain Recommendations Relating to Transit Trade, (E/CONF.46/AC.2/2) 25 September 1964, p.70.
20. United Nations Economic Commission for Asia and the Far East (ECAFF), Problems of Land-locked Countries in Asia and the Far East. (1 and IT/Sub.4/2) (Tokyo, 1956), 29 August, p.7.
21. Official Records of the Economic and Social Council, Twenty-second Session: Supplement No. 2, Para 271.
22. ECAFE/1 and T/Sub.4/2.
23. General Assembly Resolution 1028 (XI), 1957, 'Land-locked Countries and the Expansion of International Trade.'
24. Official Records of the General Assembly, Eleventh Session, Supplement No.9 (A/3159).
25. General Assembly Resolution 1105 (XI).
26. General Assembly, Eleventh Session, Sixth Committee 491st Meeting, Para 32.
27. General Assembly, 499th Meeting, Para 9.
28. Ibid., Para 25.
29. General Assembly Resolution, 1028 (XI), 1957.
30. GAOR, Eleventh Session, Supplement No.3, Doc. A/3520, Para 14(IV).
31. United Nations Conference on the Law of the Sea, Vol.VIII, Fifth Committee 1958, (A/Conf.13/C-5/21).

32. Ibid.
33. Ibid., p.7.
34. Ibid., p.25.
35. Ibid., p.36.
36. Ibid., Doc. A/Conf.13/C.5/L.1 Annex 7.
37. GAOR, Doc. A/Conf.13/C.5/L.2.
38. UN Conference on the Law of the Sea, Vol.VII, Fifth Cammittee, 1958.
39. Ibid.

5. International Conferences on Land-Locked States—II

ECONOMIC COMMISSION FOR ASIA AND FAR EAST MEETING ON THE PROBLEMS OF LAND-LOCKED STATES

The Tehran Economic Commission for Asia and Far East (ECAPE) ministerial conference held in March 1964, recommended that the subject of "principles governing international trade relations and trade policies conducive to development" be given "urgent and sympathetic consideration at the forthcoming United Nations Conference on Trade and Development (UNCTAD) with a view to formulating an adequate and effective international convention to ensure the freedom of transit trade of the land-locked countries."[1] The conference further recommended establishment of a committee of the forthcoming United Nations conference, "specially to achieve the above objectives."[2] The Tehran resolution called for presentation to the conference by the land-locked countries of the ECAFE regional documents on the right of free access to the sea (principles enunciated by the preliminary conference of the land-locked states) and the draft convention drawn up by the representatives of Afghanistan, Laos and Nepal to replace the Barcelona statute on the freedom of transit.[3]

The draft convention on transit trade drawn up by the representatives of Afghanistan, Laos and Nepal consisted of 20 Articles. As the first comprehensive treatment of the problems of the land-locked states with a somewhat exhaustive enumeration of their rights, it was a valuable contribution to the codification of international laws relating to the land-locked states.

The Tehran draft defined a 'traffic in transit' and demanded freedom of transit without any distinction. It also contained a provision for exemption from any special dues in respect of transit, an exception being the levying of such dues as were intended solely to defray expanses. On certain routes such dues may be reduced or even abolished on account of the differences in the cost of supervision.[4] The contracting states were to undertake to provide adequate means of transport for the movement of traffic in transit without delay.

FIRST UNITED NATIONS CONFERENCE ON TRADE AND DEVELOPMENT (UNCTAD I) 1964, GENEVA

The problems faced by the land-locked states were next discussed at the first United Nations Conference on Trade and Development (UNCTAD I) held at Geneva from 23 March to 16 June 1964. The fifth committee of the UNCTAD I appointed a sub-committee on the land-locked countries "to consider the proposal for the formulation of an adequate and effective international convention, or other means, to ensure the freedom of transit trade of land-locked countries and to formulate recommendations on this matter for consideration by the committee."[5]

The sub-committeee which was constituted of forty members, including Nepal, held nineteen meetings between April and May of 1964. The following land-locked countries participated in the conference, namely, Afghanistan, Austria, Bolivia, Burundi, Byelorussian, the Central African Republic, Czechoslovakia, Holysee, Hungary, Laos, Luxembourg, Mali, Mangolia, Nepal, Paraguay, Rwanda, San Marino, Switzerland, Uganda and the Upper Volta.[6]

The Sub-committeee had before it two documents issued in connection with item 10(c) of the agenda of the conference: a document entitled, "activities of the Economic Commission for Asia and the Far East (ECAFE) related to the UNCTAD, which dealt in part with the question of transit trade of the land-locked countries, and a document entitled, "problem of land-locked countries" containing a letter addressed to the Secretary General of the conference by Afghanistan, Laos, and Nepal, and five annexes with information required for the consideration of the question of transit rights of the land-locked countries.[7] These issues were put forth as follows:

Having regard to the various aspects of the problems of transit trade of land-locked states, "considering that, for the promotion of the economic development of the land-locked states, it is essential to provide facilities to enable them to overcome the effects of their land-locked position on their trade."[8]

The conference has adopted the following recommendations on principles relating to the transit trade of the land-locked states.

PRINCIPLES RELATING TO TRANSIT TRADE OF THE LAND–LOCKED COUNTRIES BY UNCTAD I

Principle I. "The recognition of the right of each land-locked state of free access to the sea is an essential principle for the expansion of international trade and economic development."

Principle II. "In territorial and internal waters, vessels flying the flag of land-locked states should have identical rights and enjoy treatment identical to that enjoyed by vessels flying the flag of coastal states other than the territorial state."

Principle III. "In order to enjoy the freedom of the season equal terms with coastal states, states having no sea-coast should have free access to the sea. To this end states situated between the sea and a state having no sea-coast shall, by common agreement with the latter, and in conformity with existing international conventions, accord to ships flying the flag of that state treatment equal to that accorded to their own ships or to the ships of any other state as regards access to sea ports and the use of such ports."

Principle IV. "In order to promote fully the economic development of the land-locked countries, the said countries should be afforded by all states, on the basis of reciprocity, free and unrestricted transit, in such a manner that they have free access to regional and international trade in all circumstances and for every type of goods."

Goods in transit should not be subject to any customs duty.

The means of transport in transit should not be subject to special taxes or charges higher than those levied for the use of means of transport of the transit country.

Principle V. "The state of transit, while maintaining full sovereignty over its territory, shall have the right to take all indispensable measures to ensure that the exercise of the right of free and unrestricted transit shall in no way infringe its legitimate interests of any kind."

Principle VI. "In order to accelerate the evolution of a universal approach to the solution of the special and particular problems of trade and development of land-locked countries in the different geographical areas, the conclusion of regional and other internationl agreements in this regard should be encouraged by all states."

Principle VII "The facilities and special rights aacorded to land-locked countries in view of their special geographical position are excluded from the operation of the most favoured-nation clause."

Principle VIII. "The principles which govern the right of free access to the sea of the land-locked state shall in no way abrogate existing agreements between two or more contracting parties concerning the problems, nor shall they raise an obstacle as regards the conclusion of such agreements in the future, provided that the latter do not establish a regime which is less favourable than or opposed to the above mentioned provisions."[9]

These principles are interrelated and each principle should be constructed in the context of the other principles. Considering that, for the promotion of the economic development of the land-locked countries, it is essential to provide facilities to enable them to overcome the effects of the land-locked position on their trade.

The land-locked countries of Africa and Asia expressed their dissatisfaction because the sub-committee had not had time to discusss the draft convention submitted by them as a working document in accordance with the sub-committee's terms of reference.

The report of the sub-committee was submitted to the fifth committee at its 31st and 32nd meetings on 19 and 22 May 1964 and the committee took note of it and decided to incorporate it in a committee's report for submission to the conference. It also proposed that the conference adopt the declaration of the principles of international economic cooperation with its interpretative note and recommended that the participating governments take these principles into account in their trade relations.

The twenty-four member expert committee appointed by the Secretary General of the United Nations, also included a representative of Nepal, who was elected its rapporteur.[10] It met in New York in October–November 1964 and prepared a draft convention. This draft convention was considered by the United Nations conference of plenipotentiaries on the transit trade of the land-locked countries, held at Geneva in 1965 which finally adopted the convention on the transit-trade of the land-locked states.

NEPAL'S PARTICIPATION IN UNCTAD I, 1964

Nepal along with the other land-locked states of the world participated in the First United Nations Conference on Trade and Development (UNCTAD I) in 1964 held in Geneva. Nepal requested the UN Conference on Trade and Development to set up a separate committee for a detailed study of the problems of trade and transit of the land-locked states. Nepal made a forceful plea for recognition of the land-locked states of the right to free access to the sea, their right of free and unrestricted transit and the right to use the ports of the coastal states.[11] She asked the representatives of the coastal states to consider the 'logical consequences' of the denial of such rights. The Nepalese delgate said that it would be equivalent to saying that those countries did not have the right to exist, develop and trade with the outside world.

The Nepalese delegate further added that international trade could not expand to its full scope if the interests of land-locked countries were ignored. The people living in these land-locked countries constitute potential consumers. The Nepalese delegate suggested that transit facilities should not be a subject of bargaining, rather they should be granted as a matter of right. Numerous complaints have been heard in the land-locked countries regarding delays in the movement of goods in transit. It hampers the pace of development of these less developed countries. For the fulfilment of the objective of integrated growth of the world economy as a whole, it is the duty of transit giving countries to see that the pace of development of the land-locked countries is not hampered. Simply because delays in movement of transit goods have taken place in their territory.[12]

UNITED NATIONS CONFERENCE ON TRANSIT-TRADE OF LAND-LOCKED COUNTRIES, 1965 (NEW YORK)

Convention on Transit-Trade of Land-locked States. The General Asesmbly of the United Nations at its 1328th plenary meeting on 10 February 1965 decided to convene an international conference of plenipotentiaries to consider the question of transit-trade of the land-locked countries and to embody the results of its work in an international convention and such other instruments as it might deem appropriate.

The United Nations conference on transit trade of the land-locked countries met at the headquarters of the United Nations in New York from 7 June to 8 July 1965.[13] The conference on transit trade was attended by delegates of fifty-eight states and observers of ten states including Iran and Peru.[14]

The conference had before it as the basis for its work the report of the committee on the preparation of a draft convention relating to transit trade of land-locked countries. The Afro-Asian draft convention, as well as all the amendments were annexed to the report.

There were vigorous debates throughout the conference on everything from whether free access to the sea was an inherent right of the land-locked states which would be reaffirmed in the convention, or whether the task of the conference was merely to resolve technical problems of transit traffic, or whether the convention should specify the procedures for clearing in transit goods through customs. While all the speakers paid lip-service to the necessity for the freest possible transit for the land-locked states, it was evident that few delegations were willing to surrender much of their own 'sovereignty' in order to achieve this. Moreover, not even the land-locked states agreed among themselves on the urgency for and scope of a new convention. Broadly speaking, the European land-locked states had few complaints, while those of Africa, Asia and South America were most vigorous in seeking broader rights and guarantees for the land-locked states.

Further, while the great majority of the participants were 'developing' countries and the emphasis throughout was on the importance of access to the sea for economic development, the 'developed' states were not always enthusiastic about aiding the developing land-locked states in the matter of free transit.

This convention consisting of a detailed preamble stating the legal right of the land-locked states, 23 articles of which came into force on 9 June 1967 and was a final legal and practical step for the solution of the problems which the land-locked countries were facing.

The state parties to the present convention, should recall that the article 55th of its charter requires the United Nations to promote conditions for economic progress and solutions of international economic problems. The convention while reaffirming the eighth UNCTAD principles relating to transit of the land-locked states, gives full recognition to the principle of the right of each land-locked state of free access to the sea. In the conference the convention on transit trade of the land-locked states consists of 23 articles explaining the practical rules of transit for the mutual benefit of the land-locked states, as well as transit states. These articles are as follows.

ARTICLES

Definitions. (a) For the purpose of this convention, the term 'land-locked state' means any contracting state which has no sea-coast.

(b) The term 'traffic in transit' means the passage of goods, including unaccompanied baggage, across the territory of a contracting state between a land-locked state and the sea when the passage is a portion of a complete journey which begins or terminates within the territory of that land-locked state, and which includes sea transport directly preceding or following such passage. The transhipment, warehousing, breaking bulk, and change in the mode of transport of such goods as well as the assembly, disassembly or reassembly of machinery and bulky goods shall not render the passage of goods outside the definition of 'traffic in transit', provided that any such operation is undertaken solely for the convenience of transportation. Nothing in this paragraph shall be constructed as imposing an obligation on any contracting state to establish or permit the establishment of permanent facilities on its territory for such assembly, disassembly or reassembly.

(c) The term 'transit state' means any contracting state with or without a sea-coast, situated between a land-locked state and the sea through whose territory 'traffic in transit' passages.

(d) The term means of 'transport' includes,

(i) any railway stock, seagoing and river vessels and road vehicles,
(ii) where the local situation so requires porters and pack animals,
(iii) if agreed upon by the contracting states concerned, other means of transport and pipelines and gaslines.

when they are used for traffic in transit within the meaning of this article.

Article 2—Freedom of Transit. 1. Freedom of transit shall be granted under the terms of this convention for traffic in transit and means of transport. Subject to the other provisions of this convention, the measures taken by the contracting states for regulating and forwarding traffic across their territory shall facilitate traffic in transit or routes in use mutually acceptable for transit to the contracting states concerned. Consistent with the terms of this convention, no discrimination shall be exercised which is based on the place of origin, departure, entry, exit or destination or on any circumstances relating to the ownership of the goods or the ownership, place of registration of flag vessels, land vehicles or other means of transport used.

2. The rules governing the use of means of transport, when they pass across a part or the whole of the territory of another contracting state, shall be established by common agreement among the contracting states concerned, with due regard to the multilateral, international conventions to which these states are parties.

3. Each contracting state shall authorize, in accordance with its laws, rules and regulations, the passage across or access to its territory or persons whose movement is necessary for traffic in transit.

4. The contracting states shall permit the passage of traffic in transit across their territorial waters in accordance with the principles of customary international laws or applicable international conventions and with their internal regulations.

Article 3. Customs Duties and Special Transit Dues. Traffic in transit shall not be subject by any authority within the transit state to customs duties or taxes chargeable by reason of importation or exportation, nor to any special dues in respect of transit. Nevertheless, on such traffic in transit there may be levied charges intended solely to defray expenses of supervision and administration entailed by such transit. The rate of any such charges must correspond as nearly as possible with the expenses they are intended to cover, and, subject to that condition, the charges must be imposed in conformity with the requirement of non-discrimination laid down in article 2, paragraph I.

Article 4. Means of Transport and Tariffs. 1. The contracting states undertake to provide subject to availability, at the points of entry and exit, and as required at points of transhipment, adequate means of transport and handling equipment for the movement of traffic in transit without unnecessary delay.

2. The contracting states undertake to apply to traffic in transit, using facilities operated or administrated by the state, tariffs or charges which, having regard to the conditions to the traffic and to the consideration of commercial competition, are reasonable as regards both their rates and methods of their application. These tariffs or charges shall be so fixed as to facilitate traffic in transit as much as possible, and shall not be higher than the tariffs or charges applied by contracting states for the transport through their territory of goods of countries with access to the sea. The provision of this paragraph shall also extend to the tariffs and charges applicable to traffic in transit using facilities operated or administered by firms or individuals, in cases in which the tariffs or charges are fixed or subject to control by the contracting state. The term 'facilities' used in this paragraph shall comprise means of transport, port installations, and routes for the use of which tariffs or charges are levied.

3. Any haulage service established as a monopoly or waterways used for transit must be so organized as not to hinder the transit of vessels.

4. The provisions of this article must be applied under the conditions of non-discrimination laid down in article 2, paragraph I.

Article 5. Methods and Documentation in Regard to Customs, Transport, etc. 1. The contracting states shall apply administrative and customs measures permitting the carrying out of free, uninterrupted and continuous traffic in transit. When necessary, they should undertake negotiations to agree on measures that ensure and facilitate such transit.

2. The contracting states undertake to use simplified documentation and expeditious methods in regard to customs, transport, and other administrative procedures relating to traffic in transit for the whole transit journey on their territory, including any transhipment, warehousing, breaking bulk and changes in the mode of transport as may take place in the course of such a journey.

Article 6. Storage of Goods in Transit. 1. The conditions of storage of goods in transit at the point of entry and exit, and at intermediate stages in the transit state may be established by agreement between the states concerned. The transit states shall grant conditions of storage at least as favourable as those granted to goods coming from or going to their own countries.

2. The Tariffs and Charges shall be established in accordance with article 4.

Article 7. Delays or Difficulties in Traffic in Transit. 1. Except in cases of force measures, all measures shall be taken by contracting states to avoid delays in or restrictions on traffic in transit.

2. Should delays or other difficulties occur in traffic in transit, the competent authorities of the transit state or states and of the land-locked states shall cooperate towards their expeditious elimination.

Article 8. Free Zones or Other Customs Facilities. 1. For convenience of traffic in transit free zones or other customs facilities may be provided at the ports of entry and exit in the transit states, by agreement between those states and the land-locked states.

2. Facilities of this nature may also be provided for the benefit of the land-locked states in other transit which have no sea-coast or sea port.

Article 9. Provision of Greater Facilities. This convention does not entail in any way the withdrawal of transit facilities which are greater than those provided for in the convention and which under conditions consistent with its principles are agreed between contracting states or granted by a contracting state. The convention also does not preclude such grant of greater facilities in the future.

Article 10. Relation of the Most-Favoured Nation Clause. 1. The contracting states agree that the facilities and special rights accorded by this convention to the land-locked states, in view of their special geographical position, are excluded from the operation of the most-favoured nation clause or a treaty between that land-locked state and the contracting state granting such facilities and special rights.

2. If a contracting state grants to a land-locked state facilities or special rights greater than those provided for in this convention, such facilities or special rights may be limited to that land-locked state, except in so far as the withholding of such greater facilities or special rights from any other land-locked state contravene the most-favoured nation provision of a treaty granting such facilities or special rights.

Article 11. Exceptions to the Convention on Grounds of Public Health. Security, and Protection of Intellectual Property. 1. No contracting state shall be bound by this convention to afford transit to persons whose admission into its territory is forbidden or for goods of a kind of which the importation is prohibited, either on grounds of public morals, public health or security, or as a precaution against diseases of animals or plants or against pests.

2. Each contracting state shall be entitled to take reasonable precautions and measures to ensure that persons and goods, particularly goods which are the subject of a monopoly, are really in transit, and that the means of transport are really used for the passage of such goods, as well as to potect the safety of the routes and means of communication.

3. Nothing in this convention shall affect the measures which a contracting state may be called upon to take in pursuance of provisions in a general convention, whether of a world-wide or regional character, to which it is a party, whether such a convention was already concluded on the date of this convention or is concluded later, when such provision relate:

(a) to export or import or transit of particular kinds of articles such as, narcotics, or other dangerous drugs, or arms, or,

(b) to protection of industrial, literary or artistic property, or protection of trade names, and indications or source of appellations of origin, and the suppression of unfair competition.

4. Nothing in this convention shall prevent any contracting state from taking any action necessary for the protection of its essential security interests.

Article 12. Exception in Case of Emergency. The measures of a general or particular nature which a contracting state is obliged to take in case of an emergency endangering its political existence or its safety may, in exceptional cases, and for as short a period as possible, involve a deviation from the provisions of this convention on the understanding that the principle of freedom of transit shall be observed to the utmost possible extent during such a period.

Article 13. Application of the Convention in Time of War. This convention does not prescribe the rights and duties of belligerents, neutrals in time of war. The convention shall, however, continue in force in time of war so far as such rights and duties permit.

Article 14. Obligations Under the Convention and Rights and Duties of United Nations Members. This convention does not impose upon a contracting state any obligation conflicting with its rights and duties as a member of the United Nations.

Article 15. Reciprocity. The provisions of this convention shall be applied on a basis of reciprocity.

Article 16. Settlement of Disputes. 1. Any disputes which may arise with respect to the interpretation or application of the provisions of this convention which is not settled by negotiation or by other peaceful means of settlement within a period of nine months shall, at the request of either party, be settled by arbitration. The arbitration commission shall consist of three members. Each party to the dispute shall appoint one member of the commission, while the third member, who shall be the chairman, shall be chosen in common agreement between the parties. If the parties fail to agree on the designation of the third member within a period of three months, the third member shall be appointed by the President of the International Court of Justice. In case any of the parties fail to make an appointment within a period of three months the President of the International Court of Justice shall fill the remaining vacancy or vacancies.

2. The arbitration commission shall decide on the matters placed before it by simple majority and its decisions shall be binding on the parties.

3. Arbitration commissions or other international bodies charged with settlement of disputes under this convention shall inform through the Secretary-General of the United Nations, the other contracting states of the existence and nature of disputes and of the terms of their settlement.

Article 17. Signature. The present convention shall be open until 31 December 1965 for signature by all states members of the United Nations or of any of the specialized agencies or parties to the Statute of the International Court of Justice, and by any other state invited by the General Assembly of the United Nations to become a party to the convention.

Article 18. Ratification. The present convention is subject to ratification. The instruments of ratification shall be deposited with the Secretary General of the United Nations.

Article 19. Accession. The present convention shall remain open for accession by any state belonging to any of the four categories mentioned in article 17. The instruments of accession shall be deposited wlth the Secretary General of the United Nations.

Article 20. Entry into Force. 1. The present convention shall enter into force on the thirtieth day following the date of deposit of the instruments of ratification or accession of at least two land-locked states and two transit states of having a sea-coast.

2. For each state ratifying or acceding to the convention after the deposit of the instruments of ratification or accession necessary for the entry into force of this convention in accordance with paragraph I of this article, the convention shall enter into force on the thirtienth day after the deposit by such state of its instrument of ratification on accession.

Article. 21 Revision. At the request of one third of the contracting states, and with the concurrence of the majority of the contracting states, the Secretary-General of the United Nations shall convene a conference with a view to the revision of this convention.

Article 22. Notification by the Secretary-General. The Secretary-General of the United Nations shall inform all states belonging to any of the four categories mentioned in article 17:

(a) of signature to the present convention and of the deposit of instruments of ratification or accession, in accordance with article 17, 18 and 19,
(b) of the date on which the present convention will enter into force, in accordance with article 20,
(c) of requests for revision, in accordance with article 21.

Article 23. Authentic Texts. The original of the present convention, of which the Chinese, English, French, Russian and Spanish texts are equally authentic, shall be deposited with the Secretary-General of the United Nations, who shall send certified copies thereof to all states belonging to any of the four categories mentioned in article 17.

In witness whereof the undersigned plenipotentiaries, being duly authorized thereto by their respective governments, have signed the present convention. Adopted at the 35th plenary meeting, 8th July 1965.[15]

If transit trade is important for all states, why should a special convention be needed concerning transit trade of the land-locked states? The answer to it is three fold.

1. Firstly, however important transit trade may be for all countries, the land-locked countries are often in a specially vulnerable position in this respect, the more vulnerable the smaller their choice of outlets. The legislative history of the convention clearly indicates that it is based on the "recognition of the need of land-locked countries for adequate transit facilities."[16] The convention is designed primarily to assure the land-locked states those links with the outside world which, under present day conditions, are indispensable for their economic life, their economic development and, in extreme cases, virtually their right of existence. In other words, the convention endeavours, first of all, to mitigate the ad-

verse consequences of the coincidences of geography of the land-locked states, and their dependence on other countries in maintaining their life-line with the outside world. This aim is not without significance for the interpretation of the convention.

2. At the same time, the convention safeguard very carefully and very extensively all legitimate interests of the transit states or, to put it more precisely, of the states, coastal or land-locked, through which traffic in transit moves to or from a land-locked state.

3. Finally, the convention covers not only the transit between the land-locked states and foreign sea-ports. It also covers transit through the land-locked states. This has potentiality of far-reaching consequence due to the conventions reciprocity clause (Art. 15). The clause underscores the function, obligation and willingness of the land-locked states to act themselves as bridges between other states, coastal or land-locked alike.

The most detailed analysis of the convention to date is that by John H.E. Fried, the legal adviser to His Majesty's Government of Nepal on assignment from the United Nations, and members of the Nepali delegation at the conference, whose conclusions are as follows:

1. The main significance of the 1965 United Nations conference which hammered out this convention was that the problems which transit involves for the land-locked states, their coastal neighbours and the "third countries" were for the first time discussed at an international plenipotentiary level. These problems have thus acquired, as it were, 'status' on the world scene.

2. Having acquired such status, those transit problems, especially of the developing land-locked countries, will probably appear more frequently on the international scene, for example, the UNCTAD. Also, the increasing awareness of transit problems in general, which were regulated in generation and a half ago in the Barcelona statute, may lead to its revision.

3. On the other hand, attitudes of states regarding transit through their territory, seem to have stiffened. This is reflected in the convention. The convention reveals stronger insistence on conditions, provisions and escope clauses, compared with such instruments as the Barcelona Statute of 1921 or the GATT of 1948. To say nothing of the 1874 Berne Postal Congress which created the great liberal transit system of the universal postal union.

4. The new convention deals with transit, not only to and from, but also through the land-locked states. It has various noticeable and beneficial features. It amply protects the countries when acting as transit states.

It contains little which is new, and no radical innovations or breakthroughs. This is largely due to the fact that the conditions of the land-locked states differ considerably from each other, as do their relations with their respective neighbours. Hence, the need for separate bilateral and, as the case may be, multilateral and regional agreements.

5. The twin notions that the transit traffic is a "burden" or "favour" and that only the land-locked countries impose such "burden" are unfounded in reality and law. Transit is an obvious and expanding feature of world trade, indispensable for the economic development and well being of all states. All are dependent on the immutable facts of geography, but some much more than others. These inequalities can only be alleviated by a spirit of solidarity.

6. Transit trade offers particularly many illustrations of interplay between international and municipal laws. The pertinent domestic laws and regulations of the countries involved and, as cannot be sufficiently emphasized, the manner in which municipal rules are actually applied by officials on the working level, are at least as crucial as are international treaties.

7. For the land-locked states, especially those with a small choice of outlets to the outside world, transit trade is a topic of grave concern. The atmosphere and debates at the 1965 conference showed it clearly. Those matters stare at the eyes the people of the land-locked states constantly. They are often felt as reminders that the land-locked countries are not truly independent.

The convention is designed to alleviate such situations. But in order to achieve this, the convention has to be strengthened and 'filled in', as said before, by separate agreements. The convention itself envisages that these provide far 'greater facilities' than are mentioned in its own, necessarily general and cautions provisions.

8. Transit trade problems are getting more, not less, importance as time goes on, because unhampered fast, reliable and economical transit is becoming ever more essential for the nations and individuals. Unless progress is made in this field, the world will be faced,

because of frustrations of the land-locked states, with a new source of dissent and complications on an international scale.[17]

In this convention the land-locked states feel that they are not free from infirmity in as much as article 15 lays down the principle that 'the provisions of this convention shall be applied on a basis of reciprocity', thereby failing to distinguish between the needs of transit of the geographically disadvantaged land-locked states and those of coastal states that serve as transit states. Whereas the transit needs of the land-locked states are elemental, it is argued, the same is not the case with the coastal states for whom the right, if at all, may best serve to facilitate transport and communication in general. Moreover, the impact of the New York convention on transit trade of the land-locked states, 1965, is not more than marginal. First, due to the fact that it is confined to a limited number of states and, secondly, that those that have ratified or adhered to it heppen to be mostly land-locked states, and that even if they be coastal states and, they are not typically transit countries.

To sum up, it is fair to say that while the convention undoubtedly represents important progress in international law, the developing land-locked states were far from completely satisfied with it. It is the latest, but not the last, word on the subject.

NEPAL'S PARTICIPATION

In the long discussions over the draft convention which took place in the committee of twenty-four and the conference of plenipotentiaries, Nepal acted as the spokesman of all the land-locked countries of Asia, Africa, and Latin America.[18] Nepal emphasized the need to have a precise definition of the term 'land-locked states', 'state of transit', and 'traffic in transit'. It was at her instance that the quasi land-locked states were excluded from the definition of the land-locked states.[19]

The representative of Nepal spoke on the matter of freedom of transit. He said, "There was a general agreement in the committee that in principle transit was to be free and unrestricted and that there would be no discrimination based on the ownership of goods or of the means of transport or on the origin, departure, entry, exit or, destination of traffic in transit. However, the terms and conditions on which the means of transport would move when in transit would be determined by the agreement between the contracting states concerned."[20]

In the conference, Nepal insisted that the convention should include a clear statement that transit goods should always be exempted from customs duties and special transit dues levied by provincial or local authorities.[21] The representative of Afghanistan supported the position of Nepal.

The representative of Nepal explained that the Afro-Asian land-locked states had thought it necessary to include a provision requiring the state of transit to provide adequate means of transport for traffic in transit. In their experience, the absence of adequate means of transport had been a major obstacle in the growth of their international trade. Representatives of the transit states feared that such an undertaking might be too onerous for the developing transit state, having regard to their own situation with respect to transportation for internal traffic. Moreover, it should be recognized that occasional delays were inevitable in a developing transportation situation and thus any obligations concerning transportation should be related to the means and conditions of the transit state.[22]

The representative of Nepal stated that free storage of goods at the points of entry, exit and intermediate stages in the state of transit, in areas or premises designated for this purpose, shall be accorded for a reasonable period of time which may be agreed upon by the states concerned. Where this period of time is exceeded owing to a delay in the movement of the goods not attributable to the fault of the owners of the goods, no demurrage shall be charged by the state of transit.[23]

The representative of Nepal along with other member states, stated that, 'traffic in transit' will not be subjected to unnecessary delays and restrictions.[24]

Replying to the criticism that recognition of the rights of the land-locked states would infringe upon the sovereignty of transit states, Nepal asserted that an enumeration of those rights in Article I of the draft convention and reference to their reaffirmation by "principles of international law," was aimed at setting an example of mutual economic cooperation. In the Nepalese view the rights of the land-looked states were reconcilable with those of coastal states. It recognized the universal truth that every right was limited and must be exercised reasonably. Nepal wanted the convention to be permeated with the legal philosophy that the 'transit goods' should be treated as though they did not pass through the transit state at all. It was made clear by Nepal that she was not suggesting that a transit state should lose any of its sovereign rights. But she considered it clearly wrong that a transit state should be able to exercise control over persons outside her own borders, simply because those persons or goods had to pass through its territory.

Nepal tried her best to make the conference adopt article I of the draft convention which referred to the recognition of the rights of the land-locked states in accordance with the principles of international law. Nepal appealed to the conference to accept it with the addition of a fourth right proposed by her delegation, namely, the right of the transit states on a basis of reciprocity to free and unrestricted transit across the territories of the land-locked states. But the article could not be adopted in the committee of twenty-four due to the opposition of several countries including India and Pakistan.[25]

There was a basic difference between the developing coastal and the land-locked states in their approach towards the rights of the latter. They held widely dissimilar views about the nature and character of the convention on the transit trade of the land-locked states. At the conference India showed a great concern for the "fundamental principle of the sovereignty of states," which her delegate called upon the conference to 'bear in mind'.[26] The Indian delegate told the conference that 'no provision of the convention' should even imply any interference with the sovereignty of the transit states. India wanted that the convention should lay down only 'guidelines' leaving the details to be worked out through bilateral and multilateral agreements.[27] It also pointed out that many transit countries were also developing countries and could not offer the same facilities as the developed countries could provide.[28]

UNITED NATIONS CONFERENCE ON TRADE AND DEVELOPMENT—(UNCTAD-II) 1968, NEW DELHI

The second session of the United Nations conference on Trade and Development (UNCTAD-II) was held in New Delhi from 1 February to 29 March 1968 in accordance with the decision of the General Assembly in its resolution No. 2206 (XXI) of 17 December 1966.[29]

UNCTAD-II established a special working group to consider

and report on the special problems of the land-locked countries. During the deliberations of this group, the representatives of the land-locked countries emphasized that their land-locked position was a factor seriously inhibiting expansion of their trade and economic development. This was so particularly on account of the high costs of transportation, the poor development of their infrastructure and other special problems such as inadequate and inconvenient transport, storage and port facilities as well as lack of opportunity to use their own transport equipment and to establish their own transport facilities. The unfavourable trend of transport tariffs and charges was also a factor hampering them in their efforts to take advantage of the international measures envisaged to promote the trade and development of all developing countries. They, therefore, emphasized that the solution of these problems required special measures in the context of global strategy of development. These measures should include free access to the sea, priority to the needs of their financial and technical assistance and the creation of a special fund designed to subsidize their additional transport costs. They considered the need for undertaking studies with regard to the feasibility of through rates, roll on and roll off facilities and identification of their most important problems.[30]

The representatives of developing transit countries recognized that the land-locked developing countries suffered from certain undesirabilities because of their distance from the sea. However, they reserved their position on matters relating to transit facilities such as transport tariffs and charges, and establishment of transport and equipment facilities by the land-locked countries in the transit states. They pointed out that though the problems of the land-locked states had some common features, their solution had to be sought on a bilateral basis in the context of the circumstances pertaining to each case. They supported the request of these countries for special attention to their needs of financial and technical assistance programme in the fields of transport and communications.[31]

The developed countries also stressed that the development of a harmonious bilateral relationship between the land-locked and transit countries was a basic necessity in the solution of these problems. They considered that in many cases the land-locked countries ranked amongst the least developed countries, and, therefore, required appropriate treatment on that account.[32]

The draft resolution on the subject approved by the working group was adopted at the plenary session of the conference. The major recommendations of the conference, as embodied in the resolution II (II) were as follows:[33]

1. In view of the special problems of the land-locked developing countries, the land-locked situation should be considered as a factor in determining the criteria for the identification of the least developed among the developing countries.

2. The governments of the developing countries in their financial and technical assistance programme in the field of transport and communication should accord appropriate attention to the special needs of the land-locked developing countries particularly with regard to the development and improvement of transport and communications needed by these countries.

3. The appropriate international financial organizations should be invited to give similar attention among their priorities to the matters referred to in the preceding recommendation.

4. The land-locked developing countries and the transit countries should enter into consultation and negotiations with a view to examine jointly the special difficulties which the land-locked countries faced in the promotion of their trade and economic development and concluding agreements designed to overcome such difficulties.

5. The governments of the developed countries should bear in mind in their assistance programme the possibility of extending loans on favourable terms to the land-locked developing countries for the development of transport and communication facilities.

6. The governments of states members of the UNCTAD should invite liner conference and insurance companies to bear in mind, informing their respective tariff policies, the special problems of the land-locked developing countries.

The conference also requested the Secretary-General of the UNCTAD to establish a group of experts for carrying and a comprehensive examination of the special problems involved in the promotion of trade and economic development of the land-locked developing countries.

The Trade and Development Board (TDB) of the UNCTAD at its eighth session (January–February 1969) appointed a group of nine experts of submit a report on the special problems of the land-locked countries.[34] This report was presented at the tenth session of the Trade and Development Board of Geneva in May–June 1970.[35] It recommended "the simplification of customs and other procedures and formalities and the limitation of documentation and through instructions of the officials concerned in the spirit of transit agreements. It also suggested the coordination and integration of transport networks." The establishment of alternative transport routes to the sea from the land-locked countries was favoured by the report.[36]

Subsequent to the appointment of the group of experts on the land-locked countries, the General Assembly adopted resolution 2569 (XXIV) of 13 December 1969 requesting the board to consider "the adoption of practical measures for the implementation of all the provisions of resolution II (II) of the United Nations Conference on Trade and Development (UNCTAD).[37] It also recommended that the governments of the land-locked developing countries and their transit neighbours should continue their joint efforts, whenever necessary, to make arrangements, bilaterally or, if mutually agreed, multilaterally, to review administrative and other relevant measures and procedures governing the flow of transit trade and the trade between the developing land-locked countries and the transit countries. With a view to facilitating the flow of traffic across frontiers, curbing smuggling the diversion of trade, and arranging for regular inter-governmental consultations to ensure that the needs and problems of both the land-locked and the transit countries.[38]

NEPAL'S PARTICIPATION

At the UNCTAD–II, held in New Delhi in February–March 1968, Nepal sponsored with eighth other land-locked countries a draft resolution which noted that the land-locked position of many developing countries was "a factor seriously inhibiting the expansion of trade and economic development of these countries," and that there were special problems involved in relation to their trade and economic development.

At the UNCTAD II the Nepalese delegate made nine suggestions. The draft resolution moved by the nine land-locked countries incorporated all these suggestions, namely:

1. Creation of a separate international compulsory fund to sub-

sidize additional higher transportation cost of the developing land-locked countries.

2. Priority by international financial agency for the development of the infrastructure of the transport project and specially of inland water navigation of the developing land-locked countries.

3. Evolution of international practice of quoting through rates in order to facilitate the international trade of the developing land-locked countries.

4. Elimination of such practices as licensing system and customs appraisal of the traffic in transit.

5. Provision for most convenient transit route and the alternative mode of transportation.

6. Stabilization of the tariff structure of surface transport by coastal countries for not less than ten years.

7. Provision for port facilities including that of terminal, transit shed, storing and hauling, etc.

8. Roll-on-roll-off facility of the railway wagons to the developing land-locked countries by coastal countries and a rebate to the land-locked countries for using their own wagons.

9. Periodic annual evaluation and meeting of experts from the land-locked countries and the international agencies.[39]

The Nepalese delegate suggested inland navigation of big rivers originating in Nepal and joining the Ganges to reduce the additional transport costs of goods in transit. The Nepalese delegate hoped that the second session of the conference would draw up specific measures to alleviate the burden of the land-locked countries. Although the convention on transit trade of the land-locked states had come into force in June 1967, it had been ratified only by the minimum necessary number of countries. He appealed to the coastal countries not to formulate reservations when ratifying or acceding to that convention.[40]

The Nepalese delegation welcomed the recommendation of the Secretary-General of the UNCTAD that unstinted technical and financial cooperation should be offered to the relatively less developed and the land-locked countries.[41]

STATEMENT ON SEA-BED, 1970

In the fall of 1967, Ambassador Arvid Pardo of Malta urged the UN General Assembly to consider the limits of national jurisdiction for the exploitation of sea-bed resources.[42] By resolution 2749 (XXV) of 17 December 1970, the General Assembly, adopted a declaration of principles governing the sea-bed and the ocean floor, and the sub-soil thereof beyond the limits of national jurisdiction.[43]

The General Assembly also took steps during its 1970 session with regard to the special problems of the land-locked countries in relation to the exploitation of the sea-bed.

In doing so, the Assembly recalled its earlier resolutions concerning the problems of the land-locked countries and bore in mind the wide support that had been indicated for the idea of convening a conference on the law of the sea at which the interests and needs of all states, whether land-locked or coastal, could be reconciled.[44] It also noted that many of the current land-locked member states of the United Nations, had not participated in the previous United Nations conference on the law of the sea, reaffirmed that the sea-bed and ocean floor beyond the limits of national jurisdiction, and the resources thereof, were the common heritage of mankind, and expressed its conviction that the exploration of the area and the exploitation of its resources must be carried out for the benefit of mankind. Taking into account the special interests and needs of the developing land-locked countries.[45]

The General Assembly then set forth the following fifteen principles which were to govern the sea-bed and ocean floor.

1. The sea-bed and ocean floor and the sub-soil thereof, beyond the limits of national jurisdiction (subsequently, referred to as, the area), and their resources, were the common heritage of mankind.

2. The area should not be subject to appropriation by any means of states or persons, natural or juridical and no state should claim or exercise sovereignty or sovereign rights over any part of it.

3. No state or person, natural or juridical, should claim, exercise or acquire rights with respect to the area or its resources incompatible with the international regime to be established and the principles of this declaration.

4. All activities regarding the exploration and exploitation of the resources of the area and other related activities should be governed by the international regime to be established.

5. The area should be open to use exclusively for peaceful purposes by all states whether coastal or land-locked, without discrimination, in accordance with the international regime to be established.

6. States should act in the area in accordance with the applicable principles and rules of international law in the interests of maintaining international peace and security and promoting international cooperation and mutual understanding.

7. The exploration of the area and the exploitation of its resources should be carried out for the benefit of mankind as a whole, irrespective of the geographical location of states and taking into particular consideration the interests and needs of the developing countries.

8. The area should be reserved exclusively for peaceful purposes. One or more international agreements should be concluded as soon as possible in order to implement effectively this principle and to constitute a step towards the exclusion of the sea-bed and ocean floor from the arms race.

9. An international regime applying to the area and its resources and including appropriate international machinery to give effect to its provisions should be established by an international treaty of a universal character. The regime should, inter-alia, provide for the orderly and safe development and rational management of the area and its resources and for expanding opportunities in the use thereof, and ensure the equitable sharing by states in the benefits therefrom, taking into particular consideration the interests and needs of the developing countries, whether land-locked or coastal.

10. States should, by various means, promote international cooperation in scientific research exclusively for peaceful purposes.

11. Acting in conformity with the international regime to be established, states should take appropriate measures for, and cooperate in the adoption and implementation of international rules, standards and procedures for the prevention of pollution, contamination and other hazards to the marine environment including the coastline, and for the protection and conservation of the natural resources of the area and the flora and fauna of the marine environment.

12. In their activities in the area, including those relating to its resources, states should pay due regard to the rights and legitimate interests of the coastal states in the region, as well as of all other states which might be affected by such activities.

13. Nothing in the declaration should affect:

(a) the legal status of the water superjacent to the area or that of the space above those waters or,

(b) the rights of the coastal states with respect to measures to prevent, mitigate or eliminate grave and imminent danger to their coastline or related interests from pollution or threat thereof or from other hazardous occurrences resulting from or caused by any activities in the area, subject to the international regime to be established.

14. Every state should have the responsibility to ensure that activities in the area, including those relating to its resources, whether undertaken by governmental agencies or non-governmental entities or persons under its jurisdiction or acting on its behalf, should be carried out in conformity with the international regime to be established. The same responsibility applies to international organizations and their members. Damage caused by such activities should entail liability.

15. The parties to any dispute relating to activities in the area and its resources should resolve such dispute by the measures mentioned in Article 33 of the charter of the United Nations and such procedures for settling disputes as might be agreed upon were in the international regime to be established.[46] These principles laid down in resolution 2749 (XXV) which was adopted by the Assembly by 108 votes to nil with fourteen abstentions.[47]

The resolution was adopted on the recommendation of the first committee, by which it was approved on 15 December 1970 by a vote of 90 to nil with 11 abstentions.[48]

The land-locked states felt that the coastal states would not give them any benefits under their new claim for enlarged maritime national jurisdiction. A joint proposal submitted by seven states, i.e. Afghanistan, Austria, Belgium, Hungary, Nepal, the Netherlands and Singapore, suggested that the National sea-bed area should not exceed either 200 metres or 40 miles from the baseline of the territorial sea and that in an additional forty mile zone called "the coastal state priority zone" no exploitation should take place without the consent of the coastal state. These countries also proposed a revenue sharing system applicable to the entire notional sea-bed.[49]

The land-locked states demanded the right for them to participate in the exploration and exploitation of the non-living resources of the sea-bed areas of neighbouring coastal states on an equal and non-discriminatory basis, and sharing of revenues by coastal states with the International Sea-bed Authority (ISBA) from the exploitation of the non-living resources of the national sea-bed. Iran made a proposal in which it was stated that the revenues derived from the exploitation of the natural resources of the continental shelf shall not be subject to any revenue sharing.[50]

There was general agreement in the first committee that an international regime should be established for the sea-bed area. A sense of urgency about this question was reflected in the statements of a number of countries, both the developed and developing, coastal and land-locked which pointed out that the sea-bed contained valuable mineral resources capable of being exploited because of recent technological advances.[51]

Austria maintained that the land-locked states having a restricted continent could participate in the exploration and exploitation of the sea-bed only through an international regime which had to extend over an area of meaningful size.[52] Afghanistan called for the quick establishment of a just international regime in which the land-locked states would have the right of participation and benefits.[53]

Several coastal states while not opposing an international regime, cautioned that it should not infringe upon the rights of the coastal states. Iceland said that it had long believed in a true and effective internationalization of the area which would permit all states to share in the benefits that would be derived from the sea-bed resources.[54]

NEPAL'S STAND

Nepal participated in the sea-bed committee and submitted proposal for the land-locked countries. Nepal welcomed the proposals of Afghanistan and she endorsed the proposal to establish an international regime and appropriate international machinery to ensure equitable sharing of such resources lying beyond the limits of national jurisdiction for the benefit of all mankind. But Nepal felt that it will be very difficult for the land-locked developing countries to share the benefits in any meaningful manner without necessary transit and port facilities. Therefore, Nepal urged the coastal states to give sympathetic consideration to make specific provisions guaranteeing the right of the land-locked countries to free and unrestricted access to and from the sea.[55]

Speaking at UN General Assembly, Mr. Rajbhandari said that the land-locked countries were facing an additional problem of exercising their right of free access to the sea. In this area, Nepal, on her part, feels that the existing international conventions and practices should serve as a basis for bilateral arrangements between the land-locked countries and their transit neighbours.[56]

While most of the coastal states are claiming wider jurisdictions in the sea and sea-bed to protect the newly found natural resources, there is a formidable group of land-locked states which is completely high and dry in the whole business. Away from the sea, they do not want to be away from the growing benefits of the common heritage of mankind. Although the coastal states have been reluctantly adjusting to the idea of a 'right of access' of the land-locked states to and from the sea, it is insisted that they have no 'right' but only 'freedom of transit', through the territories of transit states to be exercised in accordance with bilateral, sub-regional or regional agreements. But how far can they partake other benefits from the sea or the mineral resources of the coastal areas, no body can predict as yet and, indeed, will depend upon how well they play their cards. Many of these land-locked states are under severe pressure from their regions and a threat that if they do not agree, they would lose all existing transit rights and would have no chance of getting access to the living resources in the economic zone. The hidden and fairly effective sanction against these countries is that each of them will have to negotiate with its neighbouring coastal states for access to the ocean and its resources.

Instead of this, the 1970 General Assembly resolution maintained that the deep sea-bed must be explored and exploited for the benefit of mankind as a whole, and taking into particular consideration the interests and needs of the land-locked countries.

CREATION OF A SPECIAL (LAND-LOCKED) UNIT IN ECAFE, 1970

On the recommendation of the Committee on Trade (in its thirteenth session) and the Economic Commission for Asia and the Far East (in its twenty-sixth session) held in 1970, a special unit was created in the ECAFE International Trade Division to give continuous attention to the problems of the land-locked and the least developed among developing countries of the region. The unit, which is a part of the trade facilities section of the division, coordinates the activities of other substantive divisions of the secretariat dealing with various aspects of the problems of those countries.[57]

The ECAFE Ministerial Conference for Asian Economic Cooperation, at its fourth session, held in Kabul in December 1970, urged the member countries of the region to render every possible assistance to the land-locked states of the region to enable them to enjoy the right of free access to the sea, and to provide port and transport facilities, minimum and simple customs formalities, reasonable transportation charges and transit by air and over land routes. It also stressed the need to accord specially favourable treatment to import from the least developed among the developing countries, and further urged them not to allow disputes between two countries of the region to affect adversely the interest of these countries.[58]

This recommendation was endorsed by the Commission at its 27th session held at Manila in April 1971.

ACTION BY THE REGIONAL ECONOMIC COMMISSION (ECAFE), 30 APRIL 1971, MANILA

The Economic Commission for Asia and the Far-east (ECAFE), at its 27th session, held at Manila from 20 to 30 April 1971 adopted resolution 114 (XXVII) on the "special problems of land-locked countries."[59] In that resolution the commission—

1. Requests the Executive Secretary to establish a special body of the commission to make recommendation for the purpose of implementation of the Kabul declaration in regard to the land-locked countries as well as the United Nations Convention on Transit Trade of the Land-locked Countries, 1965.

2. Further requests the Executive Secretary to report to the Commission at its twenty-eighth session the result of the work of the special body.[60]

Earlier in December 1970, the Council of Ministers for Asian Economic Cooperation, at its fourth session, had unanimously adopted the Kabul declaration on Asian Economic Cooperation and Development, which inter alia urged the member and associate member countries in the ECAFE region, "to render every possible assistance to land-locked countries of the region to enjoy the right of free access to the sea and to provide port and transport facilities, minimum and simple customs formalities, reasonable transport charges and transit by air and overland routes."[61]

THE ECONOMIC COMMISSION FOR AFRICA

At its tenth session (the first meeting of the Conference of Ministers), held at Tunis from 8 to 13 February 1971, adopted resolution 218 (X) on, Africa's strategy for development in the 1970's a section of which is devoted to the special problems of the least developed among developing countries and the land-locked and Island countries.[62] The strategy states that—

1. Thirteen out of a total of eighteen land-locked developing countries can be found in Africa. The position of these countries, in particular because of the high costs of transportation, the poor development of their infrastructure, inadequate and inconvenient transport, storage and port facilities, the lack of opportunity to use their own transport equipment and to establish their own transport facilities, and the unfavourable trend of transport tariffs and charges, is a factor seriously inhibiting the expansion of their trade and economic development.[63]

2. The solution of the special problems of the land-locked and island countries requires special measures to be taken in their favour within the region and in the broader framework of the second United Nations Development Decade. The various elements of such a strategy would include the following:

(a) Detailed studies identifying their most serious bottlenecks to rapid economic development.

(b) Effective recognition of their right to, and facilitation of, free access to the sea.

(c) Priority attention to their financial and technical assistance needs, including the granting of soft-term loans and the provisions of funds designed to subsidize their additional transport costs.

(d) Application of special measures in their favour along the lines of those accorded to the least developed among the developing countries.[64]

The Economic Commission for Africa (ECA) programme of work and priorities for 1971–73, with projections to 1976, gives particular attention to the identification of basic needs of the land-locked developing countries in Africa, to the formulation of appropriate measures and to the implementation of such measures, particularly in the fields of multinational programmes and economic cooperation, trade and transport planning. One of the most important projects to be undertaken by the ECA Secretariat is entitled "Development prospects and the special problems of the least developed African countries and the measures to promote their development (1971–76)." This project, to be undertaken with the collaboration of all ECA divisions and also of the various organizations within the United Nations system will obviously embrace several land-locked countries.[65]

THE ECONOMIC COMMISSION FOR LATIN AMERICA

The Economic Commission for Latin America has also continued to place particular emphasis in its activities on the land-locked countries in the region, particularly within the fields of regional integration, trade and transport planning. The study of the problems of these countries, as well as the formulation of special measures in their favour, are included in the framework of the commission's work programme and priorities for the near future.[66]

DECLARATION OF THE MINISTERIAL MEETING OF THE ASIAN GROUP OF THE 'GROUP 77', 1971, BANGKOK

The ministers of the Asian group of the 'Group 77' assembled in Bangkok from October 5 to 7 1971. They resolved that:

Having reviewed the situation of the developing countries in the world trade international economic relations. in particular of member countries of the Asian group and having assessed the activities of the international community in assisting the promotion of the economic and social progress of their countries.

In endorsing the decision adopted at the Eleventh Session of the

Trade and Development Board, the following immediate and concrete measures are recommended:

(a) The United Nations Development Programme, specialized agencies, international financial institutions, and developed countries, should take into account the special needs of the land-locked developing countries, particularly in the field of transport, and to give favourable consideration to requests from these countries for financial and technical assistance on soft terms for fulfilment of the aims and objectives contained in the international development strategy.

(b) Invites the Secretary-General of the UNCTAD to include in his proposal for an action programme for the development of the land-locked countries the feasibility of creating a special fund for subsidizing the additional transport cost of the land-locked developing countries.

(c) Requests the Secretary-General of the UNCTAD to organize a study of the existing transit procedures obtaining in different regions and also to study the port and transport facilities available for the land-locked developing countries aimed at the improvement of such procedures and facilities in the spirit of the relevant provision of the resolution 69 (X) of the Trade and Development Board.[67]

Nepal along with the other Asian land-locked states urged the member countries of the region to assist the land-locked states of the region to provide financial assistance and, port and transport facilities.

THE DECLARATION AND PRINCIPLE OF THE ACTION OF LIMA, 1971

The ministers of the Group of 77, assembled at their second meeting in Lima from 28 October to 7 November 1971. The declaration of Lima recognized the special needs of the land-locked countries and recommended special measures for their benefit. The declaration of Lima recognized the need for subsidizing the additional transport costs of the land-locked developing countries in order to make their goods competitive in the world market. At its twenty-eighth session, ESCAFE in its resolution, had urged national, regional, and international financial institutions and the governments of the developed countries to consider creating special funds from their additional resources for the development of the land-locked countries. The Nepalese delegation fully supported the creation of such funds and also fully endorsed the provisions included in the declaration of Lima regarding programmes for the development of tourism, which could play a significant role in the development of the land-locked countries.[68]

NOTES

1. ECOSOC, Doc.E/CN. 11/657 Resolution, 51(XX), p.3.
2. Ibid., p.3.
3. Ibid.
4. UNCTAD, E/Conf. 46/88, Annex, II.
5. UNCTAD-I, Doc. E/Conf. 46/141, Vol. I, 1964.
6. Ibid.
7. Ibid.
8. Ibid.
9. UNCTAD-I, Vol. I, 1964, Final Act and Report, E/Conf. 46/141.
10. GAOR, 20th Session, Annexes, Doc. A/5906.
11. UNCTAD-I, Vol. II, 1964, E/Conf. 46/141.
12. Ibid.
13. UNCTAD-10 June, 1965, p.2. TD/Transit/R.3.
14. Ibid.
15. Ibid. See also, "Land-locked, aspects of development," Trade Promotion Centre, Kathmandu (Nepal), 1976, pp.16–24.
16. General Assembly, Res.1028(XI).
17. Indian Journal of International Law, VI (1966), pp.28–30.
18. GAOR, 20th Session, Annexes, Doc. A/5906, p. 42.
19. Ibid.
20. General Assembly, 19th Session, Annexes, 13, 1965, p.37.
21. UNCTAD, Doc. TD/Transit/SR, 4. p.8.
22. General Assembly, 19th Session, 1965, Annexes, 13, p.42, Doc. A/5906,
23. Ibid.
24. Ibid.
25. GAOR, 20th Session, Annexes, Doc. A/5906, p.45.

26. UNCTAD, Doc. TD/Transit/SR. 8, p.12.
27. Ibid.
28. Ibid.
29. Proceedings of the United Nations Conference on Trade and Development (UNCTAD–II), Second Session, (New Delhi, 1968), Vol. I. p.30, TD/79.
30. Ibid.
31. Ibid.
32. Ibid.
33. H.D. Shourie, "UNCTAD–II, A step forward." (New Delhi, 1968), p.238.
34. UNCTAD, Doc. TD/B/233, 21 Feb. 1969, p.23.
35. UNCTAD, Doc. TD/B/308, 11 June, 1970, p.50.
36. Ibid., p.51.
37. UN General Assembly, Resolution 2569 (XXIV), 1969.
38. Ibid.
39. Nepal News Royal Nepalese Embassy, (New Delhi, 1968) Vol. VII, No. 4, 10 March, pp.2, 7–8.
40. UNCTAD–II, Vol. I, 1968, p.146.
41. Ibid.
42. For the speech of Ambassador Arvido Pardo of Malta, see, UN Doc. A/C–I/PV, 1515 and 1516. 1 Nov. 1967.
43. Yearbook of the United Nations, Vol. 24, 1970, p.60.
44. Ibid.
45. Ibid., p.63.
46. Ibid., p.68.
47. Ibid.
48. Ibid.
49. P. Chandrashekhara Rao, "The New Law of Maritime Zone, with Special Reference to India's Maritime Zone," (New Delhi, 1983), pp.140-41.
50. Ibid., p.242.
51. N.43 p.61.
52. Ibid.
53. Ibid., p.62.
54. Ibid.
55. Nepal and nonalignment. HMG, Ministry of Communications, Department of Information, Kathmandu (Nepal, 1982), pp.108–109.
56. UN General Assembly, Twenty-fifth Session, 1970, Agenda Item 21, 1870th Plenary Meeting, pp.1–3.
57. ECAFE, Twenty-sixth Session, 1970, p.83.
58. ECOSOC, Doc. E/CN.11/Trade/LLC/L.1.7., Feb. 1972, p.3.

59. ECAFE, 27th Session, April 1971 p.7.
60. Ibid.
61. ECAFE, Resolution 114(XXVII), 1971, p.6.
62. "Land-locked, Aspects of Development." Trade Promotion Centre, (Kathmandu, 1976), p.47.
63. Ibid.
64. Ibid.
65. Ibid., p. 48.
66. Ibid.
67. Ibid., p.53.
68. UNCTAD, Third Session, May 1972, TD/180, pp.192.

6. International Conferences on Land-Locked States–III

THE UNCTAD, SECRETARY-GENERAL'S ACTION PROGRAMME, MAY 1972

The Trade and Development Board, at its eleventh session, requested the Secretary-General of the UNCTAD:

"To prepare a comprehensive action programme within the competence of UNCTAD, within the context of the international development strategy for the second United Nations Development Decade (General Assembly resolution 2626 (XXV) of 24 October 1970) and the relevant provisions of Board resolution 69 (X) in favour of the land-locked developing countries of 16 September 1970 and to present it to the third session of the UNCTAD."[1]

It was generally agreed that the land-locked developing countries faced special handicaps related to their geographical position and the special international action was needed to help overcome them.

TRANSPORT INFRASTRUCTURE

An Over-all Strategy for Transport. The basic transport strategy with call for technical and financial assistance for the improvement and maintenance of existing: (i) roads in both the land-locked developing countries and their transit neighbours in order to provide, where feasible, all weather transport routes for heavy vehicles, (ii) railways and rolling stock, (iii) inland waterways to improve navigability, (iv) air transport to ensure that each land-locked developing country has at least one airport fully equipped to international standards and (v) postal and telecommunications systems to raise them to modern standards.[2]

Regional Coordination Arrangements for the Transport Infrastructure. Further efforts should be made to promote regional cooperation and coordination of the policies between the land-locked countries and their transit neighbours, at least with respect to the basic transport routes, from ports through transit neighbours to each land-locked country. In particular, consideration should be given to the establishment of multinational institutional arrangements to carry out further work on the planning, financing, and execution of an integrated transit route system between each land-locked country and its transit neighbours.

Financing for Basic Transport Infrastructure. In developing a transport infrastructure for the land-locked countries, an important objective will be to reduce the effective costs, including particularly the cost involved in delays and uncertainties in the movement of goods.

ALTERNATIVE ROUTES

The land-locked developing countries, emphasized that special attention should be paid to the need for alternative transit routes and for warehousing facilities in port of transit countries, and to the availability of port and harbour facilities in transit states. Special consideration should also be given to the establishment of air transport.

Technical and financial assistance should also be provided by the developed countries and appropriate international organizations for the land-locked developing countries.

Regional cooperation can play an important role for the land-locked developing countries. It might be necessary to make use of regional and subregional machinery to facilitate the effective implementation of a programme of special measures in favour of the land-locked developing countries. The Secretary-General of the UNCTAD, should take steps to facilitate such cooperation.[3]

Nepal welcomed this concrete programme in favour of the land-locked developing countries submitted by the Secretary-General of the UNCTAD, and considered that the preparation of the programme should be completed forthwith in order to ensure its rapid implementation.[4]

UNITED NATIONS CONFERENCE ON TRADE AND DEVELOPMENT (UNCTAD) III, 1972 (SANTIAGO).

63 (III). *Special Measures Related to the Particular Needs of the Land-Locked Developing Countries.* In conformity with the General Assembly resolution 2820 (XXVI) of 16 December 1971, the third session of the United Nations Conference on Trade and Development (UNCTAD), III was held at Santiago (Chile) from 13 April to 21 May 1972.

The third session of the UNCTAD (with representatives of 131 states in attendance) was concerned, like its predecessors, with the whole complex of measures that might, by modifying the international economic and trading system, promote the economic and social advancement of the developing nations. A significant agenda included such dominant topics as commodity problems, trade policy, financial assistance, and decision taking in the international trade and monetary spheres.

The problem of the land-locked countries were clearly of less weight, but they received the attention of the special committee established to consider the agenda items on the least-developed countries (including their identification) and on the land-locked countries.[5] This committee (the sixth committee) met sixteen times from 13 April to 16 May 1972, but without reaching at any agreement on the draft resolution on the land-locked countries.

The debate in the sixth committee was dominated by the problems of the least-developed countries, but several points emerged from the discussion on the agenda item 11(b), i.e. "other special measures related to the particular needs of the land-locked developing countries." It was agreed that the land-locked countries faced special hardships calling for additional measures. The emphasis was again put on transport improvements, structural change, and financial and technical assistance on easy terms. The proposal for a special fund to subsidize transport costs received a mixed reception. Some representatives laid particular emphasis on administrative measures, including a draft convention to improve transit procedures, with some support for permanent review machinery too at regional or subregional level.

The resolution actually adopted by the Conference on 19 May 1972 is mainly the predictable outcome of the earlier resolutions, studies and declarations. Certain features must be noted, however, in addition to the by now standard proposals in regard to the transit arrangements which are as follows:

(a) The clause agreeing on the need to establish, within the regional economic commissions and UNESOB, special regional or sub-regional bodies to make suggestions with a view to implementing recommendations relating to the land-locked countries.

(b) The suggested organizations of studies of existing port and transit procedures.

(c) The requested preparation of a draft international convention on the simplification of transit, customs, and trade documents.

(d) The invitation to the governments of transit and the land-locked countries to cooperate in both administrative (e.g. inter-governmental consultation) and practical ways (e.g. provision of transit storage facilities).[6]

On 19 May 1972, the UNCTAD-III Conference adopted without dissent resolution 63 (III) proposing special measures for the particular needs of the land-locked developing countries.

The conference thereby requested the developed countries and the competent international organizations to provide technical and financial assistance to enable the land-locked countries to adopt to their particular geographical situations and to maintain and improve their transport and communication infrastructure. It recommended that the economic and social council study the desirability and feasibility of establishing a special fund for subsidizing the additional transport costs of the land-locked developing countries.

The conference also requested the Secretary-General of the UNCTAD, to appoint an expert group to study the ways and means of improving the transport infrastructure of these countries, to organize studies of the existing port and transit procedures and facilities affecting these countries, and to prepare a draft international convention or proposal on the simplification and the standardization of transit customs and trade documents.

Reservations concerning the proposal on establishing a special fund were recorded by Australia, Austria, Canada, France, Japan, the Netherland, UK and USA.[7]

Nepal along with the other land-locked countries participated in the Third UN Conference on Trade and Development (UNCTAD), and submitted her reports in the conference. Pushkar Nath Pant, Secretary, Ministry of Industry and Commerce of Nepal submitted his reports on 24 April 1972.

The Nepalese representative drew attention to the principle contained in Annex A.I.2 to the final act adopted by the conference at its first session relating to the transit trade of the land-locked countries, and to the 1965 UN Convention on Transit Trade of the land-locked states,[8] which provided for the right of access to the sea for the land-locked states. The Nepalese representative urged all member nations, who had not yet ratified that important international instrument, to do so as soon as possible.

Mr. Pant said that most of the land-locked countries were among the least developed of the developing countries. However, their problems should be dealt with separately, as they required special attention and assistance from the international community.

The Nepalese delegation said that the third UNCTAD has recommended some special measures needed in favour of the land-locked countries. Similarly, the UN General Assembly last year had adopted a resolution inviting the international organization and other developed countries to provide technical and financial assistance to the land-locked countries. As recommended by the UN General Assembly, Nepal would like to see the establishment of a special fund to subsidize the additional transport cost of the land-locked developing countries as soon as possible. These measures, though commendable, are not enough to overcome the difficulties and disadvantages felt by the land-locked developing countries. They would need substantial amount of technical and financial assistance even to complete the basic structure of development. In Nepalese view such assistance should be made available on grant basis and, if this is not possible, long term interest free loan should be extended.[9]

The Third Session of the UNCTAD was deemed to have been a modest success.[10] The foundation may have been laid for the greater participation of the developing countries in debate and decision in the fields of trade and monetary reform, progress was made in regard to action on behalf of the least developed countries. There were no breakthroughs, however, and no significant headway was made on such traditional issues as financial assistance from the donor countries. In the case of the land-locked countries, as a distinct group of developing countries, little progress was recorded.

Nepal was satisfied with the principle which was adopted in the Third UNCTAD, but she was not satisfied with the financial and technical assistance given by the developed countries. Nepal urged the international community to give immediate financial and technical assistance to the land-locked countries which is an essential prerequisite of the economic development of these countries.

THE GEORGETOWN DECLARATION, THE ACTION PROGRAMME FOR ECONOMIC COOPERATION, 1972

In the Lusaka declaration, the nonaligned countries pledged themselves to cultivate the spirit of self-reliance and to this end agreed on a firm policy of organizing their own socio-economic progress. They, therefore, decided to adopt an action programme in the field of planning and projection, trade, cooperation and development, the improvement of infrastructure, and the application of science and technology. In the two years that have followed, in spite of the adoption of the international development strategy for the United Nations Second development decade and the holding of the UNCTAD-III, not much progress has been made with regard to the international action for raising of standard of living of developing countries of the world. Rather in certain fields, there has been a distinct deterioration.[11]

These developments have made action regarding self-reliance both in and among developing countries a matter of the highest priority. The Lusaka declaration on nonalignment and economic progress indicated clearly the directions in which initiatives should be taken in this matter. The foreign ministers of the nonalignment countries, meeting in Georgetown (Guyana), decided that in order to implement that declaration concrete steps should be taken to promote economic cooperation among themselves, paying special attention to the particular problems of the least developed and of the land-locked countries.[12]

COOPERATION IN TRADE, TRANSPORT AND INDUSTRIAL DEVELOPMENT

Where possible, bilateral trade agreements, particularly between the 'more developed' and the 'less developed', nonaligned countries should provide for credit and other payment arrangements in favour of the latter. Nonaligned countries should strengthen transport links among themselves with priority given to the following actions:

(a) the establishment by integration groupings among the developing countries of multinational air, maritime, road, and rail services,
(b) where feasible, the establishment of inter-regional air and maritime services,
(c) the expansion of maritime services by the developing countries themselves, particularly those which are relatively advanced in this field,
(d) improvement of transportation facilities, including ports, on a national basis,
(e) in implementing (a) to (b) above, full account should be taken of the special circumstances of the land-locked countries who should also participate in the proposed arrangements.[13] This meeting was held in August 1972.

The Nepalese representative reiterated his country's stand on the question of providing adequate transit and port facilities to the land-locked countries. He strongly urged the coastal states, to give sympathetic consideration to make specific provisions guaranteeing the rights of the land-locked countries and to give free and unrestricted access to and from the sea.

UNITED NATIONS CONFERENCE ON TRADE AND DEVELOPMENT (UNCTAD-IV), NAIROBI, 1976 98(IV). SPECIFIC ACTIONS RELATED TO THE PARTICULAR NEEDS AND PROBLEMS OF THE LAND-LOCKED COUNTRIES

The fourth session of the United Nations Conference on Trade and Development (UNCTAD-IV), was held at Nairobi (Kenya) from 5 to 31 May 1976.

The representatives of 130 member states of the UNCTAD-IV participated in this session.[14] The resolution 98(IV) on the least developed among the developing countries, the developing island countries, and the developing land-locked countries was adopted without dissent on 31 May 1976.[15]

On the section on the land-locked developing countries the UNCTAD-IV, 1976 recommended:

(a) *Joint Cooperation.* A cooperative approach to each specific transit situation should be encouraged so that all available possibilities for improving particular routes and transit facilities could be considered together and each of the transit routes available to a particular land-locked country could be evaluated in order to determine the best available options for future progress.

(b) *Regional and Sub-regional Planning.* The land-locked developing countries can derive substantial long term benefits from the improvements and development of integrated regional and sub-regional transport infrastructure. The international organizations and financial institutions should give high priority in their assistance programme for such projects.

(c) *Commercial Policy.* In the continuous improvement of their schemes of generalized preferences, special attention should be paid by the developed countries to the possible inclusion of additional products of export interests to the developing land-locked countries.

(d) *Transport.* At the joint request of the land-locked developing countries, and their transit neighbours, technical and financial assistance should be provided for studies of the feasibility of extending and integrating the railway systems of transit countries with those of their land-locked neighbours.

Developed countries should assist land-locked developing countries in promoting the development of their air and sea transport.

(e) *Communications.* Fast and reliable communication links between the commercial centres of the land-locked countries and the transit ports on the one hand, and the overseas markets on the other hand should be developed.

(f) *Restructuring of the Economy*. The land-locked developing countries require technical and financial assistance for the restructuring of their economies. It would be worthwhile for these countries to explore the possibility of establishing import substitution industries which produce high bulk/low value goods. This would save them incurring high transport costs for their imports from other countries. International organizations and financial institutions should provide technical and financial assistance for this purpose and accord high priority for the establishment of pilot projects to achieve the aforesaid objectives.

(g) *Port Facilities and Development*. Ways and means to develop and improve the transit and port facilities should be explored and undertaken.

(h) *Flow of External Resources*. The multilateral and bilateral financial institutions, including international organizations, should intensify their efforts in raising the flow of resources for overall economic development, which is constrained by the geographical and other disadvantages of the land-locked developing countries and in particular for the development and maintenance, during a mutually agreed phasing-out period, of the transport infrastructure necessary for these countries.

(i) *Reduction of Shipping Freight and Transit Costs*. The governments of developed and developing countries should invite and urge shipowners, members of liner-conferences and insurance companies as far as is feasible, to establish freight rates and premiums for the land-locked developing countries which will encourage and assist the expansion of the export trade of these countries and to develop promotional rates for non-traditional exports of these countries. This would facilitate the opening-up of new markets and the development of new trade flows.

(j) *Air Transport and Tourism*. Bilateral and multilateral organizations, in particular the regional commissions, should assist the land-locked developing countries in the development of air transport and tourism with a view to increasing their foreign exchange earning capacity through merchandise exports and invisible.

(k) *Special Fund for Land-Locked Developing Countries.* The Secretary-General of the UNCTAD should prepare proposals on the organizational arrangements for the special fund for the land-locked developing countries including draft statutes, in accordance with the General Assembly resolution 3504 (XXX) of 15 December 1975.

(l) *Review of Progress.* The member countries of the UNCTAD, especially the developing countries should review measures which they have taken in favour of the land-locked developing countries, including the means by which such measures are undertaken.

(m) *Free Access to and From the Sea.* The developing land-locked countries reaffirmed their right of free access to and from the sea, a right earlier affirmed by the fourth conference of the Heads of state or government of the nonaligned countries (Algiers, September 1973), and by the Conference of Developing Countries on Raw Materials (Dakar, February 1975). Some developing transit countries reserved their position on this matter.[16]

Nepal participated in UNCTAD–IV Conference and submitted her reports. Nepal was fully satisfied with the principle, which were adopted in the conference. Harka Bahadur Gurung, Minister of State for Industry and Commerce who participated in the conference noted that it was a mere coincidence that most of the least developed countries were land-locked and had been largely unable to benefit from the commercial policy measures adopted by the international community to assist the developing countries in general. On the whole, the measures adopted to promote improved terms of trade had not changed the level and production of trade in those countries, whose right of access to foreign markets beyond their coastal neighbours was not fully guaranteed. As long as they did not have such a right, the land-locked countries would remain victims of their adverse geographical position. In this context Nepal welcomed the fact that her transit neighbour had recently taken the lead in recognizing the rights of the land-locked countries. Such a positive reaction and token of mutual trust certainly heralded a new era of transit arrangements conducive to the growth and development of those countries.

Nepalese delegation was convinced of the importance of economic cooperation among the developing countries, particularly neighbouring countries, and thought it essential that a special system of preferences among the developing countries be evolved, taking into account the land-locked developing countries. The New International Economic Order (NIEO) could hardly be established if efforts were not made to reshape the payment, arrangements to restructure the trading system and redefine the norms governing the flow of real resources and technology. The international community should also help to make a special fund for the land-locked countries, created by virtue of the General Assembly resolution 3504 (XXX) operational at the earliest possible date. Despite its unfavourable topography, Nepal was sure that it could succeed in that task with the assistance of the developed countries and through trade with other more favourably situated developing countries.[17]

In the discussions on the results of the fourth session of UNCTAD, in the General Assembly in 1976, many members expressed the view that whereas important decisions had been made at Nairobi, much had been left for further negotiations.

Noting the resolution adopted by the conference on the debt problems of developing countries, the General Assembly requested the Trade and Development Board at its ministerial session in 1977 to review the action taken. It also requested all organizations concerned within the United Nations system to implement as a matter of urgency the relevant special measures and specific action recommended by the conference in favour of the land-locked developing countries.[18]

UNITED NATIONS CONFERENCE ON TRADE AND DEVELOPMENT (UNCTAD–V), 1979 MANILA. 123(V). SPECIFIC ACTION RELATED TO PARTICULAR NEEDS AND PROBLEMS OF LAND-LOCKED DEVELOPING COUNTRIES

The fifth session of the United Nations Conference on Trade and Development (UNCTAD–V) was held at Manila (Philippines) from 7 May to 3 June 1979.[19]

The conference was attended by 144 member states of UNCTAD, as well as by representatives of the United Nations Secretariat, the regional commissions and other United Nations Organizations, nine specialized agencies and the General Agreement on Tariffs and Trade (GATT).

The conference on 3 June adopted without dissent resolution

123(V) on the particular needs and problems of the land-locked developing countries.[20]

By this resolution the UNCTAD agreed on specific action aimed at reducing the cost of access to and from the sea and to world markets for the land-locked developing countries, at improving their transit-transport services and at restructuring their economies to overcome their geographical limitation.

The conference reaffirmed the need for increasing external financial resources to the land-locked countries on favourable terms, and the need for close and effective collaboration between those countries and their transit neighbours, both in studying and implementing transport proposals, including proposals for specific measures to reduce transit costs.

The conference recommended as basic elements for such cooperation improved procedures and new investments to reduce the costs of access to the sea and to world markets and financial assistance from the international community to improve transit-transport infrastructures. It also called for the consideration of all aspects of the transit-transport problem, including procedures, regulations, documentation, management, training, organizational and institutional arrangements. The joint ventures study of the alternative routes, and detailed planning and economic studies of improved options were also recommended.

The conference also noted the key elements of integrated transport planning high priority by international assistance; consideration of the creation of cooperative air transport developments, and efforts to apply and possibly revise international convention to facilitate transit traffic.

The conference urged the international community to provide financial and technical support to the land-locked countries in the development and maintenance of road, rail, waterway, air transport, containerization, warehousing, transit port, dryport, communications and shipping facilities. It called for international assistance to help diversify the economies of these countries and urged that the UN special fund for the land-locked developing countries be augmented by contributions and equitable distribution.

The UNCTAD Secretary General was asked to continue the work programme on the land-locked developing countries including a review of their special economic problems and recommendations to reduce their access costs to the sea. The conference invited the UNDP and other international financial institutions to consider increasing their assistance and recommended specific action and financial and technical assistance to implement these activities.[21]

NEPAL'S PARTICIPATION

Nepal participated in the fifth UNCTAD conference alongwith other land-locked countries. The representative of Nepal said that the land-locked developing countries were more seriously affected by the current economic crisis, particularly, because most of their transit neighbours were also developing countries. There was thus need for the international community to intensify its already generous assistance to those countries.

The UNCTAD has always been in the forefront of issues relating to special measures on behalf of the least developed land-locked developing countries. Nepal would like to request the Secretary-General of the UNCTAD to undertake special responsibility for detailed preparation of crash programme in favour of the least developed and the land-locked developing countries.

The Nepalese delegation would like to extend its appreciation to the UNCTAD Secretariat for having initiated certain studies aimed at serving the needs of the land-locked countries. The transit cost studies that the secretariat has initiated in different transit corridors with a view to improving the transit situation of the land-locked countries should be continued and intensified. Substantial growth in exports would not be possible until a satisfactory solution is found to the transit transport problems of the land-locked countries.

With a view to improving the wrosening trade imbalance, the Nepalese delegation would like to reaffirm the need for free access to and from the sea for all the land-locked countries as an essential ingredient for the promotion of trade and economic prosperity in the region and beyond.

At the ministerial meeting of the 'Group of 77' held in the United Republic of Tanzania in February 1978, the Nepalese delegation had the occasion to propose a UN conference on the least developed countries to formulate a substantial action programme for these countries for the 1980's.

While the attention of the world community would now logically go to the formulation of a strategy of the third United Nations development decade, the Nepalese delegation would like to emphasize the need to treat the special case of the least developed land-locked countries as an integral part of the third development decade.

The Nepalese delegation hopes that the fifth UNCTAD conference will lay down basic and effective guidelines to ensure international cooperation in the 1980's and the establishment of a new international economic order.[22] But the UNCTAD-V, was a failure in some aspects through adoption of standstill provision.

UNITED NATIONS CONFERENCE ON THE PROBLEMS OF THE LEAST DEVELOPED COUNTRIES HELD ON SEPTEMBER 1981 AT PARIS

The General Assembly, in its resolution No. 34/203 of 19 December 1979 decided to convene a United Nations conference on the least developed countries in 1981 to finalize, adopt and support the substantial new programme of action for the 1980's for the least developed countries, outlined in the UNCTAD resolution No. 123(V).[23] The UN conference on the least developed countries was held from 1 to 14 September 1981 at Paris (France).

The least developed countries are the poorest and economically the weakest. Fifteen of the thirty-one least developed countries are land-locked and, therefore, face additional problems in their development. In order to alleviate this geographical handicap, these countries and their transit neighbours, in cooperation with each other should make, during the 1980's, immediate and intensive efforts to simplify the transit procedures and to improve transit transport storage and port facilities for their international trade, taking into account the needs and means of the land-locked least developed countries and their transit neighbours.

The representatives of several countries stated that for the land-locked countries improvement in transit transport and port facilities in the transit countries is of great importance for easy access to world markets. Consideration should be given by the donors and international agencies to the provision of concessional financial assistance for the investment schemes undertaken by the neighbouring transit countries, individually and/or jointly in association with the land-locked countries of the same region, to improve the transit infrastructure facilities.[24]

His Majesty Birendra Bir Bikram Shah Dev, King of Nepal, himself participated in the conference. Speaking on behalf of the nine least developed countries of Asia, he said that while the majority of those countries had been victims of colonialism, those that had remained independent had suffered no less for want of contact due to their land-locked or sea-locked condition. All the nine countries were struggling to preserve their identity while seeking to improve the lives of their people.

One of the major constraints that the least developed countries faced in common was the lack of basic infrastructure for development. While the land-locked countries had to bear the burden of overland trade that in time of escalating oil prices could prove like the last straw on a camel's back the poor economies of island countries with strings of islets could hardly afford their own system of transhipment. As for the land-locked countries, with their rugged terrain of mountains and high altitudes, building up infrastructure could be arduously toilsome. Afghanistan, Bhutan, Laos can be cited as examples in this connection. In the case of Nepal, although much attention in the past has been paid to the task of building roads, they have proved to be not only time-consuming but beyond the reach of ordinary means.[25]

Yadav Prasad Pant, Minister of Finance, Commerce and Supply (Nepal), led the Nepalese delegation to the UN sponsored conference on the least developed countries. He told newsmen that His Majesty's address had been noted with due seriousness and highly appreciated, not only by the developing nations, but also by a number of the developed nations. According to him, Nepal's proposal that the transit problems of the land-locked countries be solved jointly by the concerned land-locked nations and the neighbouring country through which transit facilities were sought, had been approved by the conference.[26]

He further said that for the first time, a high level conference is being held to deliberate on the problems of the least developed countries and to formulate a programme for development. From time to time, Nepal has been voicing at international conferences the need to create a world economic order based on equality and justice and, thus, to solve the problems of the developing land-locked nations. The Paris conference on the least developed countries benefitted Nepal as well as the other least and land-locked developed countries.[27]

UNITED NATIONS CONFERENCE ON TRADE AND DEVELOPMENT (UNCTAD-VI), 1983, BELGRADE

The sixth session of United Nations Conference on Trade and Development (UNCTAD-VI) was held at Belgrade (Yugoslavia) from 6 to 30 June 1983.[28]

By resolution No. 137(VI) UNCTAD agreed on the specific action related to the particular needs and problems of land-locked developing countries.[29]

In paragraph 11 of the resolution, the Secretary-General of the UNCTAD was invited to appoint a small ad-hoc group of experts from the developed and the developing countries, serving in an individual capacity to study the ways and means of improving the transit transport infrastructures and services as a part of the specific action related to the particular needs and problems of the land-locked developing countries. The report of this ad-hoc group of experts which met in Geneva from 4 to 8 June 1984, was submitted to the Trade and Development Board at its twenty-ninth session.[30]

The response of the international community to the call of the international development strategy of providing financial and technical assistance and support to the land-locked developing countries was that several major donors who had responded did not have development assistance policies in favour of the land-locked developing countries, although it was generally recognized that these countries faced problems as a result of their geographical location. The assistance programmes of several donors and institutions to the land-locked developing countries are also not always directly linked with the solution of the transit transport bottlenecks. Further, call was given to the international community to contribute generously to the United Nations special fund for the land-locked developing countries. The primary purpose of this is to provide assistance to the development and improvement of transit facilities.[31]

The UNCTAD-VI, also called for action to improve transport in fifteen land-locked developing countries, particularly, Afghanistan, Chad and Rwanda, each of which is more than 1,700 km away from the nearest seaport.[32]

NEPAL'S ROLE

Nepal actively participated in the UNCTAD-VI conference which was held in Belgrade in June 1983. Balram Ghartimagar, the Minister of Industry and Commerce, and Supplies, led Nepal's delegation. The Commerce and Supplies Secretary also represented Nepal at the official level conference preceding UNCTAD-VI.[33]

The government of Nepal, concerned with the report of the ad-hoc group of experts that there was need for mutual agreements between the land-locked and the transit countries for financing and operation of major transit projects, said that multilateral agencies should also play a major role in implementing such projects. In fact, international agencies should play a pioneering role in supporting such ventures, once they have been identified.[34]

The Nepalese delegation also said that the United Nations special fund for the land-locked developing countries could make an important contribution to these countries. The delegation believed that the international community had a serious responsibility to correct that situation.[35]

The conference provided an opportunity to reassess the consequences of being land-locked and the ways and means of minimizing the effects of this geographical disadvantage. The UNCTAD-VI agreed on further specific actions and programmes related to particular needs and problems of the land-locked developing countries and it requested the international community to provide financial and technical assistance to these countries.

In the general debate on this issue, statements were made by the spokesmen of several countries. The spokesmen for Group B said that his group maintained the position on the special fund for the land-locked developing countries. Many representatives reserved the position of his delegation on the draft resolution in view of its financial implications. Nepal's representative was fully satisfied with provisions of the UNCTAD-VI, related to the problems of the land-locked countries and she urged the international community to provide financial and technical assistance for the land-locked countries like Nepal. On the whole, UNCTAD-VI conference was successful for its policies related to the problems of land-locked states.

THE THIRD LAW OF THE SEA CONFERENCE (1973-1983)

On the basis of the work done by the sea-bed Committee, the United Nations General Assembly convened the first session of the Third United Nations Conference on Law of the Sea (UNCLOS) III, in New York from 3 to 14 December 1973.[36] This session considered matters relating to the organization of the conference.

The second session of the third United Nations Conference on Law of the Sea (UNCLOS) was held from 20 June to 29 June 1974 at Caracas (Venezuela).[37]

EXCLUSIVE ECONOMIC ZONE AND LAND-LOCKED STATES

The Caracas session of twenty-two land-locked states (LLS) and geographically disadvantaged states (GDS) submitted a joint proposal which sought recognition of the right of land-locked states and geographically disadvantaged states (GDS) to participate in the exploration and exploitation of the living as well as the non-living resources of the Exclusive Economic Zones (EEZs) of the neighbouring coastal states on equal and non-discriminatory basis.[38]

Articles 69 and 70 deal with the right of access of the land-locked states and geographical disadvantaged states, respectively, to the living resources of the Exclusive Economic Zones of other states in the sub-region or region.[39]

On behalf of the land-locked states and geographically disadvantaged states (GDS), it was argued that the EEZ concept was not consistent with the principle that the oceans were the common heritage of mankind, that the economic zone would lead to a regime of inequality, and that the zone would benefit only a small number of states at the expense of all the other states.[40] Nepal, for instance, pointed out: So let us examine how this process of erosion of the concept of common heritage of mankind benefits the developing countries. Does it benefit most of the developing countries, or even many of them? Data based on available information reveal that only 25 nations in the world would gain control of 76 per cent of the world economic zone, out of these 25 nations, 13 are developed nations such as United States, Australia, New Zeland, Canada, USSR, Japan, Norway and South Africa. These 13 developed nations will acquire 48 per cent of the world economic zone, while among the developing nations 12 among the lucky 25 will get only 28 per cent of the same. It will make the rich richer and the poor poorer, thus making the task of the establishment of the new international economic order well-nigh impossible."[41]

In the second session the draft articles sponsored by Canada, Chile, Iceland, India, Indonesia, Mauritius, Maxico and New Zealand called for an economic zone stretching to 200 miles from the coast, within which each coastal state would have sovereign rights over resources as well as other rights and duties, but where all states would enjoy freedom of navigation and over-flights. These were widely supported. Many states raised the problem of the land-locked states. Some coastal states, including the sponsors of the draft articles, committed themselves to producing proposals recognizing equitable rights of access by such countries to the living resources of the economic zones of neighbouring countries. South Africa and other states thought that detailed arrangements between the coastal states and the land-locked neighbours should be worked out bilaterally. Yet other states—Belgium, Botswana, Laos, Nepal, Paraguay, Switzerland and Zambia thought that the land-locked states and the geographically disadvantaged states should enjoy the rights of exploitation of both minerals and biological resources of the zones of their region.[42]

The land-locked states and the geographically disadvantaged states (GDS) on the one hand, and the maritime powers on the other supported each other in defending their respective position, although for different reasons. The USA proposed that the nationals of a land-locked state should enjoy the privilege to fish in the economic zone of the adjoining coastal state on the basis of equality with the nationals of that state. Similarly, the USSR and the other socialist countries proposed that the developing land-locked states should enjoy the privilege of fishing in the economic zone of a neighbouring coastal state on the basis of equality with the nationals of that state.[43]

Among other matters discussed in the second committee were the particular problems of the land-locked states. Afghanistan, Bhutan, Bolivia, Botswana, Burundi, Czechoslovakia, Hungary, Laos, Lesotho, Mali, Mangolia, Nepal, Paraguay, Swaziland, Uganda, Upper Volta and Zambia sponsored a working paper which called for the right of free access to and from the sea for the land-locked states as a legally binding principle, and the right to exploit, both the living and non-living, resources of the economic zones of their region. Czechoslovakia said that the land-locked states should enjoy the benefits of the sea on equal terms with the coastal states.[44]

India and Nigeria among others, opposed the proposals of the 17 countries and expressed the view that the question of free transit to and from the sea for the land-locked states should be settled by bilateral agreements between those states and the coastal states.[45]

Though the draft convention recognizes the right of the land-locked states and other geographically disadvantaged states to participate in the exploitation of the living resources, it requires that the terms and modalities of such participation should be established by the states concerned through bilateral, sub-regional and regional agreements. The provisions dealing with 'access' are surrounded by so many limitations that it is doubtful whether the land-locked states would ever secure a meaningful right, except with the goodwill of the coastal states concerned.

The third session of the conference was held in Geneva from 17 March to 9 May 1975. On 18 April 1975 the conference requested the chairman of its three main committees to prepare a Single Negotiating Text (SNT). The single negotiating text was converted as the revised single negotiating text.

THE REVISED SINGLE NEGOTIATING TEXT (RSNT)

The revised single negotiating text (RSNT) devotes as many as nine articles, i.e. Articles 109 to 117, to the subject of the land-locked states and their right of access to and from the sea and freedom of transit.[46] Of these, Article 110, in particular, deserves special mention in as much as it establishes the principle that the land-locked states have the right of access to and from the sea for the purpose of exercising the rights provided for in the text, including those relating to the freedom of the high seas and the principle of common heritage of mankind.

The Revised Single Negotiating Text (RSNT) is adopted in three parts.

RSNT Part I. Part I of the RSNT proposes the implementation of a regime to manage the exploitation of the deep sea-bed. The basic premise underlying part I is that the resources of the sea-bed area are the common heritage of mankind. It proposes the establishment of an International Sea-bed Authority (ISA) empowered to supervise mining operations on the ocean floor. Part I also empowers the International Sea-bed Authority (ISA) to conduct scientific research to strengthen the technological capabilities of all developing states. The developing land-locked states be given "effective participation" in the scientific activities sponsored by the ISA with regard to their needs in "over-coming obstacles arising from their disadvantaged location."[47]

RSNT Part II. Part II of the RSNT represents a distinct disadvantage to the land-locked states because only the coastal states are authorized by its provisions to exercise jurisdiction over resources. The land-locked states opposed the provisions which formally establish a 200 mile exclusive economic zone (EEZ). Although the RSNT provides that the land-locked states may participate in the extraction of living resources in EEZs of adjoining coastal states, it does not provide the land-locked states any rights to use the zones of non-adjoining states. The RSNT provides LLS (Land-locked States) access to fish in an adjoining states, EEZ on an 'equitable basis'. The RSNT provides that the land-locked states may establish rights to the EEZ resources independently through bilateral and multilateral agreements. The RSNT provides that the LLS shall partake in revenue sharing from the extraction of continental shelf resources only beyond 200 miles. The land-locked states have proposed that they be given a share of the oil revenues within the 200 mile zone.[48]

RSNT Part III. From the viewpoint of the land-locked states, the most significant part of the work of committee III, deals with scientific research within the EEZ of coastal states. Although the land-locked states may presently be unable to apply the results of the scientific research directly, such research effects them indirectly because of its effects on the future uses of the sea.[49]

The land-locked states cannot benefit from any provisions of the RSNT until it is adopted in some from by the UNCLOS III. Whereas in the past, the land-locked states have been primarily dependent upon the gratuitous concessions by the coastal states, changes in the political climate since 1958 have given the LLS more bargaining power in the world arena. Much of the developing LLS increased bargaining power derives from their present alignment with the 'Group of 77'.

The fourth, fifth and sixth sessions of the conference were held at New York in 1976 and 1977. Part X of the convention treats the subject of the land-locked states. It deals with the right of access of the land-locked states to and from the sea and freedom of transit. It is dealt in nine articles from 124 to 132.[50]

RIGHT OF ACCESS OF THE LAND-LOCKED STATES TO AND FROM THE SEA AND FREEDOM OF TRANSIT (ARTICLE 124 to 132)

The right of access of the land-locked states to the sea was covered in articles 124 to 132.

Article 125 said that the land-locked states and the transit states should together agree on the terms and modalities for exercising freedom of transit, and that the transit states had the right to take all necessary measures to ensure that the rights and facilities provided for the land-locked states did not infringe upon their legitimate interests.[51]

Article 127 provided for exemption from taxes the means of transport in transit used by the land-locked states. It extended this exemption to other facilities provided for and used by such states.[52]

Articles 129 and 130 stated that the transit and the land-locked states might cooperate in constructing or improving the means of transport and that the transit states were to take all appropriate measures to avoid delays or other difficulties of a technical nature in transit traffic.[53]

The Federal Republic of Germany maintained that freedom of transit for the land-locked states through the territory of a neighbouring coastal state should not infringe upon the sovereignty of the latter. In the absence of agreement, the national law of the coastal state regulated the transit of persons and goods. Iran was ready to recognize freedom of transit, as long as the land-locked states granted the same right on its territory to the neighbouring coastal state. Pakistan could not accept the article on the ground that it did not comply with the transit states sovereignty over its territory.[54]

Among the land-locked states, Lesotho said that aircraft, pipelines and gaslines should be included among the means of transport covered by the freedom of transit provisions. Lesotho, Swaziland and Uganda considered that the ships of the land-locked states should enjoy most favoured nation status in ports of the access state.[55]

During the eighth and ninth sessions of the conference held at New York in 1979 and 1980, the member states urged that the land-locked states and geographically disadvantaged states be granted more equitable participation in the fisheries of neighbouring state zones. The representative of Nepal said that the decisions on the distribution of the zones resources should be taken by an international organization, not unilaterally, while Bhutan said that the coastal states should take the recommendations of such organizations into account.[56]

Taking a different view, Pakistan said that she did not recognize right of any other state to the resources in the zone and voiced strong reservations on the articles pertaining to this matter.

Nepal, supported by Austria, Bhutan, Lesotho, Mali, Niger, Sierra Leone, Singapore, Swaziland, Uganda, Zaire and Zambia, urged for inclusion in the revised negotiating text of its 1978 proposal for a common heritage fund which would be redistributed to the developing countries—share of the mineral revenues derived by the coastal states from their economic zone and continental shelf.[57]

Speaking at the third UN conference on the law of the sea, the Indian representative said that India had accommodated and would continue to accommodate the legitimate interests of the neighbouring land-locked states.

India had recognized the importance of transit as the lifeline of the land-locked states and had, through bilateral agreements and in international forums, respected and protected their interests in that matter. However, the legitimate interests of the coastal or transit state should also be borne in mind. Such interests might be related to the determination of routes and the protection of the security interests of the transit state. Accordingly, the modalities of transit should be settled by bilateral or even regional agreements. The transit state should also be able to expect a favourable response to any request for transit through a land-locked state should the need arise.[58]

India had also recognized the reasonable interests of the land-locked states in the living resources of the exclusive fishery zone. However, the special rights and interests of the coastal state in the economic zone had to be kept in mind.[59]

India said that the continental shelf, which was the natural prolongation of the land territory of the coastal state, came under a separate regime in international law, and, therefore, the question of sharing its resources with another state, whether land-locked or not, did not arise.[60]

NEPAL'S PARTICIPATION

Nepal, alongwith other land-locked states participated in the third law of the sea conference and submitted a memorandum. Speaking at the conference, the Nepalese delegation said that the "Freedom of transit and free access to the sea were of course vital for the land-locked countries." The principle of free access had been established in international law and recognized in many multilateral conventions and by authorities on international law. The Nepalese delegation was happy to note that the participants in the conference were according wider recognition to the right of free access. Nepal welcomed the assurance given by the representative of India that India's neighbouring land-locked countries could rely on its continued support for their legitimate cause.[61]

Together with the other land-locked states, the Nepalese delegation submitted a paper to the sea-bed committee (A/9021 and corr. I and 3, Vol. II, sect. 5) which did not reflect the unilateral interests of the land-locked countries but took into consideration all the legitimate interests of the transit coastal states. The Nepalese delegation also supported the Kampala declaration. It hoped that the principles and guidelines would satisfy the interests of the land-locked and other geographically disadvantaged states on the one hand and the transit countries on the other.[62]

As to non-living resources, the Nepalese delegation felt that any extension of sovereignty of jurisdiction over a port of the high seas would limit the present rights of the geographically disadvantaged states. There must, therefore, be a compensatory obligation on the part of the coastal states which benefited from such extension. The states which had unilaterally extended their jurisdiction should seek to reach at an agreement with those countries who felt that their rights had been limited. The convention on the high seas stated that the high seas were open to all nations and that no state could claim sovereignty over any part of them. Any unilateral extension of jurisdiction or claims to areas of the high seas as an exclusive economic zone were tantamount to the expansion of the dominion of the coastal state over the sea and its natural resources. That would narrow the area of high seas and would be out of keeping with the principle of the freedom of the high seas.[63]

In cancelling out the few rights accorded under customary international law, articles 69 and 70 were unsatisfactory and inequitable. The articles should be improved to accommodate the needs and interests of the land-locked and the least developed countries.[64]

The Nepalese delegation urged upon the international community to show goodwill towards the land-locked states. The resources of the exclusive economic zone (EEZ) should be shared among mankind as a whole, and any decision regarding their distribution should be taken by an international organization, and not unilaterally by the coastal states alone.[65]

The Nepalese delegation said that certain of the compromise solutions found on outstanding issues did not fully satisfy them. One of the most difficult issues before the conference had been the question of the continental shelf. Nepal's position on the issue was well known and Nepal maintained its view that any extension of the national jurisdiction of the coastal state with respect to the exploitation and exploration of the natural resources of the continental shelf beyond 200 nautical miles reduced the area of the common heritage of mankind. The Nepalese delegation said that a common heritage fund should be made an integral part of the law of the sea and further proposed the principle that the oceans and their resources were the common heritage of mankind.[66]

The Nepalese delegation believed that some sharing of the immense mineral resources exploitable in the exclusive economic zone (EEZ) was in keeping with the concept of the new international economic order (NIEO).[67]

The Nepalese delegation consistently advocated that the convention on the law of the sea should respect and accommodate the concerns and interests of all states. The Nepalese delegation informed the conference that the sponsors of the proposal were prepared to consider any suggestion that would improve it and make it generally acceptable.

NEPAL APPRISES ASIAN-AFRICAN LEGAL CONSULTATIVE COMMITTEE (AALCC) OF NEED OF THE LAND-LOCKED COUNTRIES FOR SEA RESOURCES

The 24th session of the Asian-African legal consultative committee (AALCC) was held in Kathmandu (Nepal) on 13 February 1985.[68]

Nepal maintained that the land-locked countries should not be deprived of the rich national endowments, and that Nepal believed that the common heritage of mankind should be shared and enjoyed equitably by all.[69]

In a statement before the session the Nepalese delegation said that the problems confronting the land-locked countries were known to the world community, without whose attention they would remain far from the course of solution. Some of the provisions of the third law of the sea convention had provided for the right of the land-locked states to exploit the living resources of the Exclusive Economic Zone (EEZ). The question now was how to frame the modalities by which these countries could share the resources of the sea with the coastal states.

It further added that unless the coastal states cooperated in good faith and understanding, nothing provided as a matter of right to the land-locked countries would materialize.

Therefore, Nepal called for the determination of the allowable catch of the EEZ (Exclusive Economic Zone) as the first and foremost step in this regard. Since the law of the sea convention also states that the assistance of international agencies could be obtained for determining the allowable catch, Nepal believed that the Asian-African Legal Consultative Committee (AALCC) would develop the modalities for such cooperation with the international agencies and the states concerned.[70]

NEPAL AND NONALIGNMENT: FIGHT FOR THE CAUSE OF THE LAND-LOCKED DEVELOPING COUNTRIES

Nonalignment has appeared as a new strategy in international affairs over the last two decades. It is a dynamic movement with which most of the third world countries are associated. Today, nonalignment has become a powerful moral force in the conduct of international affairs. Since its formal inception in 1961 till present, eight nonaligned summits have been held.

Nepal has been a consistent champion of the nonaligned movement and under the leadership of the Crown, she has been an active participant in it since the very inception of this movement. His Late Majesty King Mahendra and the present ruling monarch, His Majesty King Birendra Bir Bikram Shah Dev have addressed the different summit conferences highlighting the noble spirit of nonalignment and also Nepal's firm commitment to its lofty principles.

Nepal has been successfully able to harmonize her support for the common struggle of the nonalignment countries against the inequitable international economic relations with her assertive voice within the movement to safeguard the legitimate interests of and to obtain equity and justice for the least developed and the land-locked developing countries.

There is a growing recognition of the need to provide special international assistance to the land-locked developing countries so as to enable them to overcome their geographical handicaps.

There has been agreement both at nonaligned and other international meetings on measures designed to assist the land-locked countries in the structural transformation of their economies. These agreements were to facilitate their access to world markets including the markets of the nonaligned and other developing countries, to alleviate their transit difficulties by procuring transport facilities, to minimize and simplify customs formalities, reasonable transport charges and transit by overland and air route and, finally, to provide assistance and cooperation for speedy implementation. The measures were adopted in favour of these countries by the nonaligned conference and other international conferences.[71]

The nonaligned summit conferences have reaffirmed the right of the developing land-locked countries to free access to and from the sea. The endorsement by an overwhelming majority at the Cairo summit in 1964 of the recommendation of the UNCTAD-I to adopt an international convention to ensure the right of the land-locked countries to free transit and access to the sea was highly encouraging. It is regrettable that some developing transit countries have not ratified this convention and continue to express their reservation on the right of free access to and from the sea.[72]

One of the positive recommendations of the nonaligned conferences was the establishment of a UN special fund for subsidizing the additional transport costs of the land-locked developing countries. The fund had already become operational but, owing to its meagre resources, it has not been able to finance even the modest projects of the land-locked countries. The nonaligned summit has appealed to the international community, the developed and developing donor countries to generously contribute to this special fund. These appeals, too, have not improved the resource situation of the fund. Nepal has been making ceaseless efforts to keep the fund alive and hopes that the donor countries will appreciate the rationale behind the fund and change their attitude.[73]

At the Lusaka conference which was held in 1970 King Mahendra appealed to the developed countries to adopt liberal trade and aid policies vis-a-vis the developing world. His Majesty stated that the land-locked countries are additionally handicapped in their development and it should not be difficult for the developing transit countries to ensure that the effects of the handicap are minimized and full and unrestricted transit rights are granted.[74]

At the Algiers summit conference in 1973, King Birendra said that the land-locked developing countries have an insufficient physical and social infrastructure to benefit from such trade and other concessions. Nepal, which falls in this category is painfully aware of such difficulties.[75]

Nepal, in cooperation with the other land-locked countries has been calling the attention of the world to this unhappy situation. The international community has recognized the depth of the problem. King Birendra referred to the recommendations of some special measures made by UNCTAD-III in favour of the land-locked countries and the resolution adopted by the UN General Assembly to provide technical and financial assistance.[76]

King Birendra expressed Nepal's wish to see the establishment of a special fund to subsidize the additional transport cost of the land-locked developing countries. He also mentioned the United Nations initiative to codify the law of the sea on the basis of new realities and new possibilities to explore and exploit the resources of the sea-bed, ocean floor, and the subsoil.[77]

The King reiterated Nepal's stand on the question of providing adequate transit and port facilities to the land-locked countries. He strongly urged the coastal states to give sympathetic consideration to make specific provisions guaranteeing the rights of the land-locked countries and to give free and unrestricted access to and from the sea in the convention.[78] His address not only provided a clear insight into Nepal's nonaligned foreign policy and its world view, but also a set of concrete proposals for the creation of a just New International Economic Order (NIEO).

NEW INTERNATIONAL ECONOMIC ORDER (NIEO) AND THE LAND-LOCKED STATES

Afro-Asian and Latin American countries have to wage new struggles—against poverty, disease and hunger. The Lusaka meeting of the Foreign Ministers of the nonaligned countries gave a call to international community to assist the land-locked developing countries in facilitating the exercise of their right to free access to and from the sea, as well as sharing the cost of transportation to the nearest sea outlet. The foreign ministers conference at Lima, also recognized the critical economic situation of the least developed and disadvantaged land-locked countries, and invited the participants "to undertake concrete and specific measures of assistance to these countries." The Lima conference adopted a strategy of 'Trade and Aid' among the countries of the movement and the developing countries with a view to promote inter-country trade.

The Lima conference which was held at the foreign minister's level just before the seventh session of the UN General Assembly 1975, proposed a "plan of action" for the promotion of the interest of all developing countries and strengthening of cooperation, solidarity and capacity for joint action by the nonaligned and the other developing countries for the establishment of the New International Economic Order (NIEO). It "called upon the developed countries to eliminate barriers of trade for developing countries and encourage their manufactured exports." It asked the developed countries "to restructure their industries in order to deploy production capacity to developing countries and to expand technical assistance programmes."[79]

The New International Economic Order is based on certain guiding principles which include the "sovereign equality of states, self-determination of all peoples, inadmissibility of the acquisition of territories by force, territorial integrity and non-interference in the internal affairs of other states."[80]

It makes special mention of the "least developed land-locked and island developing countries and those developing countries most seriously, affected by economic crises and natural calamities leading to serious retardation of development processes."[81]

One goal of the plan of action for the NIEO is regional economic integration in which all states of a region benefit from, and make concessions to, a common economic policy in which the land-locked states have the same rights in all economic activities as to other members of the economic community. In the European Economic Community (EEC) which despite its difficulties is the world's most advanced example of economic regional integration, the citizens of any state, including the only land-locked state Luxembourg have the right to fish in the waters under the jurisdiction of any other member state.[82]

Nepal is in an unenviable position in the matter of economic development. It is not only one of the least developed countries of the world but also completely land-locked. Several conferences of the United Nations have made repeated recommendations with regard to granting special assistance to the land-locked countries, including sharing the cost of transportation to the nearest sea point. Nepal, that has not been able to exploit its inland resources fully, before which the coastal opportunity becomes meaningful.[83]

NORTH-SOUTH DIALOGUE AND THE LAND-LOCKED COUNTRIES

The Brandt Commission report, which discusses the energy problems of the world in detail, is a document of exceptional merit and significance. Its main theme is the restructuring of world economic order, a better and equitable distribution of resources which will establish a cooperative relationship between the developed and the developing countries. The Brandt Commission report, in essence, aims at solving the "staggering problems of poverty, population—and pollution—the three main scourages of the world."[84]

The North-South dialogue which could provide some hope to the developing countries from current inflationary pressures generated as a result of the sharp rise in oil price and a world economy which presents a gloomy prospect in the eighties is nowhere near realization. The group of 77, the largest economic grouping of the developing countries, at a meeting in New York on the eve of the special session of the General Assembly in September 1981, noted that the economies of the least developing countries had either "collapsed" or were "on the verge of collapsing, specially countries which are land-locked or island countries." The ministers of the developing countries called upon the developed countries "to show necessary political will" and "spirit of cooperation" towards solving the problems of the land-locked developing countries. The ministers noted that "no substantial progress has been made even after six years negotiations for a New International Economic Order." On the contrary, "there have been even a tendency on the part of the developed countries to slide back from earlier agreements between North and South."[85]

At the seventh special session of the United Nations General Assembly which was held from 1 to 17 September 1976, the developed and the developing countries discussed matters relating to international trade, transfer of real resources, science and technology, international monetary reforms, industrialization, food and agriculture and measures aimed at "narrowing the gap between developing and developed countries."[86]

Nepal made a special plea for development aid, "In the least developed countries, land-locked countries, level of development is so low, their resources so poor and their problems so chronic that unless special measures are taken, they can hardly make any headway in their development."

In the past decade or so Nepal has been active in all international forums, including trade and development. There cannot be any development without strengthening national economy but so long the existing constraints continue, whether these be regarding free access to the sea and adequate transit facilities or stable price for primary commodities, the rising expectations of the masses in the vast areas of the world cannot be fulfilled. The heads of states and governments of the nonaligned countries at Algiers had recommended that "special international assistance should also be provided to the land-locked developing countries to enable them to overcome their geo-structural handicap and to derive full benefit from the resolutions adopted by the United Nations agencies in this regard."[87]

The North-South dialogue could not be successful for the land-locked developing countries because there is no willingness to reach at an understanding by the developed countries.

SOUTH ASIAN REGIONAL COOPERATION AND NEPALESE VIEWS AS A LAND-LOCKED STATE

The South Asia region comprises seven nations, India, Pakistan, Sri Lanka, Bangladesh, Nepal, Bhutan, and Maldives. In these countries Nepal and Bhutan are the land-locked states, Sri Lanka and Maldives are island states and the others share a common land-mass, which is also called the Indian subcontinent. The South Asian foreign secretaries forum has so far held five meetings in Colombo, Kathmandu, Islamabad, Dhaka and Thimpu in order to agree upon a plan of regional cooperation in various socio-economic fields. The Foreign Ministers of the seven countries in the region have met in New Delhi in August 1983. The meeting of the Foreign Ministers, the first of its kind ever held at the political level to discuss regional cooperation among South Asian partners is, by all accounts, a significant development in this part of the world in recent times.[88]

Nepal is one of the active proponents of regional cooperation which, she feels is essential for promoting the well-being and economic prosperity of South Asia. King Birendra of Nepal in his address to the opening of the Rastriya Panchayat had emphasized the need for making an all-out effort "to enlarge the areas of mutual cooperation among the nations of South Asian subcontinent and play an active role in making the regional programme a success."[89] He called at the 29 November–3 December 1982 ministerial meeting for cooperation in the industrial development of the Kingdom of Nepal, for the development of water resources of Nepal for multiple use power, flood control and navigation is a clear indication of Nepal's desire to share her resources not only for her own benefit but for the region as a whole.[90]

For a land-locked country the idea of regional cooperation comes first. Some land-locked countries have regional cooperation with their region for development. For instance, Laos, a land-locked country in South East Asia, is a member of the Mekong Basin Development Project. Another African land-locked state, Mali, is a member in the Senegal River Commission. There are also cases of inland countries retaining interests in merchant shipping. For example, Switzerland which benefits from merchant marines numbering more than 28 ships.[91]

Much more than shipping involvement are the instances of river-sea links utilized by the land-locked states in other regions. One may cite the access of Czechoslovakia to the Denube, the Elbe, and other inland waterways, the use of the Ubangi and the Cango rivers by Rwanda and the Central African Republic.[92]

All this is far from suggesting that river transport is going to be easy for Nepal. However, one survey suggests that most of the three major river systems in the land are navigable for a part of the year upto the Ganga in Patna, enjoying all year round navigability to the mouth of the sea. The barge capability of Bangladesh which proposed Nepal's inclusion in the Joint River Commission (JRC), alone is reported to be adequate to handle upto 200,000 tons of Nepalese cargoes annually.[93] A crucial role in the solution of that problem could be played by the large storage reservoir plan being mooted now, it could even add a new dimension to the regional co-operation in South Asia.

NEPAL'S PEACE ZONE PROPOSAL

Geo-political realities and economic considerations must always dictate the foreign policies of small nations. This is particularly true for those which are land-locked like Nepal.

King Birendra declared that Nepal be accepted as a zone of peace of 25 February 1975. He said that, "we adhere to the policy of nonalignment because we believe that it brightens the prospects of peace. We need peace for our security, we need peace for independence and we need peace for development. As a matter of fact, Nepal in the past had signed formal peace and friendship treaties with both our friendly neighbours. And if today, peace is an overriding concern with us, it is only because our people genuinely desire peace in our country, in our region and everywhere in the world. It is with this earnest desire to institutionalize peace that I stand to make a proposition—a proposition that my country Nepal, be declared zone of peace."[94]

Nepal raised the peace zone proposal at the different international forums. Nepal has sought support for the proposition mainly through bilateral negotiations with friendly countries. King

Birendra said that "If economic development is essential for a land-locked and least developed country, no less important for her is an environment of peace and stability. Our proposal to declare Nepal a zone of peace reflects these aspirations of the Nepalese people, who wish peace at home, in the region and the world at large.[95]

NOTES

1. "Land-locked—Aspects of Development," Trade promotion Centre, Kathmandu (Nepal, 1976), p.65.
2. Ibid., p.67.
3. Ibid., p.73.
4. UNCTAD—Third Session, May 1972, TD/180. p.192.
5. UNCTAD—Third Session, 27 July 1972, p.12, TD/178.
6. Ibid.
7. United Nations Year Book, 1972, Vol. 26.
8. United Nations Treatv Series, Vol. 597, No. 8641.
9. Nepal and Nonalignment, HMG, Ministry of Communications, Department of Information, Kathmandu (Nepal, 1982), p.108.
10. The World Today, Vol. 28, No. 9, September 1972, pp.411-320.
11. "Land-locked—Aspects of Development," Trade Promotion Centre, Kathmandu (Nepal, 1976), p.84.
12. Ibid.
13. Ibid., p.85.
14. UNCTAD—Fourth Session, May 1976, Vol. I, pp.29-31, TD/218.
15. Ibid.
16. UNCTAD—IV, Fourth Session, May 1976, Vol. I, p.30.
17. UNCTAD-IV, Fourth Session, May 1976, Vol. II, p.82, TD/218/Vol. II.
18. United Nations Year Book, Vol.30, 1976, pp.413-414.
19. UNCTAD-V, Fifth Session, Vol. I, 1979,TD/269.
20. United Nations Year Book, Vol. 33, 1979, pp.569-570.
21. Ibid.
22. UNCTAD-V, Fifth Session, Vol.II, May 1979, TD/269.
23. A. Conf. 104/22/Rev. I., Report of the UN Conference on the Least Developed Countries, Paris, 1981.
24. Ibid.
25. Proclamations Speeches, and Messages, His Majesty King Birendra

(1972-1981)—HMG, Ministry of Communications, Department of Information, Kathmandu (Nepal, 1982), p. 313.

26. Rising Nepal (Kathmandu, 1981), 15 September.
27. Nepal Press Digest, Vol. 25, No. 36, 7 September 1981, p. 359.
28. General Assembly, Thirty-seventh session, 1982–83, p. 17.
29. Idid.
30. TD/B/1002—TD/B/AC/39/3., 1984.
31. UNCTAD—Sixth Session, 7 December 1983, p. 29, TD/B/AC.36/3.
32. Times of India (New Delhi, 1983), 30 March 1983.
33. Nepal News Royal Nepalese Embassy, (New Delhi, 1983), 7 June, p.9.
34. UNCTAD—Thirtieth Session, 18 March 1985, p.4, TD/B/1040.
35. General Assembly, Thirty-eighth Session, 23 Nov. 1983, p.10, A/C.2/38/SR. 48.
36. General Assembly, Resolution 3067, (XXVIII), of 16 Nov. 1973.
37. United Nations Year Book, Vol. 28, 1974.
38. UN Doc. A/Conf. 62/C.2/L.39.
39. Third United Nations Conference on Law of the Sea, Vol. X, pp.88–95.
40. Ibid. Vol. II, p. 206.
41. UN Doc, A/Conf. 62/65.
42. Year Book of the United Nations, Vol. 28, 1974.
43. UN Doc. A/Conf. 62/C.2/L.38.
44. N. 42.
45. Ibid.
46. UN Doc. A/Conf. 62/WP.8/Rev.I, 6 May 1976.
47. Sandiago Law Review, Vol. 14, 1976, p.637.
48. Ibid.
49. Ibid.
50. N. 42, Vol. 30, 1976, p. 73.
51. N. 42, Vol. 31, 1977, p. 31.
52. Ibid.
53. Ibid.
54. N. 42, Vol. 34, 1980, p. 136.
55. Ibid.
56. Ibid.
57. Ibid.
58. N. 30, Vol. 2, 1974, p. 247, A/Conf. 62.
59. Ibid.
60. Ibid.

61. N. 30, Vol. I, Official Records, 1973-74/pp.72-73, A/Conf./62.
62. Ibid.
63. Ibid.
64. N.30, Vol.14, 1982, pp.31-32.
65. Ibid.
66. N. 30, Vol. XIII, 1980, p. 14, A/Conf. 62/OR/9th Session.
67. Ibid.
68. Nepal News Royal Nepalese Embassy, (New Delhi, 1985), 1 March, p.5.
69. Ibid.
70. Ibid.
71. Nepal and Nonalignment, CEDA, Tribhuvan University, Kathmandu (Nepal, 1982), p.64.
72. Ibid.
73. Ibid.
74. Nepal and Nonalignment, HMG, Ministry of Communications, Department of Information, Kathmandu (Nepal, 1982), p.89.
75. Ibid., p.107.
76. Ibid., p.119.
77. Ibid., p.120.
78. Ibid.
79. Dibya Deo Bhatta, "Nepal and Nonalignment," His Majesty Government Press, Kathmandu (Nepal, 1983), pp.19-20.
80. Ibid., p.22.
81. Ibid.
82. San Diego Law Review, Vol. 14, 1976, p. 637.
83. Dibya Deo Bhatta, "Nepal and Nonalignment," His Majesty Government Press, Kathmandu (Nepal, 1983), pp.18-19.
84. Ibid., pp.22.
85. Ibid., pp. 23-24.
86. Ibid., p.25.
87. Ibid., pp.26-27.
88. Indian and Foreign Review, Vol. 20, No. 20, 1-14 Aug. 1983, p. 20.
89. Ibid., p.21.
90. N.79, p.16.
91. Resources of the Sea and Regional Cooperation,—Country Study for Nepal, CEDA (Kathmandu, 1983), p.62.
92. Ibid.
93. Ibid., p.63.

94. Bhola Rana, "The Evolution of Nepal's Peace Zone Proposal," His Majesty Government, Ministry of Communications, Department of Information, 1982, p.2.
95. N.68, 16 June 1985, p.2.

7. Conclusion

After considering the international agreements and practices with regard to the land-locked states we may draw some conclusions. The present study has dealt with certain aspects of the problems of the access of the land-locked states to the sea, both from the theoretical and the practical points of view. The subject is vast and touches on a large number of related questions, such as freedom of the seas, freedom of passage across the territorial sea, the use of maritime parts open to commerce, the equal treatment of the users of those ports, communication by road, rail and air across the countries whose territories block the access of other countries to the sea.

The learned authorities have built up many theories to provide the access to the land-locked countries. Some hold that access is a right conferred by nature on every country while others consider that the principle of freedom of the sea is the foundation of right to access, and yet others take the view that a country without a sea-coast is the beneficiary of a servitude of passage across a country having a sea-coast. Sibert defends the right of access of the land-locked states to the sea as a logical consequence of the freedom of the seas:

"Since the high seas form an asset the use of which is common to all, it would appear that the right to navigate freely on the high seas should be enjoyed by all members of the international community, including those which have no coast line."[1]

In this connection, the multilateral conventions concluded under the suspices of the League of Nations at Barcelona (1921) and Geneva testify to the progress of the idea that the land-locked countries should be assured of free access to the sea and that such access should be provided for both in their interest and in the interest of the international community.

The practice of states has led to the evolution of a number of principles which find tangible expression in multilateral and bilateral treaties and of which the most important are:

1. the principle of freedom of transit,
2. the principle of non-discrimination, irrespective of the origin and destination of the goods and passengers in transit,
3. the principle that persons and goods in transit should not be subjected to any vexatious formalities and that the charges payable by or in respect of them should be the same as those payable by other users.

In principle, these rules apply to the traffic, whatever means of communication are chosen, rail, air, or river. Ever since the Congress of Vienna, rivers have been governed by various regulations. International river commissions have been setup, composed of riparian and non-riparian states, which possess virtual administrative, police and regulatory powers and a very large measure of autonomy vis-a-vis the governments which formed them. These bodies have proved their usefulness as instruments for carrying out the collective will of the states in a field which is of particular importance for the well being of all.

From the numerous treaties and conventions considered, it would appear that there are a few, but sufficiently clear, rules which could no doubt serve as a basis for the framing of new provisions granting to the land-locked states an unquestioned right of access to the ports and to the open sea, a right which these states need if they are to achieve full economic development.

In fact, access to the sea can be, and is obtained in one of three distinct ways by obtaining:

1. the right to use an international river,
2. the possession of a 'corridor' to the coast, and
3. transit rights across another country, with or without the rights of a free zone in a port of latter.

INTERNATIONAL RIVERS

There is considerable difference in the practice of the nations with regard to rivers which they share with one another. In some instances the right of navigation is reserved only to the vessels of those states which border the river, in other there is complete freedom to navigate the rivers except in time of war. We are here concerned only with the right of the upstream states to use a river as a means of reaching the open sea. During the last century and a half, by a series of international agreements the following rivers have been opened to international commerce, (a) in South America the Amazon and most of its tributaries, and the river plate and its navigable tributaries, (b) in Europe the Rhine and its tributaries Danube, (c) in Africa the Niger, the Congo, and the Zambezi are open to the ships of all nations.

In certain instances the rivers enumerated here serve as outlets for the land-locked states, and give them access to the sea. For instance, Bolivia, Paraguay, Switzerland, Austria and Czechoslovakia have no natural outlet to the sea other than through these rivers.

CORRIDORS TO THE SEA

A corridor reaching to the sea coast implies a transfer of sovereignty over an area of land in order to give to the inland state an assured outlet to the ocean. It is implied that this consideration alone is responsible for determining the boundaries of the territory in question, and that historical and ethnic factors are of no importance. It is probable, however, that no corridor has been established without at least paying lip-service to other considerations, except in the barren and uninhabited regions.

It is inevitable that a state would prefer to control a corridor rather than to have transit rights or the freedom to use a river. While theoretically all should be equally protected by international law. In fact any attempt to close a corridor would be a violation of national sovereignty, while interference with the right of passage might be more easily condoned or excused.

The most famous example in this connection is the Polish corridor established after the end of the First World War.

TRANSIT

The third and last solution to the problem of the land-locked states is that of free transit. This is the means of access upon which most of the land-locked states of the world depend. The issues involved were clarified at the Barcelona conference on the freedom of transit.

The question of the rights of the land-locked states was again taken up in 1965 by a committee on the preparation of a draft convention relating to the transit trade of the land-locked states.

While there has been no change in the legal status of transit rights during the past twenty years, the actual practice of nations has probably deteriorated on the whole. This has happened in two distinct ways. In the first place, states have used as an instrument of national policy their ability to interfere with the right of the transit of goods across their territory. The most glaring examples of this have occurred in the Middle East; Egypt's interference with the rights of Israel, the obstruction and even destruction of pipelines by other Middle East states.

The freedom of movement established between the Two World Wars by international agreements has also been prejudiced by the division of the greater part of the world into two hostile camps. The existence of the Iron Curtain has not in itself restricted the right of transit across it. The Czechoslovakia exports are currently being shipped through the port of Hamburg, and the Hungarian goods pass through the ports of Rijeka and Trieste.

The concept of the freedom of transit is dependent upon the concept of sovereignty. The land-locked states have consistently argued that the principles of state sovereignty permit them to allow or disallow all transit through their territories.

SOLUTIONS TO THE QUESTION OF ACCESS TO THE SEA

International Law. Today international law is based on equity, on general consent deriving from the recognition of the advantages to be gained by all from mutual cooperation. Admittedly, international law has not solved all international problems, it has not brought about the millenium of a prosperous, peaceful, orderly world. Yet the International Court of Justice, the International Law Commission, the United Nations itself and its specialized agencies are all making great contributions to the codification and progressive development of international law. The resolutions of General Assembly, United Nations declarations on social and economic matters, and debates on conventions developed by international conferences, even if the conventions never came into force, are coming to be accepted as contributions to international law, worthy of respect and consideration by the 'civilized nations'.

The development of international law since the Second World War illustrates its changing nature. Since the emergence of new states respect, utilize and help develop international law, at the same time objecting to certain aspects of it which they deem contrary to their interests. While recognizing that international law is vital for the establishment of an atmosphere within which free access to the sea for the developing land-locked states is encouraged and for the provision of guidelines for working out the details of such access, one cannot help but feel that it is not adequate.

Political and Economic Integration. Without any doubt, the only ideal and permanent solution to the problem of access to the sea is for the land-locked states to merge politically with their seaboard neighbours, thereby eliminating the boundaries between them. This political integration would eliminate all political impediments to the movement between the coast and the interior and the problems of transit would be reduced to the problems of transportation.

The only example of political integration involving a land-locked state since the World War II, in fact, was Ethiopia's acquisition of Eritrea giving her a sea-coast for the first time in her history.

Political integration, then, while highly desirable as a means of assuring a land-locked state her access to the sea, is exceptionally difficult to achieve, even under the most favourable circumstances. But this leaves open the question whether economic integration alone, without political union, may serve the same purpose equally well. Logically it might seem so, but again this matter requires careful investigation.

The literature on economic integration is voluminous and opinions about it are numerous. It must be recognized that no land-locked state is going to enter into a common market or free trade association or any other form of economic integration with a transit state solely in order to safeguard its access to the sea any more than it would enter into close political union for this reason alone.

The Central American Common Market and the Latin American Free Trade Association (LAFTA) were both organized in 1960, only pact in response to the organization of the European Economic Community (EEC) and the European Free Trade Association (EFTA).

Regional Cooperation and Development. In view of the manifold difficulties of organizing a common market or other type of regional economic integration among the developing countries, a reasonable alternative might be a high degree of cooperation among a group of 'sovereign' states, including both the land-locked and the transit states, for the purpose of stimulating, planning financing, and guiding the development of regional infrastructure projects for the benefit of all parties. The concept of regional cooperation raises no objections so long as it remains only a concept.

In Latin America, ECLA, (Economic Community of Latin America) and OAS (Organization of American States), the Inter-American Development Bank and other hemispheric bodies have long urged regional cooperation and have provided the stimulus, guidance, and financing for such efforts.

It may be said that while international law must provide the atmosphere, establish the framework, and set the minimum requirements for the provision of access to the sea for the developing land-locked states, it alone cannot assure such access. Political integration of interior and littoral states can do this best, but since this is so difficult to achieve, and rather unlikely until nationalism declines as a motive force in the world. The economic integration is more feasible and perhaps just as efficacious. It has worked well in the case of Uganda and has possibilities elsewhere, particularly, in West Africa where neither economic nor political integration is practicable. The solution to the question of access to the sea for the land-locked states of Africa, Asia and South America must be sought in the regional economic cooperation and regional development programmes.

INTERNATIONAL EFFORTS TO SAFEGUARDS THE RIGHTS OF THE LAND-LOCKED STATES

There is a long history of attempts made to solve the problems of the land-locked states through international conventions and bilateral as well as multilateral agreements. The first attempt can be traced back to the Peace of Westphalia in 1648, which divided the Central Europe into a large number of states, some of whom had no sea-coast. It laid down certain rules and regulations regarding free navigation and traffic charges which contributed to the development of international law on free access to the sea for the land-locked states.

There have been numerous attempts to find out a general solution to this vast question. Especially vigorous efforts were made after the First World War under the auspices of the League of Nations, which had received instructions to that effect under the treaty of Versailles and St. Germain of 1919. During the period of the Second World War, while the problems of the land-locked states had been more or less satisfactorily solved in Europe, their counterparts in Asia, Africa and Latin America were still struggling hard to obtain concessions from their coastal neighbours, mainly through bilateral agreements. The question has also been discussed from time to time in other United Nations bodies, either in the more general context of transit or, as a specific problem confronting the land-locked countries. The problems have been discussed in the various international conferences, such as the UNCTAD, the Law of the Sea, and the Nonaligned summit conferences. In these conferences many principles were adopted for the land-locked countries.

Although the land-locked countries were exercising their right of free access to the sea in varying geographical, economic and political conditions under bilateral and multilateral agreements, the joint efforts made by the land-locked countries since 1957 for the reaffirmation and safeguarding of their rights proved very useful indeed. Today the right of free access to the sea for the land-locked countries is firmly established in international law.

The land-locked states have voiced two main concerns: first, that the land-locked states be given affirmative, enforceable rights of access to the sea and extraction of its resources, and, second, that restrictions be placed upon the developed coastal states to prevent them from claiming or depleting the existing resources. The third United Nations Conference on the Law of the Sea (UNCLOS III), looking forward to having a comprehensive convention on the law of the sea that would ensure to them not only free access to the sea and to the sea-bed, but also an equitable share in the resources of the international sea-bed area that is now firmly established as the "common heritage of mankind."

Many coastal states did not recognize any other states, right to the resources in the zone and voiced strong reservation on the articles pertaining to this matter. Because of their lack of political, economic and military leverage, many land-locked states are dependent upon the potential world-wide agreement to attain enforceable rights with respect to the sea.

Remembering that poverty anywhere carries with it a potential threat to prosperity everywhere, it is in the interest of the coastal states themselves to see that the land-locked states are permitted to share the immense wealth of the sea. Again, the principle of equality of nations, which is one of the cardinal principles of the charter of the United Nations, must retain its relevance in the changed context of the law of the sea which raises great expectations in the wake of the "common heritage of mankind" doctrine. The land-locked states and geographically disadvantaged states be given an opportunity to partake of the resources of the sea along with the coastal states on an equitable basis, as partners.

The land-locked states have achieved a modest success in the conference so far. The United Nations and its agencies have played a pioneering role in drawing the attention of the international community to the unique difficulties which the land-locked states face. The national and international financial institutions should accord appropriate attention to the special needs of the land-locked states in extending adequate financial and technical assistance to projects designed for the development and improvement of infrastructure facilities needed by these countries. The following suggestions may be helpful for the solutions of the problems of the land-locked states:

1. Rehabilitation and preventive maintenance of transit facilities in the land-locked countries and their transit neighbours, including the provision of spare parts, tools, and building materials.

2. Provision of all weather transport through road transport routes linking the main commercial centres in the land-locked countries with the seaports, and the provision of vehicles.

3. Extension of the existing rail system of transit countries into the land-locked developing countries to avoid the need for transhipments, provisions of locomotives, rolling stock, and railway marshalling facilities.

4. Extension and strengthening of runways at airports, pro-

vision of adequate navigational aid and cargo handling facilities and improvement of the surface collection and distribution system.

5. Improvement of communication links between the various ports and commercial centres in the land-locked countries and between the ports and the over-seas markets.

6. Provision of storage facilities in the ports and at the rail, road and airport terminals to handle the cargo of the land-locked developing countries, and the provision of adequate berthing and handling facilities in the ports used by these countries.

The first aspects of such arrangements is the cooperation between the land-locked developing countries, and their transit neighbours, as emphasized by the integrated planning approach. The close cooperation between the land-locked states and their transit neighbours is crucial to the solution of the transit transport problem of the land-locked states.

SPECIAL CASE OF NEPAL AS A LAND-LOCKED STATE

Nepal's land-locked geographical position is aggravated by her remoteness and isolation from world market and she is also one of the fifteen least developed countries in the world. As the country is heavily dependent on external trade for her development and construction requirements, a cheaper and efficient transit transport system has become a prime need not only for trade expansion but also for speeding up the pace of her economic development. Nepal has, therefore, been particularly active in raising the problems faced by the land-locked states in the United Nations and its specialized institutions like UNCTAD, ECAFE, Law of the sea conference, etc. Nepal, in alliance with the other land-locked countries, has tried in various international conferences to press for the recognition of the "right of free and unrestricted transit" as an integral part of international law.

Ever since it became a member of the United Nations in December 1955, Nepal, alongwith Afghanistan and Laos, took the initiative in acquainting the committee on industry and trade of the ECAFE with the problems of the land-locked states. In January 1956 resolution of the ECAFE Committee on industry and trade which was incorporated in the report of the economic and social council became the basis for the General Assembly resolution of 20 February 1957. The General Assembly resolution 1028 (XI) recognized "the need of the land-locked countries for adequate transit facilities in promoting international trade," and invited the governments of the member states "to give full recognition to the needs of land-locked member states in the matter of transit trade and, therefore, to accord them adequate facilities in terms of international law and practice in this regard, bearing in mind the future requirements resulting from the economic development of the land-locked countries."

Nepal, alongwith five other land-locked countries—Afghanistan, Austria, Bolivia, Czechoslovakia, and Paraguay—moved an amendment demanding a study of the problem of free access to the sea for the land-locked states by a conference of plenipotentiaries. This recommendation was endorsed by the General Assembly in its resolution of 21 February 1957. The first law of the sea conference was held in Geneva in 1958. In this conference Nepal alongwith thirteen other land-locked states submitted a memorandum. In the conference the land-locked states including Nepal requested affirmation of the seven principles formulated by it.

In March 1963 at the ECAFE session Nepal co-sponsored the resolution on economic cooperation among the Asian countries, and in December 1963 at the ministers' conference in Manila the principle of the right of free transit for the land-locked countries was accepted due to the initiative taken by Nepal along with Laos and Afghanistan.

The first UNCTAD-I Conference was held in Geneva in 1964. Nepal requested the UN Conference on Trade and Development (UNCTAD) in Geneva in April 1964 to setup a separate committee for a detailed study of the problems of trade and transit of the land-locked states. A forty member sub-committee was appointed by the UNCTAD–I to consider the proposal for the formulation of an international convention on the transit rights of the land-locked states. The sub-committee adopted eight principles relating to the interests of the land-locked countries. On the request of this sub-committee the Secretary-General appointed a twenty-four member expert committee representing the land-locked transit and other interested states. Nepal served as a rapporteur of this committee which prepared a new draft convention on the basis of the Tehran draft prepared by Nepal together with Afghanistan and Laos.

The United Nations Conference on Trade and Transit of the land-locked states was held in New York in 1965. Nepal along with other member states demanded that "traffic in transit will not be subjected to unnecessary delays and restrictions."

On many issues the Nepalese viewpoint came into a sharp conflict with the views of India and Pakistan—her closest neighbours. Nepal acted as the spokesman of the land-locked countries of Asia, Africa and Latin America. Nepal's approach to the whole question of transit rights of the land-locked states centred around the notion that such rights were not "favours" from the transit countries but rights affirmed by the principles of international law and practice.

The second UNCTAD was held in New Delhi in February–March 1968. Nepal along with eight other land-locked states sponsored a draft resolution which called for special treatment of the developing land-locked countries as 'the least developed among the developing countries'. It also established a group of experts to carry out a comprehensive examination of the special problems and handicaps of the land-locked developing countries. The UNCTAD–II and the Algiers charter saw change in Nepal's views whereas Nepal's approach in 1964–65 had been largely legal, in 1967–68 it grew economic in orientation. Nepal's achievements in the field of recognition and extension of the rights of the land-locked states have really been noteworthy.

Many other conferences were held from time to time on the problems of the land-locked states. At the sea-bed committee held in 1970, Nepal along with seven other states—Afghanistan, Austria, Belgium, Hungary, Netherlands, and Singapore—suggested that the national sea-bed area should not exceed either 200 metres or 40 miles from the baseline of the territorial sea and that in an additional 40 miles zone called "the coastal state zone" no exploitation should take place without the consent of the coastal state. These countries also proposed a revenue-sharing system applicable to the entire national sea-bed. The land-locked and other geographically disadvantaged states demanded for them the rights to participate in the exploration and exploitation of the non-living resources of the sea-bed areas of the neighbouring coastal states on an equal and non-discriminating basis, and a sharing of revenues by coastal states with the International Sea-bed Authority (ISBA) from the exploitation of the non-living resources of the national sea-bed.

The UNCTAD–III was held in 1972 in Santiago. A special

committee established to consider the problems of the land-locked states was appointed. Nepal requested the developed countries and the competent international agencies to provide technical and financial assistance to the land-locked countries to adopt to their particular geographical situation and to maintain and improve their transport and communication infrastructure. The proposal was made to establish a special fund to subsidize transport costs for the land-locked states.

The UNCTAD–IV, V and VI respectively were held in 1976, 1979 and 1983. Nepal participated in these conferences. She has been consistently insisting in these conferences that she, as a land-locked state, should be given the right to enjoy unrestricted trade and transit facilities.

In the Nonaligned Summit conferences Nepal raised the problems of the land-locked states and demanded the international organizations and other developed countries to provide technical and financial assistance to the land-locked countries. Nepal urged the coastal countries to give sympathetic consideration to make specific provisions guaranteeing the right of the land-locked states to free and unrestricted access to and from the sea.

The third law of the sea (UNCLOS III) conference was held in 1973 at New York. It had ten meetings between 1973 and 1983. In 1973 seven land-locked states submitted a proposal to the committee with the intention to contribute to the work of the committee in adopting article relating to the land-locked states.

The land-locked states at the UNCLOS III voiced two main concerns; first that the land-locked states be given affirmative, enforceable rights of access to the sea and the extraction of its resources, and second, that restriction be placed upon the developed coastal states to prevent them from claiming or depleting the existing resources.

In March 1974 at Kampala meeting the land-locked states declared that "with respect to the exercise of jurisdiction over resources in areas adjacent to the territorial sea, the land-locked states and other geographically disadvantaged states shall have equal rights with other states and without discrimination, in the exercise of such jurisdiction." Later, at the Caracas session, 22 land-locked states and geographically disadvantaged states submitted a joint proposal which sought recognition of the right of the land-locked states and geographically disadvantaged states to participate in the exploration and exploitation of the living as well as non-living resources of the Exclusive Economic Zone (EEZ) of the neighbouring coastal states on 'equal and non-discriminatory basis'.

Nepal participated along with the other land-locked states and submitted proposal in the third law of the sea conference. The Nepalese delegation urged the international community to show goodwill towards the land-locked states. The resources of the exclusive economic zone (EEZ) should be shared among mankind as a whole, any decision regarding their distribution should be taken by an international organization and not unilaterally by the coastal states.

The coastal states did not agree with some provision in the law of the sea conference with respect to the land-locked states. Taking a different view, Pakistan said she did not recognize any other state's right to the resources in the zone. India argued strongly in the conference that the continental shelf, which was the natural prolongation of the land territory of the coastal state, come under a separate regime in international law, and therefore, the question of sharing its resources with other states, whether land-locked or not, did not arise.

UNCLOS III has provided the land-locked states with a unique forum to express their needs for enforceable rights to share in the use and exploitation of the ocean. The conference declared that the sea-bed resources should be treated as the heritage of all nations. Nevertheless, it is likely that economic and political pressures will prevent the conference from adopting any provisions which would substantially benefit the land-locked states.

Nepal hopes that the United Nations initiative to codify the law of the sea on the basis of new realities and new possibilities to explore and exploit resources of the sea-bed, ocean floor and the subsoil thereof is indeed a bold and imaginative approach. Nepal welcomes and endorses the proposal to establish an international regime and appropriate international machinery to ensure equitable sharing of such resources lying beyond the limits of national jurisdiction for the benefit of all mankind. But, Nepal feels that it is very difficult for the land-locked states to share the benefits in any meaningful manner without the necessary transit and port facilities from their coastal neighbours. Therefore, Nepal urges the coastal states to give sympathetic consideration to make specific provisions guaranteeing the right of the land-locked states to free and unrestricted access to the sea. Nepal hopes that the third law of the sea conference will have the full support for this most legitimate and just demand.

Thus, the United Nations has provided Nepal an important forum to serve her vital national interests in the family of nations. Her membership of the United Nations and its various organs and agencies has gone a long way to help her in her search for international identity and has also imparted to her a sense of security through her important contribution to the United Nations efforts to gain international recognition of the developing land-locked countries.

Nepal has been successful not only in focussing the attention of the world forum on the problems facing the developing land-locked countries, but also in obtaining juridical recognition of their transit rights through the adoption of an international convention.

Despite the recognition of the rights of the land-locked states through international conferences, Nepal is not fully satisfied on the issue of transit facilities, and, therefore, she is trying to secure maximum possible transit facilities from her neighbour (India). On this issue she continued to complain frequently about the 'inadequate transit facilities' for her external trade and India's 'lack of cooperation'.

Nepal is a land-locked state and she has to depend upon India for the development of her foreign trade. The major part of her trade is still carried on with India, but for reasons, both political and economic, Nepal decided to follow a policy of trade diversification.

Historically, Nepal's trade was confined to India. Nepal never needed foreign markets in the past because as a matter of policy her rulers tried to keep the country isolated from the world markets. Nepal's trade with other countries started only in 1951 after the fall of the Ranas.

Nepal had traditional trade relation with Tibet (China). Except some members of the Nawar trading community, who lived in Lhasa and other commercial centres of Tibet till 1950's, there was not any regular flow of Nepalese going to any part of China in search of employment. There is not even a prospect of any such development. Even now nearly 80 per cent of Nepal's trade is with India, though Chinese goods are carried through Calcutta port.

With the Royal takeover in December 1960, King Mahendra made a determined effort to diversify Nepal's foreign trade and thus reduce its dependence on India. While his efforts were directed towards expanding Nepal's trade with all countries, Nepal has entered into trade agreement with a member of friendly countries including China, Bangladesh, Pakistan, USSR, USA, etc. Despite this, the trade situation of Nepal is not satisfactory. There were numerous difficulties in the way. Nepal did not have an efficient system of internal transportation to facilitate quick and better movements of goods. More important than that was its being a land-locked state, which made it dependent upon India for the facilities of port and transit regarding trade with other countries.

The question of transit facilities was mainly related to bilateral trade relations between India and Nepal. Though India had granted transit facilities to Nepal, it still continues to face many problems. Lack of alternatives with respect to port choices, the congestion problem in Calcutta port, the inadequacy of dock storage space for Nepal, shortage of railway wagons, usual labour unrest with the danger of insecurity of commodities and the problem in the provision of containerized trucking services are among the more apparant limitations arising out of her land-lockedness.

To facilitate Nepal's access to the sea, India and Nepal concluded many Trade and Transit Treaties.

During the last part of British rule in India Nepal-India trade relations were governed by the treaty of 1923. Following India's independence, Nepal and India decided to regulate the traditional trade principles and procedures and with this objective signed a treaty of trade and commerce in 1950. However, by 1960 both Nepal and India become convinced that the existing treaty provisions were inadequate and hence a new treaty was signed on 11 September 1960 with a view to removing the unequal and disadvantageous position of Nepal vis-a-vis India in their mutual trade relations. On the expiry of this treaty, a fresh treaty of trade and transit was concluded between the two countries in 1971 for a five year period.

Though the 1971 treaty of trade and transit had lapsed in 1976, it was kept in operation till 1978 because of a continuing dead-lock in trade negotiations between Nepal and India. It was a long-standing Nepalese demand to have two separate treaties on trade and transit. The objective behind the demand was Nepal's desire to delink the problems of her trade with India from her general overseas trade that had to go through India in transit because of

Nepal's land-locked position. India was unwilling to accede to such a demand as the pre-1977 Government of Indira Gandhi felt that the question of trade had been inseparately linked with transit between India and Nepal because of the very nature of geographical contiguity and economic links between them. The Indian apprehension centred round the fact that separation of the provisions of trade from transit would further aggravate the already existing problems of illegal and deflected trade. However, the Janata Government which came to power in India in 1977 resolved to improve the country's relations with her immediate neighbours. In accordance with its declared foreign policy objective of beneficial bilateralism the Janata Government conceded the Nepalese demand for two separate treaties during Prime Minister Morarji Desai's visit to Kathmandu in December 1977. Ultimately, on 17 March 1978 two separate treaties on trade and transit and an agreement on cooperation were signed.

In accordance with the treaty of trade, India agreed to enlarge the market for Nepal's manufactured products in India in order to assist in the industrial development of Nepal. The separate treaty on transit laid down the procedures for Nepal's traffic in transit through India. India also agreed to provide an overland route for Nepal's trade with Bangladesh, as well as with other countries through Bangladesh. The trade treaty was signed for five years and transit treaty was signed for seven years.

In March 1983, the two governments held meeting for the renewal of trade treaty. Both governments agreed to extend their treaty of trade and agreement for cooperation for another five years. The scope of the new treaty has been enlarged.

The treaty of transit lapsed in March 1985. The existing Indo-Nepal transit treaty has been extended on an ad-hoc basis for a period of six months.

The original trade and transit treaty between Nepal and India provided for virtually free and unrestricted transit and transport to and from any Indian port without breaking bulk or payment of special duties. India has also provided necessary overland transit facilities through Bangladesh. Apart from this, Nepal continued to complain about the inadequate transit facilities. The Nepal Government said that the customs and other procedures in respect of goods entering Bangladesh for transit to Nepal by land are also simple in comparison to the procedure as stipulated in the improved text of the treaty of transit done between Nepal and India. The Nepalese government made it clear that Bangladesh port charges are substaintially lower than Calcutta's. Thus the routes via Bangladesh, especially Chalna, offer potentially the least costly route for Nepal's transit traffic, provided that the deserved physical and procedural facilities for railway and road transport are granted to facilitate such traffic.

However, Nepal seeks more liberal transit facilities and custom procedures from India for carrying her international trade through Bangladesh. India has provided adequate transit facilities through Bangladesh. Apart from this, Nepal demands some facilities from India. The Nepalese government said that if India provides some facilities which are mentioned below, it could improve Nepal's transit transport problems. These are:

1. The Calcutta port facilities: The Government of Nepal need to establish a centralized single warehousing facility to accommodate Nepal's traffic.

2. The reduction of average time spent in port: Now averaging 10 days per shipment for general cargo and 17 days for bulk cargoes.

3. The elimination of duty insurance: It is justified partly because the insurance rates remain above claims, current practice does not conform to normal common carrier, liability by making importers liable for losses in transit, and because it contravenes Article IV of the Transit treaty which specifies that no charges should be imposed on transit traffic which does not reflect actual costs for services incurred. The elimination of duty insurance would result in an estimated saving of Indian currency rupees eight million per year at current rates.

4. Nepalese shippers should be given the free choice of ports in India.

5. The introduction of intermodal container services and the establishment of appropriate inland freight stations at the Nepal border.

6. The extension of broad-gauge railway lines upto Nepali border.

7. On special potential benefit to all countries concerned is the reopening of selective routes through Bangladesh.

8. The introduction of barge transport along the designated waterways navigational facilities.

However, the Nepalese authorities said that many problems must be resolved, if these services can be made operational. Some government officials say that at present Nepal faces transport problems. Nepal's acute problem is the high cost of transportation and lack of efficient transport modes. According to Nepalese officials, this can be solved only through India, and India should give adequate transport facilities to Nepal.

The Indian Government argues that India has already given adequate transit transport facilities. But India has her own limitation which is a matter of her own security and sovereignty. Nepal has got recognition through international conferences to free access to the sea from her neighbouring transit countries, and India has given adequate facilities to Nepal in accordance with international conventions. Despite this, Nepal always complains about the inadequate transit facilities. The Indian Government said that the complaints of Nepal on the matter of inadequate transit facilities were 'false and misleading'. This is a political matter. India expects Nepal not to do anything which would endanger India's security and jeopardize her economic interests owing to the adoption of unfair practices by certain unfriendly countries.

However, for the purpose of maintaining harmony in the commercial relations between the two countries both should take steps affecting the other after mutual consultation. When mutual understanding and goodwill are present, wise statesmanship and efficient implementation of decisions would, it may reasonably be hoped, establish harmony in commercial field to reinforce and strengthen the friendship in the political sphere. Measures should be taken by mutual agreement to check smuggling which is a burning problem for both the countries.

Day-to-day problems could perhaps be amicably solved by establishing a 'joint trade commission' similar to the one provided for in the transit agreement between Austria and Italy. Nepal should also recognize the problems and needs of India. There is no reason why the needs and problems of both the countries cannot be fulfilled and solved.

NOTE

1. United Nations Conference on Law of the Sea, Official Records, Fifth Committee, Vol. VII 1958, p. 26.

Select Bibliography

PRIMARY SOURCES

LEAGUE OF NATIONS DOCUMENT

League of Nations Treaty Series, 1921–1927.

UNITED NATIONS DOCUMENTS

General Assembly, Official Records, General Debates, 1946–1984.

United Nations Yearbook, 1946–1981.

United Nations Monthly Chronicle, 1964–1980.

United Nations Bulletin, 1946–1980.

United Nations Statistical Yearbook, 1955-1980.

United Nations Treaty Series, 1948–1975.

United Nations, General Agreement on Tariffs and Trade, (GATT) 1946–1970.

United Nations Review, 1954–1980.

United Nations Economic Commission for Asia and the Far East (ECAFE), 1956–1970.

United Nations Economic and Social Council, Annual Reports, 1956–1980.

United Nations Economic and Social Survey of Asia and the Pacific, 1970–1984.

The Work of the International Law Commission, 1970-1980.

Documents on United Nations Conference on Trade and Development (UNCTAD), 1964–1984.

United Nations Conference on Law of the Sea, Official Records, Fifth Committee, 1958.

United Nations Conference on Law of the Sea, 1973–1982.

UNESCO Bulletin, Nepal National Commission for UNESCO, 1967–1970.

GOVERNMENT DOCUMENTS

NEPAL

His Majesty's Government, Ministry of Communications, Department of Information, Facts about Nepal, (Kathmandu, 1982).

———, Nepal in a Nutshell (Kathmandu, 1978).

———, Department of Publicity and Broadcasting, Ministry, of Foreign Affairs, Annual Reports, 1967-68, (Kathmandu, 1968).

———, Department of Publicity and Broadcasting, Ministry of Foreign Affairs, Annual Reports, 1969–71 (Kathmandu, 1971).

———, Ministry of Communications, Department of Information, His Majesty King Mahendra, Proclamations, Speeches and Measures, Vol. I to IV, (Kathmandu, 1967).

———, Minisiry of Comnunications, Department of Information, His Majesty King Birendra, Proclamations, Speeches and Messages, 1972–81 (Kathmandu, 1982).

———, Ministry of Communications, Department of Information, His Majesty King Birendra Speaks on Foreign Policy, (Kathmandu, 1981).

———, Ministry of Communications, Department of Information, Nepal and Nonalignment, (Kathmandu, 1982).

———, Ministry of Communications, Department of Information, The Evolution of Nepal's Peace Zone Proposal, (Kathmandu, 1982).

———, National Planning Commission, The Sixth Plan (1980–1985) (Kathmandu, 1981).

———, Trade Promotion Centre, Land-Locked, Aspects of Development, (Kathmandu, 1976).

———, Trade Promotion Centre, Treaty of Trade Between His Majesty's Government of Nepal and the Government of India, (Kathmandu, 1978).

———, Trade Promotion Centre, Treaty of Transit between His Majesty's Government of Nepal and the Government of India, (Kathmandu, 1978).

———, Department of Publicity and Broadcasting, Ministry of National Guidance, Nepal-Pakistan Transit Agreement, (Kathmandu, 1963).

———, Trade Promotion Centre, Nepal's Trade and Transit Agreements, (Kathmandu, 1971).

INDIA

India, Parliamentary Debates, Lok Sabha Secretariat, Treaty of Trade and Commerce between the Government of India and the HMG of Nepal, (New Delhi, 1950).

India, Ministry of Finance, Treaty of Trade and Transit between the Government of India and His Majesty's Government of Nepal, (New Delhi, 1960).

SECONDARY SOURCES

BOOKS

Aitchison, C.U., A Collection of Treaties, Engagements, Sanads Relating to India and Neighbouring Countries, Vol. XIV (New Delhi, Central Publishing Branch, 1929).

Adhikari, U.P., Some Aspects of Nepalese Economy, (Kathmandu, 1971).

Alexander, L., The Law of the Sea : Offshore Boundaries and Zones, (Ohio State University Press, 1967).

Anand, R.P., Legal Regime of the Sea-bed and the Developing Countries, (New Delhi, Thompson Press Ltd., Publication Division, 1975).

———, Law of the Sea, Caracas and Beyond, (New Delhi, Radiant Publishers, 1976).

———, New States and International Law, (Delhi, Vikas Publishing House, 1972).

Arora, V.K. and Appadorai, A., India in World Affairs (1957–58), (New Delhi, Sterling Publishers Pvt. Ltd., 1975).

Andrass, Juras, International Law and Resources of the Sea, (London, 1970).

Bhasin, A.S. (ed.), Documents on Nepal's Relations with India and China, 1949-1956, (New Delhi, Academic Books, 1970).

Bhattacharjee, G.P., India and Politics of Modern Nepal, (Calcutta, The Minerva Associates, 1970).

Banskota, N.P., Indo-Nepal Trade and Economic Relations, (New Delhi, B.R. Publishing Co., 1981).

Brecher, Michael, The New States of Asia, (London, 1963).

Bretwell, Richard, (ed.), Foreign Policy and Developing Nations, (Lexington, 1969).

Bhadur, Poorna, Nepal Behind and Screen, (Kathmandu, Nepal Youth League, 1957).

———, Foreign Eyes and Attitudes on Nepal, (Kathmandu, Nepal Youth League, 1959).

Bandyopadhyaya, J., The Making of India's Foreign Policy, (Calcutta, Allied Publishers, 1970).

Blackie, P., and others, Nepal in Crisis, (Bombay, Oxford University Press, 1980).

Baxtor, R., The Law of International Waterways, (Harvard, Harvard University Press, 1964).

Banerjee, Brojendra Nath, India's Aid to its Neighbouring Countries, (New Delhi, 1982).

Bhattacharya, D.C., An Outline of World Politics, (Calcutta, Vijay Publishing House, 1972).

Birendra, S.S. India and Her Neighbours: A Study of Political, Economic and Cultural Relations and Interactions, (New Delhi, 1984).

Brajacharya, L. (ed.), Nepal Speaks at the UN, (New Delhi, Nepal Trading Corporation).

Bowet, D.W. The Law of the Sea, (Manchester University Press, 1967).

Buzam, Barry, Sea-Bed Politics, (New York, 1976).

Chaudhari, K.C., Anglo-Nepalese Relations: From the Earliest Times of the British Rule in India till the Gorkha War, (Calcutta, Modern Book Agency, 1960).

Chatterjee, Bhola, A Study of Recent Nepalese Politics, (Calcutta, The World Press, 1967).

Charles, A. Fisher, Essays in Political Geography, (London, Mehuen and Company Ltd., 1968).

Colombos, C.J., The International Law of the Sea, (London, 1967).

Chauhan, R.S., The Political Development in Nepal, 1950–1970, (New Delhi, Associate Publishing House, 1971).

Dutt, Vidya Prakash, China's Foreign Policy 1958–62, (Delhi, 1964).

Dhakolia, R.P., The Codification of Public International Law, (Manchester University Press, 1970).

Dharmdasani, Murlidhar, Indian Diplomacy in Nepal, (Jaipur, Aalekh Publishers, 1976).

Dyke, V.V., International Politics, (Bombay, Vakils, Feffer & Simon, 1969).

Elliott, Major J.H., Guide to Nepal, (Calcutta, Newman, 1959).

Extavour, Winston C., The Exclusive Economic Zone, (Geneva, 1979).

Fisher, Margaret W. and John, V. Bondurant, Indian Views of Sino-Indian Relations, (Indian Press Digest, Monograph No. I, University of California Press, 1956).

Frankel, Josheph, The Making of Foreign Policy: An Analysis of Decision Making, (London, Oxford University Press, 1963).

Frank, E. Krenz, International Enclaves and Rights of Passage: With Special Reference to the Case Concerning Right of Passage Over Indian Territory, (Geneva, 1961).

Glassner, Martin Ira, Access to the Sea for Developing Land-locked States, (The Hague, Martinus Nijhoff, 1970).

Gupta, Anirudha, Politics in Nepal: A Study of Post-Rana Political Developments and Party Politics, (Bombay, Allied Publishers, 1964).

Gupta, Karunakar, India in World Politics, (Calcutta, Scientific Book Agency, 1969).

Gupta, K.R., GATT and Underdeveloped Countries, (Delhi, Atma Ram, 1976).

Greig, D.W., International Law, (London, 1970).

Gaige, Frederick H., Regionalism and National Unity in Nepal, (New Delhi, Vikas Publishing, 1975).

Hamilton, Francis, An Account of Kingdom of Nepal, (New Delhi, 1971).

Hussain, A. Anwar, A., Conflict in Asia: Case of Nepal, (New Delhi, 1979).

Hussain, Assad, British India's Relations with the Kingdom of Nepal (1857–1947), (London, Allen Unwin, 1970).

Hagen, Toni, Nepal: The Kingdom in the Himalayas, (Berne, Kummuly and Frey, 1961).

Hingorani, R.C., Modern International Law, (New Delhi, Oxford and IBH Publishing Co., 1978).

Jha, B.K., Indo-Nepalese Relations 1951-1972 (Bombay, 1973).

Jha, Shree Krishna, Uneasy Partners: India and Nepal in the Post-Colonial Era, (New Delhi, Manas, 1975).

Jain, Girilal, India Meets China in Nepal, (Bombay, Asia Publishing House, 1959).

Joshi, Bhuwanlal and Rose, Leo E., Democratic Innovations in Nepal: A Case Study of Political Acculturation, (Berkeley, University of California Press, 1966).

Joshi, Navin Chandra, Readings in Nepalese Economy, (Allahabad, Chugh Publications, 1978).

Karan, P.P., Nepal: A Physical and Cultural Geography, (University of Kentucky, 1960).

Karan, P.P. and Jenkins, W.M., The Himalayan Kingdoms: Bhutan Sikkim and Nepal, (Princeton, D. Van Nostrand, 1963).

Karunakaran, K.P., India in World Affairs, 1950-53, (London, 1957).

Kirpatrick, W., An Account of the Kingdom of Nepal, (London, W. Miller, 1811).

Khanal, Yadu Nath, Background of Nepal's Foreign Policy, (Kathmandu, 1964).

Kumar, Satish, Rana Polity in Nepal, 1846-1951, (Bombay, Asia Publishing House, 1967).

Kumar, D.P., Nepal: Year of Decision, (New Delhi, Vikas Publishing House, 1980).

Liska, George, Alliance and the Third World, (USA, 1968).

Manab, P.B., King Mahendra's Active Nonalignment, (Kathmandu, 1963).

Margenthau, Hans J. and Thompson, Kenneth W., Politics among Nations: The Struggle for Power and Peace, (New Delhi, Kalyani Publishers, 1985).

Mathur, Y.S., International Control of the Seas: Conflicts and Cooperations, (New Delhi, Sharda Prakashan, 1982).

Minhaly, Eugene Bramer, Foreign Aid and Politics in Nepal: A Case Study, (London, Oxford University Press, 1965).

Muni, S.D., Foreign Policy of Nepal, 1951-1966, (Delhi, National, 1973).

———, Nepal: An Assertive Monarchy, (New Delhi, Chetna Publications, 1977).

Majumdar, K., Political Relations between India and Nepal, 1877-1923, (New Delhi, Munshi Ram Manoharlal, 1973).

Mehrish, B.N., India's Recognition Policy towards the New Nations, (Delhi, Oriental Publishers, 1972).

Mishra, K.P. (ed.), Studies in Indian Foreign Policy, (New Delhi, Vikas Publications, 1969).

Mishra, P.K., India, Pakistan, Nepal and Bangladesh, (Delhi, Sundeep Prakashan, 1979).

Narayan, Shriman, India and Nepal: An Exercise in Open Diplomacy, (Bombay, Popular Prakashan, 1970).

Nath, Tribhuvan, The Nepalese Dilemma, 1960-74, (New Delhi, 1975).

Oda, S., International Control of Sea Resources, (Leyden, 1963).

Oppenheim, L., International Law, (London, 1955).

Pannikar, K.M., The Afro-Asian States and Their Problems, (London, 1959).

Pant, Y.P., Problems of Development of Smaller Countries: A Study in Problems and Prospects of Development Process, (Delhi, 1974).

———, Nepal's Economic Development on an International Basis, (Kathmandu, 1956).

———, Problems in Fiscal and Monetary Policy: A Case Study of Nepal, (N. Delhi, Vikas Publications, 1970).

Pradhan, Biswas, Foreign Policy and Diplomacy, (New Delhi, 1964).

Poudyal, Shri Ram, Planned Development in Nepal: A Study, (New Delhi, Sterling Publishers, 1983).

Pollock, N.C., Studies in Emerging Africa, (Chapter 6, Case Studies of the Transport Problems of Land-Locked Countries), (London, Butterworths, 1971).

Prasad, Bimal (ed.), India's Foreign Policy: Studies in Continuity and Change, (New Delhi, 1979).

Pathak, Shankar Raj, Facts of Nepalese Economics, (Kathmandu, 1961).

Rajan, M.S., India in World Affairs, 1954-56, (Bombay, Asia Publishing House, 1963).

Ramakant, Indo-Nepalese Relations, 1816 to 1877, (Delhi, S. Chand, 1968).

———, Nepal-China and India, (New Delhi, Abhinav, 1976).

Rawat, P.C., Indo-Nepal Economic Relations, (Delhi, National Publishing House, 1974).

Regmi, D.R., A Century of Family Autocracy in Nepal, (Banaras, 1950).

———, Ancient Nepal, (Calcutta, Firma K.C. Mukhopadhyay, 1969).

Rose, Leo E., Nepal Strategy for Survival, (Delhi, Oxford University Press, 1973).

Rose, Leo E., and Scholz, J,T., Nepal: Profile of a Himalayan Kingdom, (New Delhi, Select Book Service Syndicate, 1980).

Rao, P. Chandrashekhara, The New Law of Maritime Zones, with Special Reference to India's Maritime Zones, (New Delhi, Milind Publications, 1983).

Rene-Jean Dupuy, The Law of the Sea, Current Problems, (New York, Oceana Publications, 1974).

Shah, Manubhai, Developing Countries and UNCTAD, (Bombay, 1968).

Shaha, Rishikesh, Nepal and the World, (Kathmandu, Nepali Congress, 1955).

Shaha, Rishikesh, Nepali Politics: Retrospect and Prospect, (Delhi, Oxford University Press, 1975).

Sanwal, B.D., Nepal and East India Company, (Bombay, Asia Publishing House, 1965).

Shrestha, Sita, Nepal and the United Nations, (New Delhi, Sindhu Publications, 1974).

Shrestha, B.P., An Introduction of Nepalese Economy, (Bombay, Vara and Company, 1962).

Sinjela, A. Mpazi, Land-locked States and the Contemporary Ocean Regime, (New York, 1983).

Singh, Patwant, The Struggle for Power in Asia, (London, B.I. Publications, 1971).

Sharma, Jitendra Raj, Nepal India Relations, (Kathmandu, 1955).

Sen, Jahar, Indo-Nepal Trade in the Nineteenth Century, (Calcutta, Firma KLM Pvt. Ltd., 1977).

Shourie, H.D., UNCTAD-II: A Step Forward, (New Delhi, Indian Institute of Foreign Trade, 1968).

Tabibi, Abdul Hakim, The Right of Transit of Land-locked Countries: A Study of Legal and International Development of the Right of Free Access to the Sea, (Kabul, Afghan Book Publishing House, 1970).

Varma, S.P., Struggle for the Himalayas: A Study in Sino-Indian Relations, (New Delhi, Sterling Publishers, 1971).

Varma, S.P. and Mishra, K.P., Foreign Policies in South Asia, (New Delhi, Orient Longmans, 1969).

Vital, David, The Inequality of States: A Study of Small Powers in International Relations, (London, Oxford, 1967).

Wright, Daniel, History of Nepal, (Calcutta, Cambridge University Press, 1958).

William, H. Meneill, A World History, (New York, Oxford University Press, 1971).

Yami, Dharma Ratna, The Study of the Critical Situation in Nepal, (Kathmandu, 1958).

Zdenek, Cervenka, Land-locked Countries of Africa, (Uppsala, The Scandinavian Institute of African Studies, 1973).

SELECT ARTICLES

Acharya, M., "Foreign Trade and its impact on Economic Development of Nepal," Nepal Industrial Digest, Vol. No. 4, 1969, pp. 55–58, 67.

Ahmed, R.Y., "Indo-Nepalese Relations," United Asia, Vol. 25, No. I, January-February 1974.

Alexander, L.M. and Hodgson, R.D., "The Role of the Geographically Disadvantaged States in the Law of the Sea," San Diego Law Review, Vol. 13, 1976, pp. 558–582.

Anand, R.P., "Freedom of Navigation through Territorial Waters and International Straits," Jndian Journal of International Law, (New Delhi) Vol. 14, 1974, pp. 169–189.

———, "Limits of the National Jurisdiction in the Sea-bed," India Quarterly (New Delhi) 29, (2), April–June 1973.

Auburn, F.M. "The International Sea-bed Area." International and Comparative Law Quarterly, 20, (2), April 1971.

Ayoob, Mohammad, "India and Nepal: Politics of Aid and Trade," The Institute for Defence Studies and Analyses Journal, (New Delhi), Vol. 3, No. 2, October 1970, pp. 127–56.

Bahadur, Raj, "Indo-Nepalese Economic Relations," Commerce, July 11, 1969, p. 66.

———, "Trials and Trumphs of Indo-Nepal Cooperation in Economic Development," Vasudha, Vol. XI, No. 7, Ashad, 2025.

Bajpai, G.S., "Nepal and Indo-Nepal Relations," The Indian Yearbook of International Affairs (Madras, 1954) Vol. III.

Bhargava, G.S., "Nepal between Two Giants," Eastern World, Vol. 14, no. 9, September 1960, pp. 18–19.

Bhatta, Dibya Deo, "Soviet-Nepalese Relations," Eastern World, Vol. 18, no. 7, July 1964, pp. 11–12.

Brahmanand, "Indo-Nepalese Trade Treaties," Eastern Economist, Vol. 56, 1971, pp. 508–11.

Bhattarai, N., "Foreign Trade of Nepal: A Study of some of its Main Features," Nepal Industrial Digest, Vol. 1, No. 2, May-June 1971, pp. 93–97.

Barton, Thomas Frank, "Outlets to the Sea for Land-locked Laos," Journal of Geography, 59, (5), May 1960, pp. 206–220.

Burton, S.J., "Freedom of the Seas: International Law Applicable to Deep Sea-bed Mining Claims," Stanford Law Review, Vol. 24, 1977, p. 1135.

Caffisch, Lucius C., "Land-locked States and Their Access to and from the Sea," British Yearbook of International Law, XLIX, 1978, pp. 71–100.

Centre for Economic Development and Administration, "Trade and Transit: Nepal's Problems with Her Southern Neighbour," (Occasional Paper, No. I), Kathmandu, 1970.

Chauhan, B.R., "The Position of Land-locked States in International Law," Law Review (Punjab University) Vol. 18, 1966, pp. 422–40.

Conforti, B., "Does Freedom of Seas Still Exist?" Italian Yearbook of International Law, Vol. I, 1975, p. 3.

Cundick, R.P., "International Straits: The Right of Access," Georgia Journal of International and Comparative Law, Vol. 5, 1975, p. 107.

Daniel, Wolfstone, "Nepal takes the stage," For Eastern Economic Review, 17 March 1960, pp. 55–53.

Delupis, Ingrid, "Land-locked States and Law of the Sea," Scandinavian Studies in Law, Vol. 19, 1975, p. 101.

Devakata, B.P., "Foreign Aid and Economic Development of Nepal," Himalayan Economist, Vol. I, No. 3 October, 1971.

Dharmdasani, M.D., "India's Economic Aid to Nepal," South Asian Studies, Vol I, January 1973.

Dubey, M., "International Law, Relating to the Transit Trade of Land-locked Countries," Indian Yearbook International Affairs (Madras, 1965), pp. 22–44.

East, W. Gordon, "The Geography of Land-locked States," Trans. and Papers. Ins. British Geographers, No. 28, 1960, pp. 1–20.

Dale, E.H., "Some Geographical Aspects of African Land-locked States," Annals Association of American Geographers, 58, No. 3, 1968, pp. 485–505.

Ferguson, S., "UNCLOS III: Last Chance for Land-locked States," San Diego Law Review, Vol. 14, 1977, pp. 637–655.

Fleischer, C.A., "The Right to a 200 Mile Exclusive Economic Zone or a Special Fishery Zone," San Diego Law Review, Vol. 14, 1977, pp. 548-583.

Freith, P.R., "Rights to a Sea-bed and its Subsoil," International law Association, Report of the 43rd Conference, Brussels, 1945, pp. 168-206.

Fischer, W.E., "The Problems of Land-locked States: Some Basic Thoughts," Economic Research Paper, No. 117, Kampala, Makerere Economic Research Institute, 1967.

Fried, J.H.E., "The 1965 Convention on Transit Trade of Land-locked States," Indian Journal of International Law, Vol. VI, 1966, pp. 9–30.

———, "The New Convention on Transit Trade of Land-locked States, and the Development of Law under United Nations Auspices," Journal of the Tribhuvan University, Department of Political Science, (Kathmandu, 1966), pp. 16–29.

Gaige, Frederick H., "Nepal: More Problems with India," Asian Survey, Vol. 11, No. 2, 1971, pp. 172–56.

Ghori, Karamatullah Khan, "Nepal and its Neighbours," Pakistan Horizon, Vol, 17. No. 4, 1964, pp. 368–84.

Giri, Tulsi, "Nepal's desire to peace," Economic Weekly, 17 November 1963, p. 12.

Gupta, Jayanta Kumar, "Nepal's Relations with Outer World," Calcutta Review, June-July, August 1930

Govindaraj, V C., "Land-locked States: Their Right to the Resources of the Sea-bed and the Ocean Floor," Indian Journal of International Law, Vol. 14, 1974, p 409.

Giulino, Mario, "The Regime of Straits in General International Law," Italian Yearbook of International Law, Vol. I, 1975, p. 16.

Gupta, Ranjan, "Indo-Nepalese Ties: A New Chapter," Indian Express (New Delhi, 1970), 25 August.

Glassner, M.I., "Transit Problems of Land-locked States and the Special Case of Nepal," Foreign Affairs (Kathmandu, 1976), No. 2, May-August 1976, pp. 61–72.

Hers, Peter, "Nepal between India and China," Swiss Review of World Affairs, Vol. 17, No. 6, September 1967, p. 16.

Hussain, Zahira, "Indo-Nepal Relations," The Nepal Council of World Affairs, 1969, pp. 1–10.

Hurst, G. "Whose is the Bed of the Sea," British Yearbook of International Law, Vol, IV, 1923–23, pp. 34–43.

Hassan, T., "Third Law of the Sea Conference: Fishing Rights of Land-locked States," Lawyer of the Americas, Vol. 8, 1977, p. 686.

Ibler, V., "The Interests of Shelf-locked States and Proposed Development of the Law of the Sea," Indian Journal of International Law, Vol. 11, 1971, p. 389–410.

Jayaraman, T.K., and Shrestha, O.L., "Some Trade Problems of Land-locked Nepal," Asian Survey (California, Berkeley), December 1976, p. 1113.

Jayakumar, S., "Issue of the Rights of Land-locked and Geographically Disadvantaged States in the Living Resources of the Economic Zone," Virginia Journal of International Law, Vol. 18, 1977, p. 67.

Joshi, A., "Our Trade and Development," Vasudha, Vol. 11, No. 8, July-August 1968, pp.46–48.

Joshi, B.D.R., "Exporters Exchange Entitlement System in Nepal," Himalayan Economist, Vol. I, No. 2, August 1971, pp. 8–17.

Karki, G.B., "Foreign Policy of Nepal," Rising Nepal, 22 August 1973.

Kiran, Mishra, "Evolution of Nepalese Foreign Policy," Political Scientist, Vol. I, January 1965, pp. 101–9.

Khanal, Yadunath, "Nepal's Foreign Policy and the United Nations," The Journal of the United Nations Association of Nepal, December 1957, pp. 22–25.

Kumar, Dev R., "Nepal's Road to China," For Eastern Economic Review, Vol. 53, No. 8, 20 February 1964, pp. 619–621.

Kumar, Satish, "Nepal and China," Indian Journal of Political Science, Vol. XXIV, January–March 1963, pp. 79–93.

Khan, Rahamtullah, "The Fisheries Regime of the Exclusive Economic Zone," Indian Journal of International Law, Vol. 16, 1976, pp. 169–186.

Knall, B., "Economic Development and Foreign Trade: Import Substitution and Export Diversification in Nepal," The Journal of Development and Administrative Studies, (Kathmandu), Vol. 2, No. I and 2, June and December 1980, pp. 18–45.

Kuldharma, R., "Diversification of Trade," Vasudha, Vol. 11, No. 4, Chaitra, 2024, pp. 33–34.

Lauterpacht, E., "Freedom of Transit in International Law," Transactions of the Grotius Society, XLIV, 1958–59.

Levi, Warner, "Nepal in World Politics," Pacific Affairs, Vol. XXX, No. 3, 1957, pp. 236–48.

———, "Nepal's International Position," United Asia, (Bombay, 1960), pp. 353–5.

Louis, D. Hayes, "The Limits of Foreign Aid," The Journal of Nepal Council of World Affairs Souvenir Issue, 1977, p. 44.

Makil, R., "Transit Rights of Land-locked Countries," Journal of World Trade Law (Geneva), Vol. IV, July-August 1970, pp. 35–51.

Malhotra, R.C., "Nepal's Overseas Trade," Industrial Digest (Nepal), Vol. 2, No. I, 1968, pp. 37–49.

———, "Nepal's Role in the United Nations," Nepal Review, Vol. I, No. I, November 1968, pp. 18–27.

Malhotra, Inder, "India-Nepal Relations: Delhi's Diplomacy on Trial," The Statesman (New Delhi), 12 June 1970.

Muni, S.D , "India's Nepal Policy: Continuity and Change," Mainstream (New Delhi), Vol. 6, No 12, 18 November 1967, pp. 13–16.

———, "Kathmandu-Kodari Road: Justification and Anrciety," Mainstream (New Delhi), Vol. 6, No. 7, 14 October 1967, pp. 22–24.

———, "India's Beneficial Bilateralism in South Asia," India Quarterly, October–December 1979.

———, "India's Mutual Security Arrangement with Nepal," Institute for Defence Studies and Analyses Journal, Vol. IV, No. I, pp. 26–49.

Miles, E., "The Structure and Effects of the Decision Process in the Sea-bed Committee and the Third United Nations Conference on the Law of the Sea," International Organization, Vol. 31, 1977, pp. 159–234.

Mckinnel, R.T., "Land-locked Countries; A Test for UNCTAD-III," Journa of World Trade Law, (London, 1972), No. I.

Manjoor, World, "The Feasibility and Necessity of Waterways in Nepal," South Asia Forum, No. 4, August 1982, pp. 33-80.

Mirvahabi, F., "The Rights of land-locked and Geographically Disadvantaged States in Exploitation of Marine Fisheries," Netherlands International Law Review, 26: 130–162, No 2, 1979.

Najiullah, Syed, "Strategy Value of Nepal Lost to India," Pakistan Observer, 15 October 1970.

Narayan, Shriman, "India-Nepal," United Asia, Vol. 19, No. 4, 4 July 1967, pp. 185–86.

———, "Indo-Nepalese Economic Cooperation," Foreign Trade Review, Vol. II, No. I, April–June 1967.

Nigam, Ashok Kumar, "Chinese Claim of Suzerainty over Nepal," Modern Review, Vol. 123. 1968, pp. 570–84.

Naghmi, Shafgat Hussain, "Exclusive Economic Zone and the Land-locked States," Pakistan Horizon (Karachi), Vol. XXXIII, Nos. 1 and 2, 1980.

Oelofsen, P.D., "Third United Nations Conference on the Law of the Sea-Passage through Straits used for International Navigation," Comparative International Law Journal of South Africa, Vol. 8, 1975, p. 367

Oxman, Bernard H., "The Third United Nations Conference of the Law of the Sea: The Tenth Session," American Journal of the International Law, Vol. 76, No I, January 1982, pp. 1–23.

Pant, P.N., "Nepal's Foreign Trade," The Motherland, 13 January 1963.

Pant, Y.P., "Nepal-China Trade Relations," The Economic Weekly, 14 April 1962. pp, 621–24.

———, "Nepal's Recent Trade Policy," Asian Survey, Vol. 4, No. 7, July 1964, pp. 947–57.

———, "Nepal India Trade Relations: Some Recent Trends," The Economic Weekly, Vol. XIV, No. 8, 24 Feb. 1962, pp. 361–63.

———, "Nepal's Trade Problems," Economic Affairs, Vol. VII, April, 1962, pp. 220–23.

———, "Nepal's Trade with India," Far Eastern Economic Review, Vol. 35, No. 11, 16 March 1962, pp. 617–19.

Pradhan, B.B., "Import substitution in underdeveloped countries with special reference to Nepal," Nepal Industrial Digest, Vol. 2, No. 1, Sept. 1967, pp. 41–74.

Pathak, G.D., "Nepal's Foreign Trade before 1923," Nepal Review, Vol. 2, 5 August 1963, pp. 4–5.

Prasad, K., "Nepal's Foreign Trade," Economic Weekly, 31 October 1964, pp. 1753–5.

Przetaezni K.F., "Freedom of Navigation through Territorial Sea and International Straits," Revue de droit International Vol. 55, 1975, p. 299.

Pounds, Norman J.G., "A free and secure access to the sea," Annals of the Association of American Geographers, 49, 3 September 1959, pp. 256–268.

Perry, J.W.B. "Malawi's New outlet to the sea," Geography, 56, No. 2, 1971.

Rajbahak, R.P., "Foreign Trade of Nepal," Nepal Today, United Asia, Vol. XXX, No. 4, July-August 1967, pp. 204–210.

Rana, P.S., "Nepal's International Trade and Economic Development," Nepalese Economic Review, Vol. 2, No. 1, July 1969, pp. 36–52.

Ramakant, "Nepal's Foreign Policy and China," India Quarterly, Vol. 27, No. 3, July–September 1971, pp. 203–11.

———, "Indo-Nepal Relations: Geopolitical Compulsions," South Asian Studies (Jaipur), Vol. 6, No. 1, January 1971, pp. 49–58.

Rose, Leo E. and Dial, Roger, "Can a Mini-State Find True Happiness in a World Dominated by Protagonist Powers? The Nepal Case," The Annals of America Academy of Political and Social Science, (Philadelphia, Pennsylvania), Vol. 386, November 1969, pp. 89–101.

Regmee, Rama Krishna, "Nepal and the Law of the Sea," The Rising Nepal, 8 June 1977.

Rama Puri, "Exclusive Economic Zone: A New Dimension in the Law of the Sea," Indian Political Science Review, Vol. XIV, 1980, pp. 39-54.

Rao, K.K., "The Legal Regime of the Sea-Bed and Ocean Floor," Indian Journal of International Law, Vol. 9, 1969, pp. 1-18.

Sen, J., "Indo-Nepal Trade Through the Ages," Amrita Bazar Patrika (Calcutta), 4 October 1970.

Shah, R., "Negotiations on the Nepal India Trade and Transit Treaty: Politics of Foreign Aid and Trade," A Souvenir Issue, The Nepal Council of World Affairs (Kathmandu, 1971), pp. 42-55.

Shrestha, J.B., "Nepal's International Trade and Economic Development", Nepalese Economic Review, (Kathmandu), Vol. 2, No. 1, July 1969, pp. 46-52.

Shrestha, G.D., "Trade and Transit: Review of Nepal's Overseas Trade and Export Industries," Vasudha, Vol. 13, No. 10, September-October 1970, pp. 9-28.

Silwal, S.K., Right of Land-locked Countries: A Survey of Basic Issues," The Rising Nepal, (Kathmandu), 9 July 1980.

Suwal, Yashoda, "Nepal's Relations with her two Neighbours (1951-1971)," The Nepalese Journal of Political Science, (Kathmandu), pp. 61-76.

Shrestha, B.P., "The Least Developed and Land-locked Developing Countries," Souvenir Issue, The Nepal Council of World Affairs, (Kathmandu), June 1971.

Shumsher, Pashupati, "India and Nepal: The Political Economy of a Relationship," Asian Survey, Vol. XI, No. 7, July 1971.

Shyam Manjula, "International Straits and Ocean Law," Indian Journal of International Law, Vol. 15, 1975, p. 17.

Sinjela, A. Mpazi, "Freedom of Transit and the Right of Access for Land-locked states: The Evolution of Principle and Law," The Georgia Journal of International and Comparative Law, Vol. 12, Issue 1, 1982, p. 31.

Thapa, Bhekh Bahadur, "Foreign Aid and Economic Development in Nepal," Souvenir Issue, The Nepal Council of World Affairs, (Kathmandu), June 1971.

Trapeznikov, V., "Nepal Today," Foreign Affairs (Moscow), No. 2, February 1966, pp. 72-6.

Upadhyaya, Davendra Raj, "King Birendra and Nepal's Foreign Policy," The Rising Nepal (Kathmandu), 24 February 1975.

Wilcox, Wayne, "Regional Security in South Asia," American Review, Vol. 9, No. 2, January 1965, pp. 55-60.

Walker-Leigh, Varja, "Was UNCTAD-III a Failure?" The World Today (London), Vol. 28, No. 9 September 1972.

Young, R., " The legal status of Submarine Areas beneath the High Seas," American Journal of International Law, Vol. 45, 1951, pp. 225-239.

Young Patrik, C., "Nepal Reopened," Asian Review, Vol. 52, January 1956, p. 2041.

JOURNALS

American Journal of International Law.

American Economic Review (Washington).

Annals of the Association of American Geographers (New York).

Asian Survey (Burkeley, California).

Asian Recorder (New Delhi).

Afro-Asian and World Affairs.

British Yearbook of International Law (London).

Beijing Review (Beijing).

China Report (New Delhi).

China Quarterly (London).

Commerce.

Commonwealth Journal (London).

Dinman (Weekly) (Hindi) (New Delhi).

Eastern World

Eastern Economist (New Delhi).

Eastern Journal of International Law.

Economic and Political Weekly (Bombay).

Economic Weekly.

Far Eastern Economic Review (HongKong).

Far Eastern Survey (New York).

Foreign Affairs Journal (Kathmandu).

Foreign Trade Review

Himalayan Economist (Kathmandu).

Indian Journal of International Law (New Delhi).

India Quarterly (New Delhi).

International Studies (New Delhi).

Indian and Foreign Review (New Delhi).

India Today (New Delhi).

Indian Journal of Political Science (New Delhi).

Indian Yearbook of International Affairs (Madras).

Institute for Defence Studies and Analyses Journal, (New Delhi).

Journal of Development and Administrative Studies (Kathmandu).

Journal of International Affairs (New York).

Journal of Tribhuvan University, Department of Political Science, (Kathmandu).

Journal of World Trade Law (London).
Journal of Maritime Law and Commerce.
Keesing's Contemporary Archives.
Link (New Delhi).
Lawyer.
Lawyers of the Americans (New York).
Law Review (Chandigarh).
Mainstream (New Delhi).
Nepalese Journal of Political Science (Kathmandu).
Nepal Today (Calcutta).
Nepal News (Royal Nepalese Embassy, New Delhi).
Nepal Press Digest (Kathmandu).
Organiser (New Delhi).
Pacific Affairs.
Political Studies (London).
Pakistan Horizon (Karachi).
Seminar (New Delhi),
South (London).
South Asia Forum (Kathmandu).
Sunday (Calcutta).
South Asian Studies (Jaipur).
San Diego Law Review.
Scandinavian Studies in Law.
The Annals of American Academy of Political and Social Sciences (Philadelphia).
The Journal of Nepal Council of World Affairs (Kathmandu).
The International and Comparative Law Quarterly.
The Illustrated Weekly of India (Bombay).
The World Today (London).
United Asia (Bombay).
Vasudha (Kathmandu).
Virginia Journal of International Law,
World Focus (New Delhi).
Yearbook of the International Law Commission.

NEWSPAPERS

Amrita Bazar Patrika (Calcutta).
Financial Express (Bombay).

Gorkhapatra (Kathmandu).
Naya Samaj (Nepali) (Weekly) (Kathmandu).
Northern India Patrika (Allahabad).
Nepal Times (Kathmandu).
Matribhumi (Weekly) (Kathmandu).
Motherland (Kathmandu),
Nepal Sandesh (Hindi) (Patna).
The Commoner (Kathmandu).
The Hindu (Madras).
The Hindustan Times (New Delhi).
The Indian Nation (Patna).
The Pioneer (Varanasi).
The Rising Nepal (Kathmandu).
The Times of India (New Delhi)·
The Statesman (Calcutta).
The Times (London).
The Bangladesh Times (Dhaka).
The Indian Express (New Delhi).
The Pakistan Times (Lahore).
The Patriot (New Delhi).
The Sunday Times (London).
The Telegraph (Calcutta).
The Tribune (Chandigarh).

Index

Abdul Hakim Tabibi, 42, 121
Abecheport, 3
Abidjan, 24
Adriatic sea, 5
Afghanistan, 2, 3, 6, 15, 21, 73, 100, 113, 124, 125, 141, 149, 150, 172, 174, 177, 204, 205, 206
Africa, 2, 4, 7, 16, 22, 41, 106, 127, 129, 140, 198, 205, 206
Albania, 102, 116
Algeria, 17, 168, 186, 189
Amazon, 198
America, United States of, 7, 5, 8, 107, 162, 177, 178, 210
Amlekhgunj, 58
Andora, 3, 7, 18, 27
Andorra Lavella, 27
Argentina, 18
Angola, 17
Annapurna, 45
Antofagasta, 26
Antwerp, 27
Aricca, 26
Ariniko Raj Marg Highway, 57
Asia, 2, 3, 5, 7, 15, 21, 41, 73, 106, 113, 125, 129, 140, 173, 201, 202, 206
Asian-African Legal Consultative Committee [AALCC], 184
Asian Economic Cooperation, 152
Asian Telecommunication Network, 61
Asuncion, 26
Australia, 61, 107, 162, 176
Austria, 3, 7, 18, 27, 40, 73, 102, 113, 149, 150, 162, 181, 213
Austro-Hurgarian Empire, 3

Bahadur Shah, 48
Balabhadra Marg, 57
Bangkok, 21, 59, 63, 154
Bangladesh, 50, 61, 62, 67, 74, 90, 95, 190, 191, 210, 211, 212
Barauni, 83, 92
Barcelona, 27, 102, 106, 124, 138, 196, 199
Barcelona Conference, 122
Barge Transport, 63, 212
Barhni, 86
Bay of Bengal, 60
Beira Nalala, 24, 25
Belgium 19, 27, 102, 107, 149, 177, 206
Belgrade, 174, 175
Bendar Abbas, 21
Benin, 17
Berne, 28
Berne Postal Congress, 132
Berth Kidderpore Dock Shed, 87
Bhadrapur, 86
Bhairawa, 52
Bhaktapur, 52
Bhakti Marg, 57
Bhantawari, 87
Bharatpur, 59
Bhasin, A.S., 98
Bhatgaon, 47
Bimsen Thapa, 48
Bhimnagar, 86, 92
Bhitamore, 87, 92
Bhojpuri, 46
Bhola Rana, 195
Bhutan, 2, 7, 21, 29, 30, 37, 50, 173, 177, 181, 190
Bikhanathori, 86
Bijalpura, 58
Bir Shumsher, 48

Biral, 62, 75
Biratnagar, 59, 64, 82
Birendra Bir Bikram Shah Dev, 49 173, 185, 190, 192
Birganj, 52, 95
Bista, Nirmal K., 86, 97
Bolivia, 3, 7, 18, 26, 29, 32, 37, 102, 113, 125, 177, 198, 205
Bonapale, 75
Botswana, 2, 17, 22, 29, 32, 37, 177
Brandt Commission, 188
Brazil, 18, 102, 107
Brewery, 52
Britain, 48, 210
Budapest, 27
Buffer state, 4
Buienos Aires, 26
Bujumbura, 22
Bulgaria, 67, 116, 102
Burma, 72
Burundi, 2, 17, 22, 29, 32, 37, 125, 177
Byelorussia, 7, 114, 116, 125

Cairo, 185
Calcutta, 21, 63, 70, 74, 81, 85, 92, 190, 209, 210
Calcutta Jetty Shed, 87
Camiri, 26
Camroon, 15
Canada, 7, 107, 162, 176, 177
Canton of Geneva, 100
Caracas, 176, 206
Capetown, 22
Central African Republic, 2, 16, 29, 39, 125, 191
Central American Common Market, 200
Central Bank of Nepal, 87
Central Europe, 202
Chad, 2, 7, 16, 30, 39, 50, 174
Chalna, 62, 75, 76, 91, 97, 212
Chana, 25
Char Koshe Jhadi, 45
Charles De Visscher, 9
Chihati, 75
Chile, 18, 102, 107, 161, 177
China, 4, 22, 44, 57, 62, 67, 82, 95, 102, 210
Chittagong Port, 62, 74
Churia, 45
Coastal State, 117, 177, 182, 206, 208
Colombia, 102
Colombo, 59, 63
Combodia, 15
Comecon, 5
Congo, 23, 191, 198
Contraven Imparting Trade Control Restrictions, 80
Costa Rica, 102
Cotonou, 24
Cuba, 102, 107
Customs Transit Declaration (CTD), 88, 89, 93
Czeehoslovakia, 3, 7, 19, 27, 40, 102, 107, 112, 117, 125, 177, 178, 191, 198, 199, 205

Dadra, 10
Dakar, 24, 168
Daman, 10
Dang, 59
Dar-es-Salaam, 22
Daraundi, 46
Darchula, 59
Darsana, 75
Denmark, 102
Denube, 191, 198
Desai, Morarji, 90, 211
Developing countries, 129
Dhaka, 59, 63, 90, 91, 190
Dhanagadhi-Dadeldhura, 57, 59
Dhankuta, 58
Dharan-Dhankuta, 57
Dharsing, 58
Dibya Deo Bhatta, 194
Dinajpur, 85
Dom Dusadh, 46
Douala, 23
Durban, 22
Dutch, 8

East-Pakistan (Bangladesh), 85, 96
ECAFE, 111, 113, 122, 124, 151, 152, 204

Economic Commission for Africa, 31, 153
Economic Commission of Latin America, 154, 201
Economic Survey of Latin America, 31
EEZ, (Exclusive Economic Zone), 12, 176, 179, 184, 208
Egypt, 67, 199
Elbe, 191
Eritrea, 5, 200
Esthonia, 102
Ethiopia, 5, 100, 200
Europe, 2, 18, 41, 198, 202
European Economic Community, 188, 201
European Free Trade Association, 201
European Mediterranean States, 5

Farakka dam, 63
Federal Republic of Germany, 180
Finland, 102
First Law of the Sea Conference 1958, 113
First World War, 199, 202
Fort Archambault, 3
Fort Lamy, 3
France, 8, 61, 73, 102, 107, 162, 172
Freedom of fly over the high seas, 119
Freedom of fishing, 119
Freedom of laying submarine cables and pipelines, 119
Freedom of navigation, 119, 177
Freedom of transit, 131, 151, 178, 180, 182, 197, 199
French Indo-China, 3

Gaborone, 22
Galgalia, 86, 91
Gandaki, 46, 60, 63, 72
Gandhi, Indira, 90, 211
Ganesh, 45
Ganga, 46, 60, 146, 191
Garighat, 59
GAOR, 121, 122, 123
Gauriphanta, 86, 92
Gaungzhou, 62
GDR, 18
Geographically Disadvantaged States (GDS), 177, 182
Georgetown, 164
General Agreement on Tariffs and Trade (GATT), 107, 110, 122, 169
General Assembly, 113, 122, 145, 147, 151, 186, 189, 193, 199, 205
General Assembly Resolution 1028 (XI), 111, 204
General Assembly Resolution 2820 (XXVI), 161
General Assembly Resolution 3504 (XXX), 168, 169
Geneva, 100, 107, 125, 128, 145, 175, 178, 196, 205
Germany, 61, 73
Genoa, 27
Ghana, 17, 117
Gobi, 44
Gorkhas, 47
Great Britain, 100
Greece, 102
Group of 77, 154, 171, 180, 189
Guatemala, 102
Guinea, 17
Guyana, 164

Hague, the, 28
Haiti, 102
Haldia, 74, 89
Hamburg, 21, 27, 199
Harare, 25
Harka Bahadur Gurung, 168
Hatauda, 52, 58, 63
Havana Charter, 109, 110
Himalayan Kingdom, 4
Himalayas, 44, 49
Holysee, 7, 114, 125
Honduras, 102
Hongkong, 63, 82
Hungary, 3, 19, 27, 40, 114, 117, 125, 149, 177, 206

IBRD, 40
Iceland, 117, 150, 177
Import Entitlement Scheme, 82
India, 3, 22, 44, 51, 63, 67, 70, 94, 102, 107, 142, 177, 181, 190, 206, 208, 209, 210, 211
Indian Customs Officer-Incharge, 88
Indian Economic Aid, 53
Indian Ocean, 61
Indian Subcontinent, 190
Indira Gandhi, 90, 211
Indo-Aryan, 46
Indo-Nepal Treaty of Trade and Commerce, 78, 211
Indo-Nepalese Trade, 61
Indonesia, 117, 177
Indravati, 46
Inter-American Development Bank, 201
International Court of Justice, 10 136, 199
International Law, 8, 13, 114, 182, 183, 198, 204, 208
International Law Commission, 114, 148, 199
International Sea-bed Authority [ISBA], 150, 179, 206
International Trade Organization (ITO), 110
Iran, 21, 129, 150
Iron Curtain, 199
Island Countries, 153
Israel, Fred L., 7, 121, 131, 151, 199
Italy, 8, 61, 73, 102, 213
Ivory Coast, 17

Janakpurdham, 58
Janata Government, 89, 90, 211
Japan, 61, 82, 102, 162, 176
Jarwa, 75, 92
Jayanagar, 58, 86, 75
Jefferson, Thomas, 8
Jhulaghat, 86
Jogbani, 72, 86, 91, 92
Joint River Commission (JRC), 191
Joint Trade Commission, 213

Kabul, 21, 152
Kakavita, 75, 87
Kalikat, 59
Kampala, 25, 182, 193
Kampuchea, 50
Karachi, 21, 63, 96
Karan, 97
Karnali, 46, 60, 63, 72
Katarniaghat, 87
Kathmandu, 22, 46, 50, 69, 90, 96, 184, 190, 193, 211
Kathmandu-Kodari Road, 46, 51, 58
Katihar, 75, 95
Kenya, 17, 22, 165
Kerong, 47
Khulna, 62, 75
Kidderpore Dock, 91
Kigali, 24
King George's Dock, 87
King Yaksha Malla, 47
Kirats, 47
Koilabas, 85
Kosi, 59, 60, 63, 72
Krishna Nagar, 86
Kshatriya, 47
Kumbhakarana, 45
Kuti, 47

La Paz, 26
Lagos, 3
Lalitpur, 52
Land-locked states, 177, 179, 190, 196, 199, 204, 208, 209
Land-locked developing countries, 184, 186, 189
Land reform, 53
Land routes, 53
Laos, 2, 15, 21, 30, 39, 50, 100, 111, 114, 117, 124, 125, 173, 177, 190, 204, 205
Latin America, 106, 140, 201, 202, 206
Latin American Free Trade Association (LAFTA), 200
Lotiria, 102
Law of the Sea, 181, 183, 202, 204

League of Nations, 9, 101, 104, 106, 202
Leningrad, 21
Lesotho, 2, 7, 16, 30, 39, 177, 181
Lhasa, 66, 209
Libya, 16, 17
Lichchhavis, 47
Likhu, 46
Lima, 155, 187
Lithuania, 102
Lome, 24
Lusaka, 25, 164, 186
Luxembourg, 3, 7, 19, 27, 102, 107, 114, 115, 125, 188

Machhapuchhare, 45
Mahendra Bir Bikram Shah Dev, 49, 185, 186, 209
Mahendra Nagar, 86
Mahendra Raj Marg, 57
Mahabharat Range, 45
Mahottari, 58
Malawi, 2, 16, 24, 30, 39
Maldives, 69, 190
Mali, 2, 17, 24, 30, 39, 46, 125, 177, 181, 190
Mallas, 47
Malta, 146
Mangolia, 2, 3, 15, 22, 30, 125, 177
Manjoor World, 65
Manila, 152, 169
Mare Liberum, 2
Margenthau, Hans I., 43
Maritime Flag, 115
Maritime Ports, 117
Maputo, 22, 25
Maseru, 23
Mataranu, 26
Matatirtha, 58
Mauritania, 16
Mauritius, 177
Mexico, 177
Mombasa, 22
Mongaloid, 46
Montevideo, 26
Mozambique, 16
Mugu, 59
Mustang, 45

N'Djamena, 23
N. Korea, 67
Nagar Haveli, 10
Nairobi, 165
Nalala, 24
Namibia, 16, 17
Narayani, 46, 59
Narayanghat-Gorkha highway, 57
National Panchayat, 89
Nautanwa, 75
Nawar Trading Community, 209
Naxalbari, 87
Nepal, 2, 7, 22, 30, 39, 44, 73, 79, 81, 84, 85, 88, 99, 106, 114, 117, 124, 125, 128, 138, 140, 145, 149, 150, 162, 166, 169, 173, 176, 177, 181, 184, 190, 193, 206, 208
Nepal Government Railway (NGR) 58
Nepal Press Digest, 69
Nepal Rastra Bank, 71
Nepalganj-Jumla, 57, 59
Netherland, 27, 28, 102, 107, 149, 162, 206
New Delhi, 59, 79, 94, 142, 190, 194, 206
New International Economic Order (NIEO), 183, 187, 189
New Jalpaiguri, 75
New York, 114, 128, 129, 176, 180, 181, 189, 205, 207
New Zealand, 102, 107, 176, 177
Newars, 46
Niamey, 24
Niger, 2, 16, 17, 24, 30, 39, 178, 198
Nonaligned, 7
Nonaligned Summits, 185, 202, 207
North Atlantic, 10
North-South Dialogue, 188, 190
Norway, 102, 107, 176
NTC (Nepal Transport Corporation), 93
NTWC (Nepal Transit and Warehousing Corporation), 93

OAS (Organization of American States), 201

Ocean floor, 147
OECD, 31
OPEC, 38
Ouagadougou, 25
Oulan-Bator, 22
Overseas Trade, 66

Pakistan, 15, 67, 81, 95, 142, 180, 190, 206, 208, 210
Paksey, 75
Panama, 102
Papal State, 7
Paraguay, 3, 7, 18, 26, 30, 39, 102, 112, 117, 125
Parbatipur, 75
Paris, 172
Peace of Westphalia, 201
Persia, 102
Peru, 5, 129
Petrapal, 75
Phalehung, 87
Philippines, 169
Point Noire, 3
Pokhari, 86
Pokhra Valley, 57
Poland, 9, 67, 102
Port Elizabeth, 22
Port Harcourt, 23
Portugal, 10, 100, 102
Prague, 27
Prithvi Raj Marg, 57

Radhikapur, 62, 74, 81, 85
Railway risk rate, 81
Raja of Gorkha, 48
Rajapur, 86
Rajapur, Mandi, 87
Rajbiraj, 59, 86
Ram Shah, 47
Rana Jung Bahadur, 48
Ranas, 48, 209
Rastriya Panchayat, 190
Raxaul, 58, 60, 63, 91
Revised Single Negotiating Text, 178, 179
Right to Flag, 117
Rijeka, 199
Rimmi, 28
Rohanpur, 75
Romania, 18, 102
Rome, 18
Rotterdam, 27, 80
Royal Nepal Airlines Corporation, 59
Royal Nepalese Consul General (RNCG), 83, 88, 93
Rukum, 59
Rupaidhia, 86
Russia, 57
Rwanda, 2, 17, 24, 30, 39, 125, 174, 191

Salle, 59
San Lonenzo el Real, 8
San Marino, 3, 7, 20, 28, 114, 125
Sanghai, 62
Santa-Cruz-Corambe, 26
Santa-Cruz-Yacuiba, 26
Santiago, 161
Santos, 26
Sapta Koshi, 46
Sardinia, 100
Sarh, 23
Sarlahi, 86
Saudi Arabia, 117
Scavengers, 46
Scheldt, 8
Sea-bed 1970, 146
Second World War, 200, 202
Senegal River Commission, 17, 190
Serb-Croal-Slovenestate, 102
Serbla, 5, 9
Seti, 46
Shah, Prithvi Narayan, 47, 48
Shohratgarh, 86
Shrestha, A.K., 77, 98
Sibert, 196
Sicasica, 26
Sidhartha Raj Marg, 57
Sierra Leone, 181
Sikkim, 44
Simra, 59
Sindhuli-Chisapaui, 58
Singapore, 149, 206
Singhabad, 75

Single Negotiating Text (SNT), 178
Sitamarhi, 92
Sitasrestha, 65, 97, 122
Smuggling, 213
Sonauli, 86
Sonbarsa, 86
South Africa, 16, 107, 176
South America, 2, 7, 18, 41, 129, 198, 201
South Asia, 120, 191
South Asian Countries, 69, 96
South Asian Regional Cooperation, 190
South Korea, 67
South East Asia, 190
South-West-Asian Countries, 61
Soviet Union, 15, 100
Spain, 3, 102
Spainish American Empire, 4
Sri Lanka, 59, 67, 72, 90
Sriman Narayan, 64
Statesman's Year Book, 20
St. Germain, 202
Sudan, 16
Surkhet-Pokhra Rajpath, 57
Sukhia, 86
Sukhiapokhari, 87
Sunkoshi, 46
Sursand, 87
Swaziland, 2, 17, 25, 30, 39, 177, 181
Sweden, 102
Swiss Confederation, 100
Switzerland, 3, 7, 19, 40, 73, 102, 114, 117, 125, 177, 191, 198

Tamakoshi, 46
Tamor, 46
Tanakpur, 86
Tanzania, 16, 17, 171
Tarai Hindus, 46
Tarai region, 45
Tehran, 124, 205
Tekudown, 58
Tema, 25
Thai International Airlines, 72
Thailand, 15, 21, 59, 72, 100
Thakuris, 47
Thapa, N.B., 65
Thimpu, 21, 190
Thori, 86
Tibet, 4, 62, 66, 69, 95, 209
Tientsin, 22
Tikonia, 86
Tista, 45
Tistamukhghat, 75
Togo, 17
Trade and Development Board (TDB), 144, 145
Trade and Transit Treaty, 76, 205, 210
Trade Promotion Centre (TPC), 69
Traffic in Transit, 1, 92, 102, 124, 130, 140, 206
Triagar, 87
Trans-Himalayan, 47
Transhipment, 1, 10, 92, 102, 108, 133
Transit State, 2, 13, 130, 201
Transit trade, 7, 129, 139
Transit transport, 170, 213
Transport infrastructure, 159
Tribhuvan, 49
Tribhuvan airport, 59
Tribhuvan Raj Marg, 57
Trieste, 27, 199
Trishuli, 46
Treaty of Segouli, 48
Tunis, 153
Tunisia, 117

Uganda, 2, 17, 25, 30, 39, 125, 177, 181, 201
UK, 57, 67, 107, 162
UN General Assembly, 67
UNCTAD, 20, 122, 124, 125, 130, 138, 144, 145
UNCTAD-I, 1964, 125, 128, 185, 205
UNCTAD-II, 1968, 142, 206
UNCTAD-III, 161, 164, 176, 179, 186, 206
UNCTAD-IV, 165, 166, 168, 174, 175, 207
UNCTAD-V, 169, 172
UNCTAD-VI, 193

UNDP, 171
UNESOB, 162
United Nations Economic and Social Council, 31, 202, 203, 204
Upper Volta, 2, 17, 25, 30, 39, 125, 177
Uruguay, 102
USSR, 7, 57, 67, 107, 176, 177, 210
Uttar Pradesh, 44

Vaduz, 27
Varanasi, 63
Vatican City, 3, 7, 20, 28
Venezuela, 102, 112, 176
Versailles, 101, 202
Vienna, 27, 197
Vientiane, 21
Vietnam, 15

Waga, 81
West Africa, 201
West Bengal, 44, 85
West Germany, 18
Westphalia, 100

Yacuiba, 26
Yugoslavia, 5, 67, 174

Zaire, 16, 181
Zambezi, 198
Zambia, 2, 16, 17, 25, 31, 39, 177, 181
Zia-ul-Haq, 96
Zimbabwe, 2, 16, 18, 25, 31, 39